Communicating Environmental RISK in Multiethnic Communities

Communicating Effectively in Multicultural Contexts

Series Editors: William B. Gudykunst and Stella Ting-Toomey

Department of Speech Communication
California State University, Fullerton

The books in this series are designed to help readers communicate effectively in various multicultural contexts. Authors of the volumes in the series translate relevant communication theories to provide readable and comprehensive descriptions of the various multicultural contexts. Each volume contains specific suggestions for how readers can communicate effectively with members of different cultures and/or ethnic groups in the specific contexts covered in the volume. The volumes should appeal to people interested in developing multicultural awareness or improving their communication skills, as well as anyone who works in a multicultural setting.

Volumes in this series

1. **BRIDGING JAPANESE/NORTH AMERICAN DIFFERENCES**
   William B. Gudykunst and Tsukasa Nishida
2. **INTERCULTURAL COMMUNICATION TRAINING: An Introduction**
   Richard W. Brislin and Tomoko Yoshida
3. **EFFECTIVE COMMUNICATION IN MULTICULTURAL HEALTH CARE SETTINGS**
   Gary L. Kreps and Elizabeth N. Kunimoto
4. **MULTICULTURAL PUBLIC RELATIONS: A Social-Interpretive Approach**
   Stephen P. Banks
5. **COMMUNICATING EFFECTIVELY WITH THE CHINESE**
   Ge Gao and Stella Ting-Toomey
6. **MANAGING INTERCULTURAL CONFLICT EFFECTIVELY**
   Stella Ting-Toomey and John G. Oetzel
7. **COMMUNICATING ENVIRONMENTAL RISK IN MULTIETHNIC COMMUNITIES**
   Michael K. Lindell and Ronald W. Perry

Communicating Environmental RISK in Multiethnic Communities

Michael K. Lindell
Texas A&M University

Ronald W. Perry
Arizona State University

SAGE Publications
International Educational and Professional Publisher
Thousand Oaks ■ London ■ New Delhi

For information:

Sage Publications, Inc.
2455 Teller Road
Thousand Oaks, California 91320
E-mail: order@sagepub.com

Sage Publications Ltd.
6 Bonhill Street
London EC2A 4PU
United Kingdom

Sage Publications India Pvt. Ltd.
B-42, Panchsheel Enclave
Post Box 4109
New Delhi 110 017 India

Library of Congress Cataloging-in-Publication Data

Lindell, Michael K.
Communicating environmental risk in multiethnic communities / by Michael K. Lindell and Ronald W. Perry.
p. cm.
Includes bibliographical references and index.
ISBN 0-7619-0650-9 — ISBN 0-7619-0651-7 (pbk.)
1. Environmental impact statements. 2. Pollution-Social aspects. 3. Environmental policy.
I. Perry, Ronald W. II. Title.
TD194.5.L56 2004
363.1′056—dc22 2003018364

03 04 05 06 07 08 09 10 9 8 7 6 5 4 3 2 1

Acquiring Editor: Margaret H. Seawell
Production Editor: Claudia A. Hoffman
Copy Editor: Jamie Robinson
Typesetter: C&M Digitals (P) Ltd.
Indexer: Molly Hall

Contents

Preface

Many of the ideas underlying risk communication have a long history, but the identification of risk communication as a distinct subject matter has occurred only in the past two decades. The current era in risk communication can be defined as beginning with a risk communication conference held in Washington D.C. in 1986, which brought together speakers and an audience from a broad range of organizations and disciplines with an interest in this topic. The speakers at this conference included representatives from Congress, federal and state government agencies, chemical companies, law firms, nongovernmental organizations, environmental groups, the news media, and universities.

The emergence of risk communication as a field seems to have stemmed from the increasing recognition that there are many problems in which people must exchange information—about their beliefs and evaluations of undesirable outcomes, about the actions that can be taken to avoid those outcomes, and about the social roles (especially rights and responsibilities) of the parties involved. Accordingly, risk communication arises in a number of distinct areas, including lifestyle choices (e.g., diet and exercise), occupational activities (e.g., use of industrial solvents), food and drugs (e.g., pesticide residues on fruit), consumer products (e.g., automobiles), technological facilities (e.g., production, storage, and transportation of chemicals), and occupancy of geographic areas prone to natural hazard impacts (e.g., floodplains).

There are some important differences between some areas of risk communication, but there are also useful similarities between others. Thus, this book is not about risk communication in general but, rather, about *environmental risk communication.* In particular, we are persuaded that the technological risks of hazardous facilities and transportation are quite similar to the risks of natural hazards in terms of their exposure mechanisms and, equally important, their often being addressed by the same government agencies (especially emergency management agencies). For example, there are both technological and natural hazards that can be classified as chronic environmental risks involving the release of low levels of hazardous materials whose effects accumulate over time. Similarly, there are both technological and natural hazards that involve catastrophic risks—typically involving the rapid release of large quantities of hazardous materials or energy. Catastrophic materials hazards include releases of toxic chemicals, such as chlorine or radiological materials from a nuclear power plant, but can sometimes result from natural sources, such as volcanic eruptions. Catastrophic energy hazards can result from releases of flammable or explosive materials, such as liquefied natural gas, as well as from natural sources, such as ground shaking in the case of earthquakes and wind forces in the cases of hurricanes and tornadoes.

For a broad group of practitioners that we refer to as environmental hazard managers, such hazards raise broad scientific questions about the magnitudes of the events that could occur in a specific community. This includes the types and quantities of hazardous materials that might be released from specific facilities or transportation routes, the maximum probable magnitude of an earthquake, and the recurrence intervals of different flood discharges. Other questions, especially regarding hazardous materials, include environmental transport processes through soil, groundwater, surface water, and the atmosphere. There also are concerns about both natural and technological hazards regarding the nature of the biological effects on those exposed and the variations in the sensitivity of different population segments to these exposures.

These environmental hazards need to be explained to those at risk, but they also raise questions about the management of these hazards by stakeholders in the community. These stakeholders include any industries that are the sources of risk, government agencies that must respond to these hazards, and households and businesses that are vulnerable to the hazards. Risk communication is needed by stakeholders to work toward a consensus regarding the proportion of the community's resources allocated to each of the four principal methods of environmental hazard management—hazard mitigation, emergency preparedness, emergency response, and disaster recovery. Risk communication also is needed to determine the nature of each stakeholder's contribution to environmental hazard management, that is, what the specific responsibilities of government and industry and of households and businesses will be.

We have made two significant theoretical choices in writing this book. First, we adopted the classic communication model (Source-Channel-Message-Receiver-Effect-Feedback) as the best way to explain the fundamental dyadic relationship that underlies all communication. We are aware that some scholars (e.g., Kasperson & Stallen, 1991) have characterized the classic communication model as inadequate, but its limitations are more apparent than real. Claims that the classic communication model is only unidirectional are countered by noting that there is a feedback loop in the model that is a shorthand way of saying that the roles of source and receiver can be reversed. Thus, the initial receiver can use the same or a different channel to transmit a message to the initial sender.

Moreover, claims that the classic communication model cannot adequately represent the flow of information through complex social networks are likewise unfounded. In principle, each link (more precisely known in network theory as an arc or edge) directly connecting a source and a receiver (known as a pair of nodes or vertices) in a communication network can be described in terms of the channels that define that link and the messages that are transmitted over it. Thus, a network generalization of the classic communication model can account for multiple receivers from a single source, multiple sources for a single receiver, and indirect paths from a source (via intermediate sources) to an ultimate receiver. We do not contend that practitioners should attempt to develop detailed network models, but we do discuss the ways in which they can adapt their risk communication plans and procedures to the demands that complex networks will place on them.

Second, we have relied on the Protective Action Decision Model (PADM) as the most suitable way to explain the relationship between communicated information and protective behavior. The PADM, which has been developed from research conducted over the past 25 years, is similar in some respects to other attitude-behavior models (such as the Health Belief Model, Theory of Reasoned Action, Protection Motivation Theory, and Person-Relative-to-Event Theory) in its adoption of an expectancy-valence model of decision making. It also has elements in common with Janis and Mann's Conflict Model of Decisionmaking. We believe that the PADM contains the most useful features of each of these models (or the earlier research on which they were based), as well as some distinctive aspects that are particularly well suited to explaining people's attempts to protect themselves, their families, and their property from environmental hazards.

This book is intended to overcome two major limitations of previous books on environmental risk communication. The first of these is the low priority, if not outright neglect, of risk communication about natural hazards. Most of the books and articles on risk communication have addressed chronic releases from technological facilities—an important topic to be sure, but one that involves many issues that are different from issues such as informing people about the long-term risks of natural hazards (which usually are a low priority for public officials and citizens alike) and warning them of an imminent threat.

The other neglected issue concerns the challenges involved in communicating environmental risks to multiethnic communities. As succeeding chapters will show, ethnic diversity is an important part of the community context that affects the processing of information during the protective action decision-making process. Multiethnic communities are already a fact of life in many parts of the country and, as minority populations grow, will become a challenge in more communities in coming decades.

This book was written principally for professionals in emergency management, community planning, public administration, and environmental health, as well as students in those fields. It also will be useful to risk communication scholars in departments of anthropology, communication, geography, marketing, political science, psychology, and sociology. Accordingly, we have sought to provide a review of the most relevant literature on environmental risk communication and to briefly summarize relevant propositions from the fundamental theories of communication and decision making that are relevant to this topic. Chapter 1 provides an overview of environmental hazard management and summarizes the role of ethnicity in community functioning. Chapter 2 reviews the principal theories from social science that are relevant to risk communication. Chapter 3 summarizes the literature on disaster response, focusing on people's reactions to disaster warnings, and identifies the implications of these findings for the design and implementation of warning systems. Chapter 4 reviews and summarizes the literature on the adoption and implementation of *hazard adjustments*—risk reduction actions consisting of hazard mitigation actions taken to provide passive protection at the time of hazard impact, emergency preparedness actions taken to support active response after hazard impact, and recovery preparedness actions (e.g., hazard insurance) taken to provide the financial resources needed to recover from disaster impact. Chapter 5 identifies the tasks that environmental hazard managers should perform in each of three stages—the continuing hazard stage, an escalating crisis, and an emergency response—to explain the environmental hazards to which their community is exposed, the actions public authorities and local industry are taking to manage these risks, and the actions that households and businesses can take to reduce their vulnerability.

The ideas that are presented in the following chapters come from many sources. Those derived from the research literature are cited in the conventional manner throughout the text. Other ideas were derived from work that we have done for a variety of other organizations, including Boston Edison; GAF Chemical; Long Island Lighting; Smith-Kline Chemical; the Phoenix Fire Department; the Arizona Division of Emergency Management; Local Emergency Planning Committees for Ingham and Muskegon Counties; State Emergency Response Commissions for Illinois, Indiana, Michigan, and Ohio; the Texas Governor's Division of Emergency Management; the Federal Emergency Management Agency; the U.S. Nuclear Regulatory Commission; and the International Atomic Energy Agency.

We gratefully acknowledge that many of the concepts in this book come from research projects that were funded by the National Science Foundation (most recently, by Grants CMS0219155 and CMS9796297). However, the conclusions and recommendations presented in the following chapters do not necessarily reflect the positions of any of the organizations mentioned above. The interpretations of the research literature and our work experiences are our responsibility alone.

1

Risk Communication, Culture, and Ethnicity

Risk can be defined broadly as a condition in which there is a possibility that people or property could experience adverse consequences. Some people, by virtue of their access to data or their specialized expertise in interpreting that data, have more information than others about the risk of a particular hazard and about ways in which that risk can be managed. These risk analysts have the responsibility to convey their assessments to decision makers who must determine what action to take in response to the risk that the analyst has characterized. These assessments typically (1) define risk in terms of the likelihood that an event of a given magnitude will occur at a given location within a given time period and (2) describe the expected consequences that the event will inflict on people and property. The decision makers to whom the analysts communicate this information can be either the population at risk or hazard managers who are responsible for protecting the population at risk. In either case, the principal reason for risk communication is to initiate and direct protective action.

Risk communication has become a common concept in recent decades—appearing in many contexts (e.g., infectious diseases, food additives, natural hazards, routine effluents, and technological accidents) and referring to many target groups (e.g., employees, citizens, households, minority groups, and legislators, to name only a few). With such diversity of contexts and target groups, it is critical to any scientific treatment of risk communication that the meaning of the term be established clearly. This volume will address risk communication about the hazards of extreme events that originate in the natural environment or are transmitted through it. Our principal concern will be with events that, because of their rapid onset and the large amounts of energy or materials released, have the potential to kill a large number of people in a very short period of time unless timely and effective action is taken to protect public safety.

Some of these extreme events originate in the natural environment and thus are known as *natural hazards.* The ones that involve the release of substantial amounts of energy can cause the immediate destruction of buildings and infrastructure that are not designed to resist extreme meteorological (hurricanes and tornadoes), geological (earthquakes and volcanic eruptions), and hydrological (floods) forces. These environmental hazards also can cause traumatic injuries to people through the direct effects of extreme temperatures or pressures or through the indirect effects of structural collapse. Some natural hazards, such as volcanic eruptions, can release materials that cause adverse health impacts to people. In some cases, these health effects are immediate, whereas in other cases they may take years to manifest themselves.

Some types of natural hazards are not addressed here because their speed of onset is slow (e.g., droughts), because they take place in rural areas where the size of the threatened population is small (e.g., avalanches), or because the population at greatest risk is geographically dispersed (e.g., extreme heat and cold). Nonetheless, many of the principles of risk communication described in this volume are likely to apply to these hazards as well.

In addition to the extreme events that originate in the natural environment, there are also those that are transmitted through the natural environment. These include some, but not all, of what are commonly referred to as *technological hazards.* Like the natural hazards, the technological hazards that are addressed here include sudden and massive releases of energy and hazardous materials. These hazards—which include explosions, releases from nuclear power plants, and chemical releases from fixed-site facilities or during transportation—all can have a very rapid onset and have the potential for killing a large number of people in a very short period of time unless there is a prompt and effective emergency response.

There are, as well, technological hazards that are not addressed here, especially those that involve the cumulative effect of routine air- or water-borne releases from technological facilities or contamination of food and drugs. Many exposures to these hazards unfold over an extended period of time and the adverse health effects are even more delayed—frequently producing low incidence rates of disease in the affected population. Here, too, many of the same principles of risk communication are likely to apply even though these hazards are not explicitly addressed here.

A temporal distinction that is central to the organization of this volume is the amount of time between the detection of the hazard and the onset of exposure. A risk communication effort that addresses the imminent threat of an extreme event is referred to as a *warning,* whereas one that addresses the potential for such events to occur is often known as a *hazard awareness program.* As we shall see in the following chapters, the (unfortunately quite distinct) research literatures on natural and technological hazards have produced similar conclusions about warnings, but there has been an important difference in the case of hazard awareness programs because natural hazards seem to arouse substantially less concern than technological hazards. Consequently, risk communication programs about the long-term threat of natural hazards generally have sought to *increase* public concern, but risk communication programs about the long-term threat of technological hazards have more frequently sought to *decrease* public concern. Research on technological risk perception has sought to explain why some hazards elicit more concern than others, and it appears that the difference in response is due, at least in part, to such hazard characteristics as the voluntariness and controllability of hazard exposure and the degree of dread about its consequences (Slovic, 1987).

One important function of risk communication is, explicitly or implicitly, to promote appropriate protective behavior by those to whom the information is directed. One can think of such behavior changes as "adjusting" to long-term threats by modifying the hazard, modifying the hazard's impact by preventing specific effects, moving to another location, changing the land use to reduce hazard vulnerability, sharing the loss, or bearing the loss (Burton, Kates, & White, 1978, 1993). Alternatively, one can think of such behavior changes as "responding" to an imminent threat by, for example, evacuating, sheltering in-place, expedient respiratory protection, or food interdiction (Drabek, 1986; Mileti, Drabek, & Haas, 1975). In general, our emphasis will be on communicating information to those who are actually at risk of exposure to a hazard, but we also recognize the need for communicating to those who *think* they are at risk of exposure to the hazard. In the latter case, messages are sometimes needed to convince people that they do not need to take protective actions because they will not be exposed to the hazard or because the actions being taken by authorities will be sufficient to protect them. Alternatively, such messages might be designed to convince people that hazard managers do not need to implement protective actions because the costs of responding outweigh the risk. Moreover, authorities are occasionally knowledgeable enough about citizens' concerns that a one-way communication flow from them to citizens will produce results that are satisfactory to all concerned. In practice, however, authorities frequently need feedback from citizens and should expect such feedback whether or not they believe that it is needed. For most environmental hazards, the risk communication process should be based on a hazard analysis that identifies risk areas—the geographical locations in which the environmental extremes are expected to occur—and the mechanisms by which exposure can occur. The risk communication process also should be guided by a vulnerability analysis that identifies the populations and property located in those risk areas. These analyses provide the basic data on which messages can be formulated that describe the vulnerability of different population segments and the protective responses that are appropriate to reduce these risks.

It is important to recognize that in generating risk messages, one cannot focus exclusively on the risk analyst's definition of the situation. Unfortunately, many well-intended attempts at risk communication are based on the assumption that risk area populations make decisions that differ from analysts' protective action recommendations largely because they misperceive the risk or misunderstand the analysts' recommendations. The premise of this approach is that disseminating scientific information about the hazard agent will motivate people to take appropriate protective action (which might be to take no action). This assumption is correct in some cases, but it substantially oversimplifies the risk communication process because it ignores the roles of the information source, the channel by which the information is transmitted, and the individual differences among those who receive the information. In addition, this naive approach to risk communication also ignores the effects of impediments to information processing, such as competing demands for attention, the use of cognitive heuristics, and conflicts with people's existing beliefs. Furthermore, such an approach fails to place risk communication in the context of behavioral decision theory (e.g., Yates, 1990) and neglects the social structural (community) and cultural environments in which communication processes are immersed (Gudykunst, 1998).

Instead, risk communication should be a process by which stakeholders share information about hazards affecting a community. The use of the term *sharing* is important because risk analysts and hazard managers, if they are to be effective in communicating with their audience, must understand how different segments of the population at risk think about a hazard. These population segments include businesses and households that are vulnerable to a specific hazard, as well as community and industry personnel who are responsible for managing a hazard in ways that reduce the risk to an acceptable level.

In this volume, we will address risk communication broadly by examining the social processes that determine who receives risk information, the social-psychological processes by information sources and receivers interact, the cognitive processes by which people interpret risk information, and the cultural context that influences the broader beliefs that determine the way in which specific information is interpreted. We will also touch on a few of the economic issues that are involved in judging the cost of protective action and the political issues that are involved in adopting and implementing measures that provide community-wide protection. Our general perspective is based on Burton and colleagues' (1978, 1993) conception that natural hazards arise from the interaction of physical event systems and the human use system. The physical environment is characterized by forces (geological, meteorological, and hydrological) that vary over time and produce extreme events at irregular intervals. We also acknowledge that the complexity and close coupling of advanced technology can produce "normal accidents"—events whose frequency and magnitude seem to defy the best intentions of systems designers (Perrow, 1984). When extreme events of nature or technology exceed the capacity of the human use system, they produce negative impacts on people and their property; the most damaging of these extreme events are called *disasters* (Quarantelli, 1995). Following Blaikie, Cannon, Davis, and Wisner (1994), we recognize that disaster impacts are not distributed equitably but, rather, tend to be experienced disproportionately by ethnic minorities and the poor. Indeed, because ethnic minorities frequently are the poor, those at greatest risk often have the least access to information about the risks they face and to the resources they need to protect themselves from exposure to these hazards.

To further articulate our perspective, the remainder of this chapter describes the basic structure of environmental hazard management and explores the contingencies associated with managing such hazards in a multicultural society. Subsequent chapters deal with major features of risk communication. Chapter 2 addresses the theoretical foundation of effective risk communication by examining research on persuasive communications and attitude-behavior relationships. Chapter 3 is devoted to applying the theoretical model to situations where risk communication focuses on promoting protective response to an immediate threat, that is, compliance with disaster warnings. Chapter 4 addresses protective behaviors undertaken in response to a long-term threat, that is, the adoption of hazard adjustments in response to hazard awareness programs. All of these chapters are based on the notion that the risk communication process operates in a multicultural society where there are systematic differences among subgroups in their beliefs, values, norms, and access to other community groups. Finally, Chapter 5 summarizes what is known about practical strategies of risk communication for promoting citizen adoption of hazard adjustments.

❖ RISK COMMUNICATION IN ENVIRONMENTAL HAZARD MANAGEMENT

One very useful approach to risk communication comes from the field of *emergency management,* which, in the most general terms, is the practice of identifying, anticipating, and responding to the risks of catastrophic events in order to reduce to more acceptable levels the probability of their occurrence or the magnitude and duration of their social impacts. In the United States, emergency management generally has been conceptualized as a problem—and, increasingly, the legal responsibility—of local, state, and federal government. In recent years, several factors have increased the salience of emergency management. One factor is the apparent legal liability of governments for the protection of citizens from natural and technological threats (Kubasek & Silverman, 2000; Rabin, 1978). A second factor is the growing professionalization of emergency managers, which arises from the recognition of needs for specialized training and development of credentialing processes. This has resulted in the development of an organized body of specialists who understand how to appraise and cope with environmental threats. Still a third factor is the public's growing sensitivity to environmental hazards, which is driven by the attention of the media to periodic catastrophes associated with the forces of nature and technology. Taken together, these factors have generated a social environment in which governments' social expectations and legal obligations to protect citizens have increased in priority, demanding explicit attention to emergency management.

Research and operational experience with disasters has conceptualized emergency management in terms of four relatively distinct but clearly interrelated phases: mitigation, preparedness, response, and recovery. This conceptualization was originally proposed by the National Governor's Association Emergency Management Project led by Hilary Whittaker (National Governor's Association, 1979). As this group grappled with what it means to manage emergencies, they generated considerable discussion and some controversy in both the disaster research and hazard policy communities. After reviewing the many formulations of disaster phases proposed during the 1950s and 1960s, they developed a standardized terminology and identified specific activities that environmental hazard managers could undertake within each of these phases. In addition to the advantages provided by standardizing terminology, this conceptualization clearly indicates the cyclic nature of hazards. Mitigation and preparedness are generally thought of as taking place prior to the onset of any specific disaster, whereas response and recovery are usually undertaken in connection with a particular event.

Nonetheless, it is increasingly recognized that there are problems with this formulation. The four phases are indistinct because it is not possible to unequivocally establish the beginning and end of each phase. The phases also overlap because mitigation and preparedness activities take place concurrently before disaster impact, yet after a disaster, mitigation and recovery activities might be taking place concurrently with each other (and also with response activities). Finally, the phases are interdependent because the nature and extent of a community's mitigation actions can influence the type and range of the preparedness actions needed. Accordingly, mitigation, preparedness, response, and recovery are more accurately considered to be emergency management *functions* rather than phases. Nevertheless, we will refer to them as *phases* rather than functions because the former usage is so well established.

Figure 1.1 Relationships Among Primary Emergency Management Functions

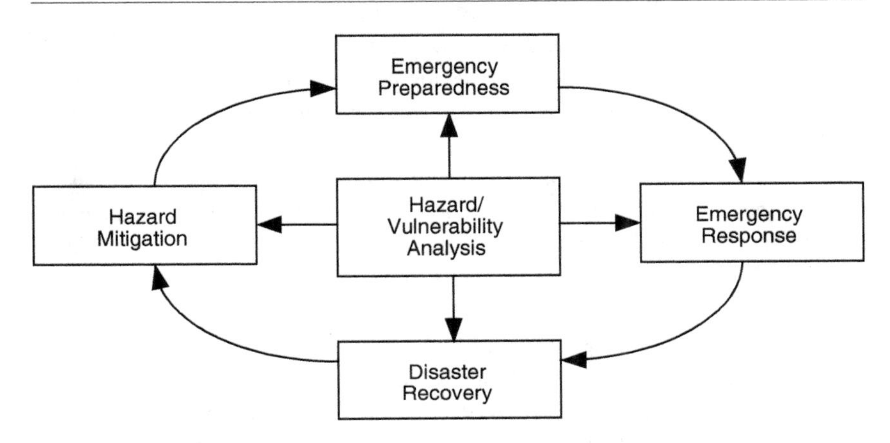

In addition, it also is important to recognize that hazard/vulnerability analysis is a vital function that is not explicitly included in the conventional four-phase typology of emergency management, even though this activity provides important information that is needed for hazard mitigation, emergency preparedness, emergency response, and disaster response. Accordingly, we find it useful to display the interrelationships of these functions in terms of Figure 1.1. Finally, the term *emergency management* is somewhat misleading because three of the four functions—hazard mitigation, emergency preparedness, and disaster recovery—do not take place during emergencies. Instead, hazard mitigation and emergency preparedness might more accurately be characterized as *hazard management*, with emergency response and disaster recovery labeled *disaster management*. Indeed, the terms *environmental risk management* and *environmental hazard management* are more accurate labels for this field, but the term *emergency management* has such widespread currency among researchers and practitioners that we will use it interchangeably with our preferred term, *environmental hazard management*.

Emergency Management Activities

Ideally, risk communication is based on information drawn from systematic risk assessments. During the pre-impact period, hazard and vulnerability assessments should be conducted that identify the potential impact of extreme environmental events on human use systems. These analyses should identify the geographic areas and demographic segments at risk and describe the anticipated physical (damage and casualties) and social (psychosocial, sociodemographic, socioeconomic, and sociopolitical) impacts of events of varying intensity and location (Federal

Emergency Management Agency, 1997; Lindell & Prater, in press). Once the analyses have been completed, they should guide authorities' mitigation and preparedness actions and, once these are under way, messages from authorities should inform the public about the geographic areas and demographic segments at risk, the potential impacts of different event intensities, and the mitigation and preparedness measures that should be undertaken by those at risk.

Mitigation activities are directed toward eliminating the causes of a disaster, reducing the likelihood of its occurrence or limiting the magnitude of its impacts if it does occur. The ways in which mitigation activities can reduce a hazard can best be understood in terms of the Burton and colleagues (1993) model mentioned earlier—the human impact of an environmental extreme can be altered by modifying the physical event system or the human use system or both. In the case of floods, for example, installing community protection works, such as dams or levees that confine flooding, can reduce the probability of loss of life or property. However, it is much more difficult, if not impossible, to control meteorological and geophysical systems.

By contrast with natural event systems, technological systems are inherently controllable (although experience teaches us that this is only *imperfectly* so). For example, explosives, toxic chemicals, and radioactive materials can all be produced, stored, and transported in ways that avoid adverse effects on plant workers, local residents, and the public at large. Dangerous technological systems can be avoided or, if constructed, can be sited in remote locations or constructed at small scales that minimize the threat to other segments of society. In addition, the likelihood of a release of toxic chemicals from a fixed site facility can be reduced by means of diverse and redundant system design, by reliable and efficient operations and maintenance procedures, and by effective worker selection, training, and supervision.

For both natural and technological hazards, control of the human use system is generally more feasible than control of physical event systems. As Burby and colleagues (1998) have noted, human use systems can be modified by altering land use practices (e.g., limiting the density of development in areas of high risk) and by altering building construction practices to reduce hazard vulnerability (e.g., elevating flood prone properties and implementing floodproofing). Similarly, human exposure to technological hazards can be controlled by prohibiting the construction of schools, hospitals, and other structures with high occupant density in areas close to hazardous facilities.

The choice of mitigation action, controlling the hazard agent, or controlling the human use system, depends on political and economic decisions about the relative costs and benefits of exercising these two types of control. Further issues include whether the adoption and implementation of mitigation actions is based on regulations, market forces, or informational approaches (Lindell et al., 1997). As is the case with controls over the physical event system, issues arise concerning who can control the human use system, what degree of control can be maintained, and what incentives exist for the maintenance of control over the human use system. The principal objective of risk communication in connection with hazard mitigation is to explain the effectiveness of alternative mitigation measures in protecting people and property. Specific risk communication issues include comparisons of the relative effectiveness of alternative mitigation measures, comparison of the effectiveness of a mitigation measure to its cost (i.e., assessment of cost-effectiveness), and comparison of the effectiveness of a mitigation measure to an absolute standard.

Preparedness activities are those that are undertaken to protect human lives and property in conjunction with threats that cannot be controlled by means of mitigation measures, or from which only partial protection may be achieved. Thus, preparedness activities are based on the premise that an extreme event is likely to occur and that plans, procedures, and resources must be established in advance to support a timely and effective response to any threat that arises. In anticipating the needs that will arise later during the response phase, preparedness programs must address four emergency response functions—emergency assessment, expedient hazard mitigation, population protection, and incident management (Tierney, Lindell, & Perry, 2001). Risk communication is important in conjunction with all four of these functions. Emergency assessment requires detecting an event, classifying it, and disseminating information to emergency response organizations. Expedient hazard mitigation involves actions taken during the disaster to protect property. Population protection includes warning the population at risk about the timing and extent of disaster impact and implementing protective actions such as evacuation, search and rescue, and medical care. Incident management includes alerting members of emergency response organizations and providing information about the event to those population segments who are not at risk but might think they are in danger because of their proximity to the hazard. Each of these functions requires organizations to prepare in advance of disaster impact because of the need for physical (e.g., sirens and tone-alert radios) and administrative mechanisms for timely and effective risk communication. In the immediate pre-impact period (when there is advance information about the timing and location of disaster impact), risk communication should focus on timely warning and rapid implementation of protective measures that minimize casualties and, to the extent possible, reduce property damage.

Emergency response activities are conducted during a time period that begins with the detection of the event and ends with the stabilization of the situation following disaster impact. In some cases—an earthquake, for example—detection of the event may be no more technically sophisticated than noticing that high rise office buildings are swaying in an alarming manner, whereas in other cases, such as floods along the lower Mississippi River, there may be an extensive system of instrumentation integrated into a model for forecasting the timing and magnitude of the flood crest. Stabilization of the situation means that the threat to life and property has de-escalated back to "normal" levels. Emergency response activities focus on protecting the affected population, as well as attempting to limit damage from the initial impact and minimizing damage from secondary or repeated impacts.

Some of the more visible response activities undertaken to limit the primary impact include securing the impact area, evacuating threatened areas, conducting search and rescue for the injured, providing emergency medical care, and sheltering evacuees and other victims. Operations mounted to counter secondary threats include fighting urban fires and hazardous materials releases after earthquakes, identifying contaminated water supplies or other public health threats following flooding, identifying contaminated wildlife or fish in connection with a toxic chemical spill, or preparing for flooding following glacier melt during a volcanic eruption. During the response stage, environmental hazard managers must also assess the damage and coordinate the arrival of converging equipment and supplies so that they may be deployed to those areas most in need. The principal objective of risk communication in connection with emergency response is (1) to explain which areas and which people within those areas are at greatest risk and (2) to describe when it is safe to discontinue protective actions, for example, by reoccupying evacuated areas. Other important risk communication objectives include explaining to those who are not at risk that they can continue normal activities, that they should avoid the impact area, and the most appropriate ways of providing assistance to victims.

Recovery activities begin after the disaster impact has been stabilized and extend until the community is restored to an acceptable level of functioning—which may require a very long period of time, especially for marginalized segments of the population (Peacock & Girard, 1997). There has long been controversy over the "static" versus "dynamic" views of society implied by definitions of recovery. Following Stallings (1998), we contend that even a "static" community is characterized by social, economic, and political processes that are in dynamic equilibrium. In most communities, this equilibrium changes over time and disasters constitute an external shock that reduces the level of community functioning by destroying physical resources and altering human interaction patterns. The level of post-disaster functioning is unlikely to be identical to pre-impact functioning, but there will come a time when temporary arrangements are no longer necessary; this point marks the close of the recovery period. The immediate objective of recovery measures is to restore housing for households, businesses, and governmental agencies, as well as the community's infrastructure, but the ultimate goal is to restore an acceptable quality of life that can be further improved on as time passes. *Recovery* has been defined in terms of short-term (relief and rehabilitation) measures versus long-term (reconstruction) measures. *Relief and rehabilitation* activities usually include demolition of damaged structures, clearance of debris, and restoration of infrastructure (water/sewer, fuel/electricity, telecommunications, and transportation), reestablishment of basic economic (commercial and industrial) activities, restoration of essential government and community services, and provision of an interim system for meeting the basic needs of victims—especially their housing, clothing, and food. *Reconstruction* activities include the revitalization of the area's economic system and, in some communities, the implementation of community plans for hazard mitigation to promote sustainability. Such an approach to reconstruction was documented after the great Alaska earthquake of 1964 (Anderson, 1969), the eruption of Mt. Usu in Japan (Perry & Hirose, 1991), and the Loma Prieta and Northridge earthquakes in California (Lindell & Perry, 1996, 1997). A major challenge for risk communication during recovery is to provide information about the potential for continuing aftershocks (Mileti & O'Brien, 1992) and secondary threats from diseases (Lillibridge, 1997; Toole, 1997).

Risk communication in connection with recovery activities addresses continuing threats from recurrence of the primary hazard (e.g., earthquake aftershocks), delayed consequences (e.g., building collapses during reoccupancy), secondary hazards (e.g., the risk of fires caused by damaged gas and electrical service), and ways of adapting to a changed environment while restoration is in progress.

Structuring Risk Communication

As indicated in the previous discussion, the need for effective risk communication permeates all four emergency management functions—mitigation, preparedness, response, and recovery. Emergency managers, environmental authorities, and public health officials engage in a wide variety of activities to assess and reduce environmental hazards in their communities. These local officials need to be effective in communicating the results of these activities so that their constituents can understand what actions are being taken to protect them and what actions they need to take to protect themselves. However, risk communication should not be restrictively viewed as existing solely between environmental authorities and citizens. It also can be established between anyone knowledgeable about environmental hazards and any other stakeholders, including businesspeople, government officials, environmental activists, risk area residents, and plant workers.

People's attentiveness to risk communication varies across the four phases of emergency management. Decades ago, Fritz (1968) observed that most of the money and resources for emergency management are expended in connection with response and recovery activities. This is consistent with a cycle, well known to disaster researchers and emergency management professionals, of citizen and governmental interest in disasters. Immediately after impact, the attention of both the public and elected officials is riveted on the physical devastation and social disruption

(May, 1985; May & Williams, 1985). Although considerable resources are made available, the compelling needs at that time are shelter, food, clothing, and financial aid for victims and the clearance of debris and physical restoration of infrastructure and critical facilities in the community. However, public attention declines significantly as time passes and, because considerable time is required to translate public concern into government budget allocations and coherent programs, many mitigation and preparedness programs have simply failed to be implemented (Birkland, 1997; Prater & Lindell, 2000).

In particular, risk communication that emphasizes mitigation activities is at an inherent disadvantage because these are protective measures that have, at best, a very long-term payoff. They are actions for those at risk to take far in advance of disaster impact, either in response to a previous disaster or after the community has been found to be vulnerable to a particular hazard. Interestingly, in the history of attempts at emergency management in the United States, the smallest proportion of resources seems to be devoted to mitigation activities. Like mitigation measures, preparedness activities are conducted or undertaken in advance of a particular disaster event, providing capabilities for protecting life and property when disasters do strike. Preparedness activities, like mitigation activities, have historically received significantly less support than response and recovery activities.

In summary, two points should be reiterated regarding emergency management activities. First, although the distinctions among them are not sharp, the four activities are noticeably time phased. Mitigation and preparedness measures take place in advance of any specific disaster impact, whereas response takes place during and recovery occurs following disaster impact. Therefore, practical problems accompany risk communication regarding mitigation and preparedness strategies because such communication must usually be accomplished during periods of normal activity, when environmental threats are not a high priority. Historical evidence indicates that it has been difficult to mount efforts to engage in these sorts of activities (Rossi, Wright, Webber-Burdin, Pietras, & Diggins, 1982). Response and recovery take place in the context of a disaster impact—clearly an unusual time—and benefit from the operation of an emergency social system, as well as from the high level of community cohesiveness that usually emerges in the short-range aftermath of such an event (Fritz, 1961b).

The second point is that previous research indicates that far more resources have been allocated to response and recovery activities than to mitigation and preparedness. To a certain extent, this differential emphasis has been a function of the difficulty citizens and political officials have in maintaining a high level of concern about disasters during times when they seem so remote. To do so requires that both citizens and officials dwell on negative events that might or might not occur sometime in the future—a task that is almost universally regarded as unpleasant and thus elicits procrastination. Consequently, risk communicators should be aware that the timing of a message might be as important as its content, because there typically is only a brief window of opportunity that is opened by a *focusing event* (Birkland, 1997) that puts vulnerability to environmental hazards on the political agenda (Prater & Lindell, 2000).

It also is important to recognize the limitations posed by the state of technical knowledge regarding various hazards, because this constrains the types of mitigation and preparedness activities that can be undertaken. If disaster onset cannot be detected or if the technology for doing so is crude (as in the case of predicting earthquakes and volcanic eruptions), some response actions such as evacuation may be precluded and the corresponding preparedness measures rendered unnecessary. Thus, in the past it might not have been possible to devote resources to anything other than response and recovery.

In cases where forewarning is not possible, mitigation is essential—regardless of the difficulty. For these and other reasons, the Federal Emergency Management Agency (FEMA) has adopted a more aggressive emphasis on mitigation, particularly since 1995 (Allbaugh, 2002; Witt, 1995). The more aggressive stance has included, for example, the allocation of mitigation funds to the purchase of property located in floodplains, thus allowing vulnerable areas to revert to less intensive uses. This policy is supported by cost-benefit analyses indicating that carefully researched mitigation measures can be considerably less expensive than policies based on disaster relief, which involve redistributing losses following an event but do nothing to decrease hazard vulnerability. Government acquisition of property in high hazard areas is particularly important for properties suffering repetitive losses, where some flood insurance policyholders have rebuilt substantially damaged homes as many as five times or more. Here, as well, risk communication is needed to develop the support of local voters and politicians for property acquisition and to convince the property owners to sell.

The important differences between the imminent threat associated with response and recovery and the long-term threat associated with mitigation and preparedness—especially the significant differences in the behavior that risk communicators should expect from those at risk—suggest that there should be corresponding differences in the risk communication processes associated with these two different types of situations. This dichotomy between imminent and long-term threats does not imply that two completely different theories are needed to guide risk communication for these threats. In fact, most of the same theoretical principles are relevant to both situations, so a single theoretical model can account for short-term warning response and long-term hazard adjustment. Nonetheless, each of these situations requires some specific modifications of the overall model. For this reason—and because researchers have traditionally segregated their

Figure 1.2 Classical Persuasion Model

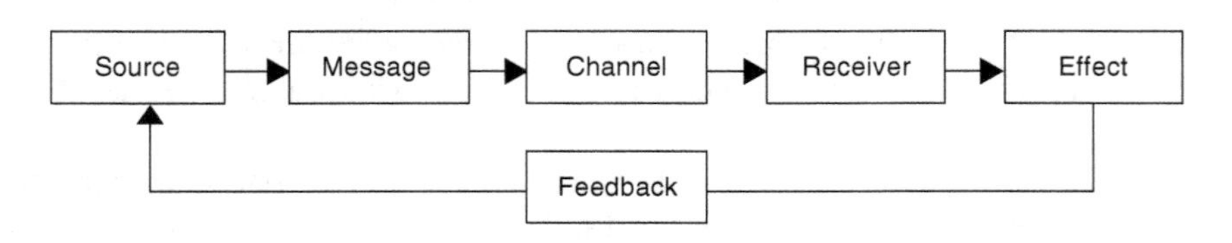

research along these lines—the treatment of risk communication in this volume deals with disaster warning and hazard adjustment in separate chapters.

❖ RISK COMMUNICATION, ETHNICITY, AND CULTURE

According to Lasswell (1948), all communication should be analyzed in terms of who (Source) says what (Message), via what medium (Channel), to whom (Receiver), and directed at what kind of change (Effect). This Classical Persuasion Model, which is depicted in Figure 1.2, was further articulated by Hovland, Janis, and Kelley (1953) and has remained the predominant conceptual approach in the field of communication, and especially research on persuasive communication (McGuire, 1969, 1985; O'Keefe, 1990).

Research guided by this model has found that sources are perceived in terms of two principal characteristics, expertise and trustworthiness, as well as others such as status, likability, and attractiveness. *Expertise* is defined by information about the situation and about cause-and-effect relationships in the environment. By contrast, *trustworthiness* refers to a source's willingness and ability to provide accurate information and take actions that protect the receiver without seeking hidden advantage for himself or herself.

Messages vary in a large number of ways that will be discussed more thoroughly in Chapter 2. Very briefly, however, these include style (clarity, forcefulness, speed of delivery, and the use of figurative or humorous language), inclusions and omissions (of a person's own arguments, rebuttals of opponents' arguments, and/or implicit or explicit conclusions), ordering of message contents, and amount of message material (McGuire, 1985).

The information channels available for use include print media such as newspapers, magazines, and brochures; electronic media such as television, radio, telephone, and the Internet; and face-to-face interaction through personal conversations and public meetings. The distinctions among these information channels are important because the channels differ in the ways in which they accommodate the information processing activities of the receivers. For example, orally presented information is ephemeral and will be lost unless otherwise recorded, whereas written information inherently provides a record that can be referred to at a later time. Moreover, many types of risk information can be presented in a verbal, numeric, or graphic format. Sometimes one mode of presentation is more effective for a particular type of information, but there are individual differences among receivers so that some presentation modes are effective for some people but not others.

Receivers differ in many respects, but the most important of these respects are psychological characteristics that have direct effects on the communication process. For example, receivers differ in their perceptions of source credibility, access to communication channels, prior beliefs about hazards and protective actions, ability to understand and remember message content, and access to resources needed to implement protective action. The effects of a message on a receiver include attention, comprehension, acceptance, retention, and behavioral change. Indeed, researchers agree that message effects should be characterized in terms of multiple stages—but the boundaries of these stages are not well defined, so differences exist among various researchers in their typologies and some theorists have varied in their definitions of these stages over time (McGuire, 1969, 1985).

Finally, feedback is an important component of the communication model because some attempts are unidirectional, whereas others are interactive. Unidirectional communications are appealing to many risk communicators because they appear to be less time consuming—and sometimes this actually is the case. Frequently, however, interactive communication is needed for receivers to indicate that they have not comprehended the message that has been sent or that what was sent by the source did not satisfy their information needs.

The Classical Persuasion Model makes it clear that risk communication is an activity with relatively clearly defined parameters regarding source, message, channel, and intended effect. In most cases, the source is an authority, the message focuses on environmental risk, and the intended effect is a change in receivers' behavior. However, receiver characteristics have very important influences on each of the stages in the communication process. For example, the effect of a given information source is determined by receivers' perceptions of that source and the effect of a given message is determined by receivers' willingness to attend to and ability to comprehend and retain the information. Moreover, the effect of a given channel is determined by receivers' access to and preference for that channel, and the amount of feedback depends on receivers' willingness to attend to and ability to provide it. Unfortunately, authorities often fail to recognize the importance of these factors and sometimes fail to design risk communication programs in accordance with the principles of effective communication even when these issues are recognized (Perry & Lindell, 1991).

It is important to recognize that some scholars (e.g., Kasperson & Stallen, 1991) have criticized the classical persuasion model as providing an incomplete

Figure 1.3 Communication Network Model

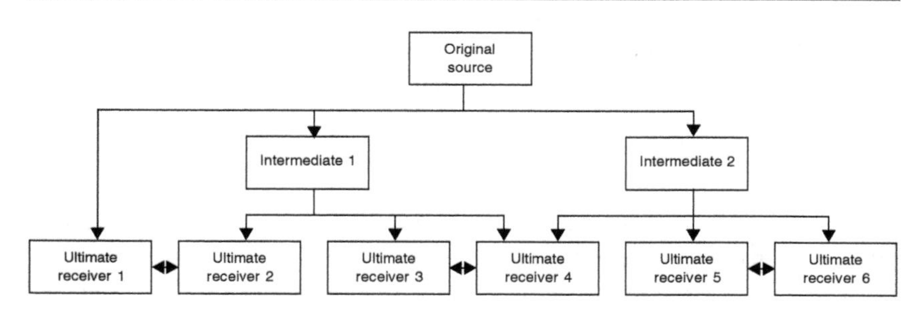

representation of the risk communication process. The major limitation of the model is that the feedback loop in it implies a dyadic relationship that is limited to contact with the original information source. In fact, people often engage in information-seeking activities that are directed to other sources as well. More generally, risk communication should be represented by a network in which there are multiple sources that are linked to the ultimate receivers through intermediates that receive information and relay it to the ultimate receivers (Figure 1.3). The original sources could be linked to few or many intermediates and, indeed, could be linked directly with some of the ultimate receivers. Similarly, the intermediates could be linked to few or many of the ultimate receivers and the ultimate receivers could be linked to each other.

Another apparent limitation of the Classical Persuasion Model is that receiver characteristics have pervasive effects on the other components of the model. Thus, receiver characteristics are of critical importance in determining the success of risk communication programs, but many of them are psychological in nature and thus not readily observed. Nonetheless, receivers do have some readily identifiable characteristics—such as sex, age, education, income, race, and ethnicity—that are related to relevant psychological characteristics and can therefore provide some indications as to how receivers will respond. One particularly important demographic characteristic is ethnicity, because it provides an indication about receivers' cultural background and, thus, their beliefs, values, and social norms. The term *culture* is often used as a broad label for a variety of receiver characteristics, although the logic for attributing differences in interpretation of risk communications to culture is not often elaborated (Johnson, 1991). Indeed, one prominent treatise managed to address the role of culture in risk communication without ever explicitly defining the term *culture* (Douglas & Wildavsky, 1982). The following discussion makes explicit a definition and vision of culture, its connection to ethnicity, and the notion of risk communication in a multiethnic community.

The Cultural Context

Definitions of culture vary widely and anthropologists—to whose discipline culture is a central construct—have long argued about its precise meaning (Oliver-Smith, 1996, 1998). There remains much controversy over whether culture is primarily cognitive in nature and thus should be defined as shared meaning (Geertz, 1973; Sahlins, 1976) or is principally a function of material objects and relations (Harris, 1979). Indeed, anthropologists' consensus regarding the definition of culture is only slightly greater now than it was a half-century ago when Kroeber and Kluckhohn (1952) identified 164 different definitions of culture.

The problem of risk communication does not require all of the fine distinctions made by anthropologists. Instead, a definition of culture used in interpersonal (Gudykunst, 1998) and intercultural (Gudykunst & Kim, 1997) communication may be adopted here. Specifically, Keesing (1974) has defined *culture* as

> a system of competence shared in its broad design and deeper principles . . . a system of knowledge, shaped and constrained by the way the human brain acquires, organizes, and processes information and creates "internal models of reality." (p. 89)

In this definition, culture consists of shared beliefs that encompass both people's interpretations of the world and their notions of how one deals with (responds to and attempts to influence) that world. Gudykunst and Kim (1997) have contended that culture is the individual's "theory of the 'game being played' in our society . . . [which tells us] how to communicate with others and how to interpret their behavior" (p. 17).

When talking about ways in which risk communication is shaped, there are several ways in which the impacts of culture need to be made explicit. One of the most important of these is that culture implies small, but not necessarily zero, variation among individuals who are said to share a given culture. Cultural norms are essentially *guidelines* for how one should and should not behave, with the distinction that norms are based in morality (Gudykunst, 1998, p. 42). Olsen (1978) has pointed out that "culture influences and guides—but does not fully determine—people's collective activities by providing them with interpretations of social life, role expectations, common definitions of situations, and social norms" (p. 107). Consequently, cultures are heterogeneous and it is not reasonable to expect that all individuals sharing a culture will interpret or behave in precisely the same fashion.

Another important aspect of this conception of culture is that it usually refers to a system of knowledge shared by a fairly large number of people. That is, cultures are commonly seen as coinciding generally (though not exclusively) with political boundaries between countries and, thus, are often associated with nationalities. However, collections of people representing different cultural systems often coexist within national boundaries. Such groupings are traditionally called *subcultures*, although subcultural identification is not just dependent on variations in culture as defined here; one can also talk about ethnic subcultures, computer user subcultures, and student subcultures, as well as elderly subcultures and others. Gudykunst and Kim (1997) have defined a subculture as a "set of shared symbolic ideas held by a collectivity within a larger society"(p. 18). In one sense, subcultures represent a means of viewing a society and subunits such as communities in terms of a socially significant variable. Subcultures may be defined along a variety of dimensions, but one of the most significant of these for risk communication is ethnicity. Yinger (1994) has described the following three characteristics of ethnicity, each of which is sufficient to define membership in an ethnic group: (1) others in the society perceive group members to be different, (2) members identify themselves as different, and (3) members participate in shared activities related to their perceived common origin or culture (p. 3). National origin, race, and religion all meet these conditions, so ethnic groups are often defined in terms of these variables (Gudykunst & Kim, 1997). However, it is important to recognize that race is defined by anatomical differences, whereas ethnicity is defined by cultural differences. Because the variables that influence risk communication are cultural rather than biological, ethnicity—not race—is the focus here.

When focusing on communities within the same society, ethnicity can be seen as an important explanatory variable, capturing a variety of cultural and ancestral influences on individuals. *Community* is used here in the sociological (not political) sense, to mean a group of individuals ("insiders") who identify and interact with each other more than they do with others ("outsiders"), and this usually takes place within a geographically localized human settlement. The notion of ethnic subcultures provides a rationale for grouping individuals in terms of both their cultural history and traditions and their individual expressions of their history and traditions. Wong (1999) has noted that accounting for ethnicity when studying the United States involves identifying within-community variation due to traditions and worldviews that have arisen from factors such as ancestral nationality or local history. This issue has been voiced in a variety of contexts, but it is exemplified by concerns expressed when Mexican Americans and Cuban Americans are combined in the single ethnic category of "Hispanic" (Boswell & Curtis, 1984). Gudykunst (1998) has pointed out that all panethnic terms imply the homogeneity of the groups included under the term and are consequently misleading and may veil both national variation and cultural variation (p. 84). Although it is important to be attentive to these "aggregation errors," general knowledge of ethnic subcultures is useful in enabling analysts to view a constellation of influences of culture, race, and national ancestry. It is not appropriate, and perhaps not possible, to develop rigid rules regarding the number or types of ethnic subcultures that an analyst "should" identify when characterizing a particular community or society. Instead, it should be expected that, within a given society, the number and types of ethnic groups vary across communities.

Ethnic subcultures clearly operate within the context of the larger culture. Indeed, Gudykunst (1998) has observed that subcultures "are groups within a culture whose members share many of the values of the culture, but also have some values that differ from the larger culture" (p. 43). In addition to value and tradition differences, ethnic subcultures may also be distinguished by distinctive argots or even language. Like cultures, however, ethnic subcultures are not entirely homogeneous; there is variation among members within a subculture regarding adherence to and endorsement of subcultural norms and values. As Feldman (1999) has indicated, "people make up their lives as they go along" (p. 44), thus introducing situational variants in behavior, values, and attitudes that can change over time and make an individual distinct from the rest of his or her group. Hence, the degree of ethnic identification—a person's commitment to and exhibition of ethnicity—can vary. Ethnicity is a part of an individual's social identity that can be embraced in varying degrees by different ethnic group members; to the extent that an individual is conscious of ethnic customs, symbols, traditions, and group membership, that individual's ethnic identity is high and can be expected to influence his or her lifestyle. Alternatively, ethnic identity can be low, as is sometimes observed in new immigrants seeking to assimilate to a new culture and nationality. Indeed, time and the forces of assimilation can minimize or sometimes even "erase" ethnic distinctiveness and identification. It has been argued that many immigrant Americans with European ancestry have lost their specific ethnic identities over the years—they recognize their general heritage but lack a "clear-cut identification with and/or knowledge of a specific European origin" (Lieberson, 1985, p. 159).

This raises the question of how ethnic and other cultural differences are viewed. *Assimilation* describes the process through which a person gives up one culture while adopting another, whereas *pluralism* describes a condition where individuals retain ethnic identity—producing a community in which many different cultural traditions coexist. The terms *assimilation* and *pluralism* have specific scientific meanings, but they have also acquired evaluative connotations. The notion of assimilation implies an increasingly homogeneous society in which immigrants abandon past cultural ways to adopt new ones. The view of the United States as a "melting pot" for many cultures expresses an extreme form of assimilation that is currently embraced by very few because empirical evidence supporting homogeneity is sparse, and also because immigration continues to widen variation even as assimilation narrows it. A pluralist vision of American society is more widely embraced and much emphasis has been placed on respecting cultural differences; a variety of ethnic subcultures coexist and are mutually accepted, even if they cannot be said to interact in perfect harmony. In general, the pluralist model provides a better description of American society than does the assimilationist model. This is especially true if one allows for the individual variation associated with ethnic identification, meaning that individuals sometimes choose to assimilate—temporarily or permanently—with groups with which they have no ancestral ties. Of course, the notion that ethnic subcultures are "accepted" is equivocal, since evidence suggests that prejudice and discrimination still exist both between majority and minority groups and among minority groups (Bonilla-Silva, 1999). Certainly, the simple presence of ethnic subcultures is less equivocal. Bond (1999) has pointed out that "almost all contemporary nations are de facto multicultural" (p. 20). For our discussion, the terms *multiethnic* and *multicultural* will both be treated as indicating the presence of multiple ethnic subcultures.

The picture of a multiethnic community is potentially complex. At one level, outsiders can identify candidates for membership in ethnic subcultures on the basis of exhibited cues, including anatomical features, language, dress, lifestyle, and family name. The extent of participation in an ethnic subculture is also subject to identification, but it is an individual preference that might not be easy for a risk communicator to identify. As we argue in Chapter 4, however, risk communicators do not need to identify all of the ethnic groups that exist in a community and classify the ethnicity of all community members with perfect accuracy. The needs of risk communication in environmental hazard management require only that ethnic subcultures be identified phenotypically and in terms of traditional categories. Subtle subcultural distinctions could be made, but few are needed for effective risk communication. As will be seen below, the crucial ethnic distinctions needed by risk communicators are defined by the risk communication model.

Ethnic Subcultures and Risk Communication

With respect to risk communication within a given community, ethnic subcultures form a context whose importance stems from two lines of reasoning, both of which are supported by empirical studies. First, ethnic groups vary in terms of cultural traditions that have implications for risk communication (Vaughn & Nordenstam, 1991). These include differential expectations of family and family role obligations that may be manifested in many ways, such as extended family households (McAdoo, 1999). Household structures are important because language mastery has been found to affect the speed and effectiveness with which people respond to disaster warning messages. Thus, people's safety can be endangered in the absence of a readily available bilingual person in a household containing many members who do not understand the language used in a warning (Lindell & Perry, 1992; Perry, Lindell, & Greene, 1982a). However, ethnicity can also affect the success of risk communication in more subtle ways. For example, definitions of kin and household structure have been shown to affect the likelihood that families will even receive hazard-relevant information (Smith & Johnson, 1988), as well as the ways in which they perceive and interpret danger and environmental uncertainty (Mirowsky & Ross, 1980; Turner & Kiecolt, 1984; Weber & Hsee, 1998; Wright & Phillips, 1980).

Another important aspect of culture used to explain intercultural differences is the concept of "individualism-collectivism" (Triandis, 1995; see also Gudykunst, 1998). In general, individualist cultures are those in which individual goals are emphasized over group goals, while collectivist cultures reverse this priority. For example, the United States is an individualist culture and Japan is usually classified as collectivist. In individualist cultures, individuals are generally seen as responsible for themselves and their immediate families, while in collectivist cultures, individuals are seen as having a personal loyalty to the group (collective), which is responsible for caring for the individual (Hofstede & Bond, 1984). While macrosocial concepts like individualism-collectivism cannot provide deterministic predictions of individual behavior (Gudykunst, 1998), they can be indicative of individual tendencies. For example, Perry and Hirose (1991), in comparing warning response behavior in Japan and the United States, found that Japanese are more likely to feel a sense of responsibility to a larger number and range of family and friends (the collective) when relaying warning information than are Americans. Thus, to the extent that subcultures reflect such cultural characteristics as individualism and collectivism, it may be anticipated that similar beliefs would arise among Japanese Americans who strongly identify with their ethnic heritage.

A second line of reasoning associated with the importance of ethnic subcultures for risk communication lies in the extent to which ethnicity is associated with other personal characteristics that affect the individual's risk environment. In the United States particularly, ethnicity is related to income and education (Wilkson, 1999), which, in turn, influence housing quality and location, access to community resources, preference for communication channels, and ability to comprehend environmental threats in the context of scientific information. It has been reported, for example, that ethnic minorities tend to experience higher levels of deaths, injuries, and property loss in disasters, which is attributed to their higher probability of living in less disaster-resistant structures and in areas more prone to disaster impacts such as floodplains or proximal to hazardous materials transport and storage facilities (Blaikie et al., 1994; Bolin & Bolton, 1986; Hershiser & Quarantelli, 1976; Ives & Furuseth, 1980; Perry, 1987; Trainer & Hutton, 1972). More hazardous areas and structures are often accepted because they are more affordable than safer locations and structures. Furthermore, in connection with hazard awareness programs, Perry and Nelson (1991) found that ethnic groups differed in their access to and preferences for message channels that were more likely to contain information disseminated by government.

It has also long been known that there is a difference in the way that American minority and majority citizens assess the credibility of warning sources, and that this difference exists both between minority and majority groups and among minority groups (Lindell & Perry, 1992; Perry & Lindell, 1987). There is also evidence that ethnicity is related to warning responses (Drabek, 1983; Dynes & Quarantelli, 1976; Perry, 1979a).

Research also indicates that ethnic minority groups are less likely than the majority to be aware of and apply for the range of governmental assistance available following disasters (Girard & Peacock, 1997), as well as less likely to be immersed in community networks through which information about hazards and disaster assistance flow (Cohen & Kapsis, 1978; Georgas, 1999; Midlarsky, 1968; Olsen, 1970). They also differ in their patterns of resource seeking and norms regarding the acceptance of help during recovery and mitigation activities (Bolin, 1976; Bolin & Bolton, 1986; Peacock & Girard, 1997).

Developing a Theory-Based Approach

In summary, there is empirical evidence that ethnic subcultures vary systematically in ways that affect the process and outcomes of risk communication. This observation raises fundamental questions regarding how ethnic subcultural differences should be integrated into both the knowledge of and management of environmental hazards. The first issue concerns the scientific meaning of the findings themselves. Are we dealing with real differences among ethnic groups? Statistically significant differences have been found between ethnic groups in the few studies that have examined this variable, but the number of studies is small. Moreover, when ethnicity has been included in such studies, measurement of the concept has been crude and respondents' ethnicity was simply included as another variable to be correlated with disaster response or hazard adjustment. In many of these studies, ethnicity appears to be acting as a surrogate or proxy variable that spuriously captures variance that should have been properly attributed to causal variables that are correlated with ethnicity. Thus, controls for other relevant variables, such as income and education, have been neglected because researchers have failed to use this variable in multivariate, multistage models that make it possible to explain the mediating mechanisms by which ethnicity affects hazard adjustment and disaster response (Lindell & Perry, 1992; Perry & Lindell, 1991; Perry et al., 1981). To understand the impact of ethnicity on risk communication and people's subsequent adoption of protective behaviors, it is important to map the processes through which ethnicity exerts its effects on hazard adjustment and disaster response. Although the studies cited above provide many useful ideas about the role of ethnicity in all four phases of emergency management, there is another study, by Perry and Montiel, that illustrates the need for carefully analyzing the presumed effects of ethnicity through the use of multivariate models. Perry and Montiel's (1997) study of ethnic minority members' response to a flood risk communication program found that formal education obtained in the United States mediated Mexican American's understanding of environmental risk information. Specifically, those with higher levels of education tended to rate levels of risk from flooding conveyed in a specific message more similarly to environmental hazard managers than those with lower levels of education. Thus, the results of this study indicate that statistically controlling for the confounding effect of education shifted the likely locus of causality from ethnicity to education.

Finally, even though observed ethnic differences are real, it remains to be determined whether those differences significantly affect the outcomes of risk communication. Normally, the sparseness of data on a given topic can be compensated for by looking to broader theories as a means of answering significant questions. In the case of ethnicity and environmental hazards, the theories are almost as sparse as the empirical data. We contend that to sort out the issues of ethnicity in communicating the risks of environmental hazards and determine what this relationship means for environmental hazard management, it is necessary to create a theoretical framework that provides a basis for interpreting the data that do exist and for determining what new data are needed. To accomplish this goal, we will focus on the task of risk communication in two specific risk communication situations, short-term warning response and long-term hazard adjustment. In examining these situations, we will integrate the effects of a wide variety of factors—including ethnicity—into our conceptual framework. Ultimately, the goal of this book is to accomplish three objectives. First, based on a range of existing theories and empirical studies, we will articulate a theory of decision making called the Protective Action Decision Model (PADM) as an explanation of protective response to the hazards of environmental extremes. Second, we will use this framework to carefully examine the empirical literature and show how the PADM can address individuals' decisions to comply with disaster warnings and to adopt hazard adjustments. Finally, we will use the theory, guided by empirical findings, to illuminate strategies for environmental hazard managers to use in promoting both emergency response and long-term hazard adjustment.

2

Theoretical Bases of Risk Communication

We have argued that risk communication is a process that should have the clearly defined purpose of sharing information about an environmental hazard that can be used to protect those at risk. In some cases, this means that authorities will attempt to influence those at risk to undertake individual protective action. In other cases, those who consider themselves to be at risk will attempt to persuade authorities to take collective protective actions. We also have described the risk communication process in terms of the Classical Persuasion Model (with its four components of Source, Channel, Message, and Receiver) and the environment in which messages are sent and received, especially the presence of ethnic subcultures.

To understand the way in which risk communication affects the protective response process requires theory, but many pronouncements have been made regarding what theories are and how they relate to models. As in all things academic, there is much variation among alternative definitions of the terms, in this case, *theory* and *model*. However, there is a general agreement on the utility of Kaplan's (1964) view of theory as a deductively structured collection of propositions (interrelating concepts or variables as determinants and results) whose purpose is to explain one or more phenomena (Bunge, 1998). Some scholars have attempted to differentiate theories from models (Reynolds, 1971), but for the most part a model has the same basic structure and goals as a theory (Blalock, 1969; Brodbeck, 1968). Since risk communication and not philosophy of science is the topic of interest here, we will use the terms *model* and *theory* interchangeably.

One crucial function of theory is to create a parsimonious explanation, that is, one that explains a phenomenon with the smallest number of variables and assumptions. One implication of parsimony is that theory should isolate the most specific variables that account for or cause other variables. Consequently, we will look for psychological variables that mediate the correlations of communication components and demographic variables with protective action. For example, we want to understand what beliefs, values, and norms account for differences in ethnic groups with regard to protective action and incorporate those variables into our theory. Measuring the variables that intervene between ethnicity and protective action will not cause ethnicity to disappear completely from the model. However, it will clarify the differences among ethnic groups in their responses to risk communication and will avoid the necessity for devising a separate theory of risk communication for each ethnic group. The latter tactic would, at a minimum, ignore the fact that commonalities exist across ethnic subcultures in the same society and also would violate basic scientific principle of parsimony. Thus, our approach will be to understand the protective action adoption process well enough to characterize the commonalities in all individuals, while at the same time taking into account any distinctions that must be made to accommodate ethnic subcultural variations.

In this chapter, we will examine theories that are relevant to risk communication and protective action, encompassing those situations that involve near-term or imminent threats (disaster response) and those that address long-term or chronic threats (hazard adjustment). In so doing, we hope to explain three related issues—what people believe about environmental hazards, the consequences of those beliefs for individuals' adoption of protective actions, and how such beliefs are affected by risk communication variables. Historically, risk communication, risk perception, and protective action adoption have been only loosely linked in the research literature, so it is necessary to develop an integrative theoretical framework that encompasses all of them. Our review of theoretical models therefore will begin with a brief discussion of research on social influence, focusing on persuasive communication and conformity. Next, we will examine literatures dealing with behavioral evaluation and choice, especially behavioral decision theory, attitude-behavior relationships, and information seeking. Then, we will review theories that integrate cognitive and behavioral processes, including theories of protective action and innovation. The final section will show how the Protective Action Decision Model (PADM) integrates the concepts from these literatures through a theoretical structure that explains individual protective action decisions in the context of situational variables, such as the environmental cues and social context. This model then becomes the basis for evaluating the process of risk communication. The next two chapters examine the empirical literature with respect to communicating disaster warnings and hazard awareness.

❖ SOCIAL INFLUENCE

Social influence is most prevalent when people lack opportunities to learn directly from their physical environment (Festinger, 1957). When the physical environment is complex or rapidly changing and supplies only subtle cues for predicting threats to people and property, physical reality testing tends to give way to social reality testing. That is, people are less able to test the appropriateness of their actions in terms of accuracy in predicting important events in their physical environment, so they try to assess the need for protective action in terms of agreement with important people in their social environment.

The literature on social influence indicates that people's actions can be affected by one of two means: informational influence and normative influence (Turner, 1991). *Informational influence* reflects personal acceptance or internalization of information as a valid description of objective reality. By contrast, *normative influence* reflects compliance with the expectations of others, based on their power to reward or punish. The role of informational influence has been addressed primarily in research on persuasive communication, whereas the role of normative influence has been addressed in research on conformity.

Persuasive Communication

As noted in the previous chapter, the use of persuasive communication—informational influence—has a long history of use as a technique to change attitudes and behaviors (McGuire, 1969, 1985). The classical approach to the study of persuasive communication is to view it in terms of a series of inputs and outputs, where the input or independent variable is the persuasive communication, and the output or dependent variable is attitude or behavior change. A recently developed alternative perspective on persuasion, the Elaboration Likelihood Model, was proposed by Petty and Cacioppo (1986a, 1986b, 1990), who postulated that people subjected to persuasive messages process information, and thus change attitudes, using two routes. The first route is the central route, in which the person attends to and is influenced more by the cognitive contents of the message. The second route is the peripheral route, in which a person attends to and is influenced more by superficial cues available in the persuasive context (e.g., the attractiveness of an information source). The Elaboration Likelihood Model postulates that people are motivated to hold correct attitudes, and it implies that individual differences in message processing arise from people's ability and willingness to think about the arguments in the message. This suggests that in situations of low threat (e.g., pre-impact hazard awareness), there will be some people who take the threat seriously and process the contents of risk messages, but there will be others who will be influenced by superficial cues. However, one would expect an increase in the amount of central processing of warning messages in situations of moderate threat (e.g., a hazard onset with substantial forewarning such as hurricane), but a decrease in the amount of central processing of warning messages in situations of high threat (e.g., a hazard onset with minimal forewarning, such as tornado or flash flood). Another significant finding from research on the Elaboration Likelihood Model is that repetition has been found to initially increase and then decrease agreement with a message. The increase comes from having additional opportunities to process the message, but a decrease occurs when tedium sets in.

A somewhat similar model has been proposed by Chaiken (Chaiken, 1980, 1987; Chaiken, Liberman, & Eagly, 1989), whose Heuristic Model of persuasion distinguishes between systematic processing (i.e., influence due to cognitive elaboration of the persuasive augmentation) and heuristic processing (i.e., attitude change due to invoking heuristics such as "experts can be trusted" and "more arguments are better"). She contended that heuristic and systematic processing are parallel rather than mutually exclusive processes and that receiver factors (such as inattention, anxiety, or lack of the knowledge required to comprehend arguments) tend to impede systematic information processing more than they do heuristic processing. Moreover, some of the factors that impede recipients' ability to process the information may also adversely affect their motivation to try to comprehend it.

These information processing approaches to persuasion also report that people who have pre-existing organized knowledge structures (known as *schemas*) regarding an issue tend to counterargue messages that disagree with their existing beliefs and to bolster messages that are congruent with their beliefs. Moreover, if recipients are told in advance that they will receive a message that disagrees with their attitude toward an issue, they use the period between the receipt of the warning and the actual message to rehearse counterarguments to the anticipated message content. Most important, these information processing theories demonstrate that attitude changes resulting from the central route (processing issue-relevant arguments) are more persistent over time, more accurately predict behavior, and are more resistant to counterpersuasion than are attitude changes resulting from the peripheral route. Petty and Cacioppo (1986a, 1986b) have attributed the superiority of central processing to the fact that the issue-relevant attitude schema can be accessed, rehearsed, and manipulated more times. This strengthens the interconnections among the components and renders the schema more internally consistent, accessible, enduring, and resistant than is the case when persuasion is addressed via the peripheral route. In particular, attitudes derived from personal experience are more predictive of behavior, probably because personal experience involves more central processing of the information. This effect is consistent with other evidence showing that vivid verbal descriptions of single cases have more impact on people's decisions than do pallid statistical data about a large sample of cases, even when the latter are far more diagnostic (Feldman & Lindell, 1990). Here as well, the explanation seems to be that a more vivid description produces a more elaborate cognitive representation at the time of message reception. In turn, the more elaborate cognitive representation is more likely to remain salient and to produce further thought and discussion. Moreover, because these attitudes are more readily retrieved when an opportunity arises for relevant action, the correlation between attitudes and behavior is stronger.

Another important issue in persuasion research is the identification of factors that influence the response at each stage, especially what motivates people to continue to think about the message, to seek additional information, and to take action. One key explanatory variable is known as *personal involvement* or *perceived relevance* (Johnson & Eagly, 1989; Petty & Cacioppo, 1990).

Research on persuasion theory can be summarized by the following propositions that are relevant to risk communication:

1. The risk communication process can be conceptualized in terms of the classical persuasion model of Source-Message-Channel-Receiver-Effect-Feedback.

2. The effectiveness of risk information sources varies with their credibility, that is, their perceived expertise and trustworthiness.

3. Risk communication messages vary with respect to a number of different characteristics, including style (clarity, forcefulness, and speed of delivery, and the use of figurative or humorous language), inclusions and omissions (of a person's own arguments, rebuttals of opponents' arguments, and/or implicit or explicit conclusions), ordering of message contents, and amount of message material (repetition and number of different arguments).

4. The ability of a risk information channel to provide a record of the communication can have a significant effect on the retention of information and, thus, its long-term impact.

5. Receivers differ in many ways that affect all stages of the risk communication process, including perceptions of source credibility, message comprehension, channel preferences, and willingness to provide feedback.

6. The cognitive processing of risk communication takes place in stages, beginning with exposure to a message, and followed by attention, comprehension, acceptance, and action.
7. People tend to interpret new information about risk in terms of preexisting schemas, counterarguing messages that disagree with these schemas and bolstering messages that agree with them.
8. People who expect risk communication messages that disagree with their current positions on an issue devote attentional resources to rehearsing counterarguments, which can prevent them from attending to incoming information.
9. Some characteristics of risk information sources affect message acceptance through central processing (e.g., expertise and trustworthiness), whereas other characteristics affect acceptance through peripheral processing (e.g., attractiveness).
10. Source characteristics have their greatest effects under conditions of low motivation (e.g., low personal relevance) and low ability (high distraction, high time pressure, or low message comprehensibility) for systematic processing.
11. Message length, number of persuasive arguments, and reactions of others have greater effects under conditions of low motivation and ability for systematic processing.
12. Attitude changes resulting from systematic processing are more persistent over time, more consistent with behavior, and more resistant to attack than those resulting from heuristic processing.
13. A vivid description of a single case often has a greater impact on individuals' judgments than do pallid statistical data about a large sample of cases.
14. Attitudes derived from personal experience are more predictive of behavior than attitudes derived from other sources.
15. The perceived relevance of a risk, and personal involvement with it, motivates people to think more extensively about a risk communication message.
16. Repetition has a nonlinear effect on agreement with risk communication messages.

Social Conformity

The findings of research on bystander intervention indicate that people are uncertain how to react to ambiguous situations even when these appear to be threatening (Latané & Darley, 1970). In such circumstances, the presence of similar others provides social models that help to define what behavior is appropriate, so people are more likely to take emergency action if they see others doing likewise. Conversely, they are less likely to take emergency action when they are with others who fail to act than when they are alone. One of the reasons for this phenomenon is that groups—even groups of strangers—experience forces toward uniformity among members, and these forces can reflect explicit or implicit social pressure (Festinger, 1957). A critical tension exists between physical reality testing and social reality testing, with social reality testing dominating when physical reality testing is not possible. Social reality testing is particularly potent when the core members of a reference group achieve a group consensus on an issue and group members are strongly attracted to the group (Turner, 1991). Compliance with the observed behavior of others can result from either informational influence or normative influence. Informational influence reflects a deep personal acceptance of the validity of the rationale for an action, whereas normative influence reflects a superficial behavioral compliance that is intended to avoid the social pressure that is directed toward anyone who deviates from a group norm. Accordingly, compliance is most common when significant others can observe any deviation and have the power to punish deviance. Indeed, compliance (but not necessarily personal acceptance) with the views of powerful others is sometimes found even when these conflict with physical reality (Asch, 1951). However, pressures toward social conformity are weakened significantly when there is a lack of consensus in the group; in some cases, the agreement of a single other is sufficient to prevent an individual from complying with the views of a dominant majority. Indeed, there are situations in which the minority can change the opinions of the majority through informational influence, especially when their position is obviously superior (a "Eureka" effect; Lorge, Fox, Davitz, & Brenner, 1958) or when members of the minority are consistent in their position over time (Moscovici & Faucheux, 1972).

These findings lead to the following propositions.

1. Social conformity is more likely in ambiguous situations where physical reality testing is not possible.
2. In ambiguous situations, people tend to look to reference groups for guidance on how to respond, but they can be influenced even by total strangers.
3. Compliance is most common when core members of the group can observe any deviation and have the power to punish deviance.
4. Pressures to conform are weakened when the group is divided on how to act.
5. People have the ability to resist pressures to conform when they view themselves, and others view them, as competent and confident individuals rather than just members of the group.

6. An innovative or consistently presented minority opinion can change the beliefs and actions of the majority.

❖ THEORIES OF BEHAVIORAL EVALUATION AND CHOICE

The process by which people choose to take protective action has been approached from two quite different perspectives. The first of these approaches, deductively derived from the axioms of mathematical economics, has examined the degree to which individual decision processes conform to the tenets of normative theory. Studies guided by behavioral decision theory have generally sought to compare observed decision processes to a theoretical standard of how a perfectly rational individual ought to decide. Many early studies within this framework were conducted in laboratory settings to probe the limits of decision makers' cognitive ability to process uncertain information. An alternative approach has sought to assess the correspondence between attitudes and behavior, as well as to identify the variables that influence the strength of this relationship. The studies using this latter approach have a less rigorous theoretical foundation, but many of them have been executed in field settings with research participants who are making consequential life decisions.

Finally, there is research in a third area, information seeking, that has drawn on attitude theory, but it is distinctly different from research on attitude-behavior relations. Instead of focusing on decisions to implement protective actions, research on information seeking emphasizes the conditions under which people search for additional information that they believe is needed to justify protective action.

Behavioral Decision Theory

Rational decision theories, which can be traced to Bernoulli's work in the early 18th century, argue that a decision maker should choose among alternative courses of action on the basis of value maximization. As an example, Keeney (1982) called for a decision maker to (1) identify and assess the problem, (2) identify alternative courses of action, (3) assess each alternative with respect to its (subjective) probability of achieving the decision maker's goals, (4) adopt and implement one or more of those alternative actions, and (5) evaluate the implemented actions to assess the degree to which they actually were effective in achieving the decision maker's goals. Thus, a simple theoretical framework for deciding whether to adopt a hazard adjustment such as earthquake insurance would require a decision maker to analyze the ratio of benefits to costs by assessing the probable losses to a given property in a specific year and calculate the relative costs of purchasing insurance in advance versus paying for repairs after the fact (Kunreuther, 2001; Kunreuther et al., 1978). For this *expected value* principle to not only guide the ideal practice but also predict the observed practice, a decision maker must seek to maximize net benefits and possess all the relevant information about costs and benefits. Unfortunately, these conditions apply only in trivial choice situations. Consequently, theorists have developed the Subjective Expected Utility Theory (Edwards, 1954), which relies on subjective rather than objective probabilities and replaces objective values with subjective ones (called *utilities*). However, even with this modification, empirical studies dating back to Friedman and Savage (1948) have shown that decision makers fail to act in conformity with the principles of normative decision theory. Rather, the degree to which decision making is rational seems to be *bounded* by cognitive limitations (Simon, 1957). Decisions regarding hazard mitigation are especially problematic because they must be made under conditions of extreme uncertainty regarding the probability of occurrence, likely impact of disaster, and effectiveness of adjustments. Indeed, Kunreuther and colleagues (1978) found that potential hazard insurance purchasers had inaccurate beliefs about the hazard and about insurance, and that they did not even combine their inaccurate information in accordance with the tenets of utility theory.

Slovic, Kunreuther, and White (1974) assessed the descriptive validity of Subjective Expected Utility Theory in terms of its relevance to the adoption of natural hazards adjustments. The evidence they gathered leads to the conclusion that decision makers tend to rely on standard operating procedures, incremental changes, and short-term feedback (Cyert & March, 1963; Lindblom, 1959; Simon, 1959), which might work well in static environments but are poorly suited to coping with the risks of environmental extremes. Bounded rationality leads people to underestimate the risks of natural hazards and, in turn, leads to underadjustment, followed by a crisis orientation after disaster does strike. Slovic and colleagues (1974) argued that psychological research provides much evidence of decision makers' limited ability to effectively utilize probabilistic information. Specifically, people often misperceive random sequences of data (Jarvik, 1951), believing that if a low probability event has occurred recently, it is unlikely to occur again soon (the gambler's fallacy). In a related phenomenon known as *illusory correlation*, decision makers frequently infer that variables are related even when there is nothing more than a chance relationship between them (Chapman & Chapman, 1969). Decision makers also have an inadequate appreciation for the amount of error and unreliability in small samples of data (Tversky & Kahneman, 1971), leading them to draw conclusions with as much confidence from small samples as from large samples.

After studying such systematic errors, Tversky and Kahneman (1974) concluded that decision makers arrived at judgments of probability through the use of *heuristics,* which are simple cognitive shortcuts that are prone to systematic errors. Since Tversky and Kahneman's initial work, researchers have identified a number of heuristics and conditions under which they are used (for more detailed summaries, see Feldman & Lindell, 1990; Sherman & Corty, 1984; Yates, 1990). One of these heuristics, *representativeness*, refers to the degree to which an event appears to be similar to the category to which it belongs or the process by which it is generated. Conversely, characteristics of the category or underlying process are attributed to the events they generate. For example, environmental phenomena such as the weather tend to be thought of as (and to a significant degree are in fact) periodic. The fact that this periodicity is probabilistic rather than deterministic is less salient or altogether unrecognized. The resulting tendency to think of rare events as occurring in long cycles leads to the well-known misconception of 100-year floods as occurring only at 100-year intervals rather than having a 1% chance of occurrence in any given year.

Another heuristic, *availability*, occurs when judgments of event frequency are determined by the ease of retrieving specific instances from memory. Events that are more easily recalled are judged to be more probable than events that are not easily recalled. The availability heuristic has some validity because more frequent events are more easily recalled, but this heuristic can produce significant errors because factors other than the actual frequency of an event influence recall. These include recency, situational salience, and emotional impact. In addition, availability in memory also can be affected by the vividness of others' descriptions of events. That is, residents who live in an area that is earthquake-prone but lack personal hazard experience would be expected to judge an earthquake as more likely if they have heard earthquake victims' vivid descriptions of their experiences than if they have heard geologists talk about tectonic processes.

Again, it appears that the notion that individuals follow Subjective Expected Utility Theory in calculating the costs and benefits of various alternatives and deciding on some set of rational adaptations to the environment does not fit the empirical reality of decision making. Not only do individuals lack complete knowledge of alternatives, but there are also many other factors, including patterns of consistent "errors" in risk calculation, that affect decision making. The flaws in human decision performance have led to the development of a number of revised theories of human decision making. One of these theories, Prospect Theory, contends that decision problems are solved in phases. In the first phase, one frames a problem in terms of a relevant set of alternative actions and the potential consequences of those alternatives. The set of options is edited by translating the potential consequences of a decision into subjective values and the probabilities of those outcomes into decision weights. The subjective values and decision weights are combined into a prospect value in the second phase, while the third phase uses the prospect value to produce an evaluation (if there is only one alternative) or a choice (if there are two or more prospects).

Despite the fact that a number of aspects of Prospect Theory have been supported in experimental studies (Tversky & Kahneman, 1981, 1986), it has failed to provide a completely satisfactory account of human decision processes (Yates, 1990). Consequently, decision theorists have continued to search for models that better account for the available research results. Another response to the invalidity of Subjective Expected Utility Theory has been to propose contingent decision models (Beach & Mitchell, 1978; Payne, 1982). These models assert that decision makers use complex strategies such as Subjective Expected Utility Theory *only* if the complex strategy's benefits exceed its costs. Specifically, Beach and Mitchell (1978) contended that people's decision strategies could be classified as aided-analytic, unaided analytic, and nonanalytic. *Aided-analytic* strategies are formal procedures involving rigorous methods for formulating a problem and defining the relevant data, as well as precise computational tools for calculating an optimal solution. By contrast, *unaided analytic* strategies rely on insight to identify a problem's most important features, to generate some possible solutions, and to think systematically about the advantages and disadvantages of these solutions and on decision heuristics (rules of thumb) to choose among the alternatives. Finally, *nonanalytic* strategies rely on intuitive processes to classify a relatively familiar situation, which almost automatically elicits simple preformulated rules (e.g., "don't change horses in midstream" to justify a habitual response or "don't make waves" to justify compliance with social convention).

Beach and Mitchell (1978) argued that the strategy applied in a given situation is chosen only after the decision maker has recognized the existence of a problem and evaluated the task to be accomplished. They further proposed that strategy selection was followed by information processing, strategy implementation, and choice of a course of action. This led them to conclude that strategy implementation depends on characteristics of the decision problem, the decision environment, and the decision maker. Characteristics of the decision problem include its familiarity (due to experience); the ambiguity of goals, alternatives, and constraints; the complexity of alternatives and criteria; and the instability of the solution attributes. Characteristics of the decision environment include time and money constraints, decision irreversibility, decision significance, and decision maker accountability. Characteristics of the decision maker include knowledge and ability, as well as the motivation to maximize the accuracy of the decision versus minimizing the time, effort, and resources required to make it. Many of the elements of this model and its more recently elaborated successor (known as Image Theory) have been supported in subsequent research (Beach, 1990; Mitchell & Beach, 1990). Image Theory elaborates on the earlier contingency model in its emphasis on the prevalence of routine or automatic decisions (i.e., nonanalytic strategies) in everyday life.

The relevance of behavioral decision theory to environmental hazard adjustment has received relatively little scrutiny by hazard researchers, although the research on hazard insurance purchase by Kunreuther and colleagues (Kunreuther et al., 1978; Kunreuther, Ginsberg, & Handmer, 1993) is a notable exception. Kunreuther has argued that the way in which people process the complex trade-offs between the probability of the event and its likely outcomes depends on the context of the problem and the mode in which information is communicated. Furthermore, people often weight these dimensions differently than would be suggested by normative models of choice such as Subjective Expected Utility Theory or benefit-cost analysis. Moreover, people's tendency to treat a very low probability as a zero probability is simply a conclusion that "it can't happen to me." These problems with people's decision processes are exacerbated by their "myopic" time horizon for hazard planning, which is usually only a few months or years rather than the actual time of probable exposure to the hazard—perhaps as long as a lifetime (Kunreuther, 1993). Indeed, the widespread failure by homeowners to purchase earthquake insurance is a specific example of what Hogarth and Kunreuther (1993) have labeled "decision-making under ignorance," where both costs and benefits are unknown to the decision maker. In such conditions, these authors argue that "people determine choices by using arguments that do not quantify the risk and may reflect concerns that are not part of standard models of choice under uncertainty" (Hogarth & Kunreuther, 1993, p. 2). Instead, people use arguments to justify their decisions when those decisions seem farfetched or distant from rational models of choice.

Research on behavioral decision theory can be summarized by the following propositions that are relevant to risk communication.

1. People often lack the information needed to make a rational decision about hazard adjustment, yet they fail to seek even the information that is readily available.

2. People have poor conceptions of probability, relying on heuristics such as representativeness and availability to estimate the likelihood of events.

3. Information processing is characterized by bounded rationality—which leads people to *satisfice* by seeking satisfactory outcomes in the short term rather than optimal outcomes over the long term.

4. People's strategies for decision making (analytic, unaided analytic, nonanalytic) depend on the characteristics of the decision problem (especially unfamiliarity), the decision environment (especially irreversibility and significance), and the decision maker (especially motivation to maximize accuracy).

Attitude-Behavior Theory

At one time, the relationships among beliefs, values, attitudes, and behavior were considered to be quite controversial. As recently as 30 years ago, some researchers contended that attitudes were only slightly related or even unrelated to behavior (Wicker, 1969). However, theoretical developments subsequent to Wicker's pessimistic review produced models that provide much more satisfactory levels of behavioral prediction. In particular, Fishbein and Ajzen's (1975; see also Ajzen, 1987, 1991; Fishbein & Stasson, 1990) Theory of Reasoned Action has had an especially significant impact in this area. According to their model, people's volitional behaviors are largely a function of their *behavioral intentions.* Intentions differ from observed behavior largely as a result of unanticipated impediments to the intended action or unexpected circumstances that facilitate unintended behaviors (Triandis, 1980). In turn, people's behavioral intentions are determined by their *attitude toward the behavior* and their *subjective norm* for that behavior. These two determinants of behavioral intentions correspond to the two types of influence, informational and normative, respectively.

Empirical data indicate that people's attitude toward a specific behavior and their subjective norm for that behavior take the form of an expectancy-valence model in which judgments are defined in terms of expected consequences. Specifically, an attitude toward a behavior is defined by the attractiveness (also known as *valence*) of its outcomes, each of which is weighted by its subjective likelihood of occurrence. The higher an alternative is evaluated, the more positive the attitude toward that behavior. Similarly, people's subjective norms reflect their beliefs about how specific others would view their engaging in that behavior, weighted by the decision maker's motivation to comply with each of those others' views. Although not a part of Fishbein and Ajzen's (1975) model, it is clear that some behavior is determined directly by habits that might at one time have been subject to conscious thought but, over repeated occasions, have become automatic processes that can bypass conscious awareness altogether (Eagly & Chaiken, 1993).

There are a number of important characteristics of the Theory of Reasoned Action. First, the initial part of the model—the attitude toward the behavior—is identical in form to earlier expectancy-valence models proposed by Rosenberg (1956) and Vroom (1964), which have had the strongest empirical support among all attitude models (see Kennedy, Fossum, & White, 1983; Wanous, Keon, & White, 1983). Second, acknowledging the subjective norm recognizes the importance of normative (social) influence from others that affects behavior independently of beliefs about the consequences of a behavior. The Theory of Reasoned Action is compatible with Raven's (1965, 1993) findings that legitimate power, expert power, and referent power act on the subjective norm (Fishbein & Ajzen, 1981). That is, other people have normative influence because they are perceived as having a right to expect to have an influence (legitimate power) or because their similarity to the decision maker warrants their consideration as an important frame of reference (referent power). Two other forms of social influence are information power and expert power. Sources have *information power* to the extent that they are perceived as having specialized knowledge that provides relevant data about the state of a person's environment. By contrast, *expert power* is based on a source's perceived ability to explain the *intrinsic* (naturally occurring) consequences of a particular course of action (Raven, 1993). Finally, Raven's two remaining bases of power—*reward power* and *coercive power*—are *extrinsic* consequences that are arbitrarily imposed by another. These extrinsic consequences supplement the intrinsic consequences in influencing a person's attitude toward a behavior.

The Theory of Reasoned Action and other expectancy-valence models often have significant predictive accuracy, but reviews of the research literature have found evidence that such models sometimes fail to provide reasonable predictions of behavior across individuals and situations (Sheppard, Hartwick, & Warshaw, 1988). Such variations in predictability of behavior have led researchers to look for other variables that might affect the relations between people's beliefs and their behavior. One of these factors is the correspondence between the level of specificity of the attitudinal and behavioral measures, with general behaviors (overall hazard adjustment) being best predicted by general attitudes and specific behaviors (insurance purchases) being best predicted by specific attitudes (Perry, 1976). Another factor that improves behavioral prediction is consideration of the conditions under which an attitude has been developed, with attitudes developed from personal experience better predicting behavior than attitudes developed from vicarious experience (Fazio, 1985). Moreover, it is important to recognize that attitudes toward an object (e.g., an earthquake) are not necessarily equivalent to attitudes toward an action in response to that object (e.g., a hazard adjustment such as insurance purchase). Thus, adoption of hazard adjustments would be more accurately predicted by attitudes toward the hazard adjustment than by attitudes toward the hazard itself. Finally, Fishbein and Ajzen have contended that an individual's attitude toward a behavior is a function of the consequences of the behavior that are salient to the respondents, not necessarily the consequences that are salient to an investigator. Similarly, an individual's subjective norm is determined by the people who are salient to the respondent, but these people might be different from those whom the investigator has assumed to be relevant.

One limitation of the Theory of Reasoned Action is that it only describes the attitude toward an act only in terms of very general types of information, such as "salient beliefs" or "the consequences of an act," without specifying the salient beliefs or consequences that people are likely to expect. This is not a flaw in the model, per se; the Theory of Reasoned Action was proposed as a very general model whose details would need to be specified in each area where it was applied.

Research on attitude-behavior relationships can be summarized by the following propositions that are relevant to risk communication:

1. People's behavior is correlated with their intentions, but situational impediments and facilitating conditions distort the relationship; the greater the time interval between the formation of a behavioral intention and the opportunity to act, the lower the likelihood that the behavior will occur.

2. Behavioral intentions are a function of people's attitudes toward that behavior (which are a function of beliefs about the intrinsic consequences of that behavior) and their subjective norms (which are a function of beliefs about significant others' attitudes toward that behavior).

3. Behavioral intentions will be more strongly correlated with actual protective behaviors to the extent that attitudes toward those behaviors are developed from personal rather than vicarious experience and from vivid descriptions rather than statistical data.

4. Behavioral intentions will be more strongly correlated with the perceived characteristics of the behavior than with perceived characteristics of the attitude object.

5. Behavioral intentions will be most strongly correlated with the perceived characteristics of the attitude object and with the perceived characteristics of the behavior that are salient to the individual.

Information Seeking

One reason why people fail to take protective action is that they believe that they lack sufficient information about the hazard or about the protective actions to justify the commitment of time, energy, and money that is required. In such cases, according to Janis and Mann (1977) vigilance is an appropriate coping pattern that could involve monitoring the news media, contacting authorities, or seeking out friends, relatives, neighbors, and coworkers. It is important to recognize that information is often sought out by those at risk who are trying to establish an accurate appraisal of the hazard. However, new information also can be used to provide protection against negative thoughts and feelings stimulated by hazard information. The effect desired by the individual (accuracy or reassurance) corresponds to one of the two types of actions that Lazarus and Folkman (1984) identified as "problem-focused" or "emotion-focused" coping, respectively. The type of goal, together with expectations regarding the likely outcome of information search, affects the sources contacted and the amount and type of information sought. The basic idea underlying selective reception can be illustrated by noting that, unlike systematic processing (which involves unbiased exposure, undivided attention, and extensive processing) and heuristic processing (which involves haphazard exposure, minimal attention, and superficial processing), selective reception involves biased exposure and attention to defend existing schemas (belief systems) by deliberately avoiding potential sources of counterattitudinal information.

Frey's (1986) review of psychological research on selective exposure to information noted that a substantial amount of the work in this area was instigated by Festinger's (1957, 1964) Theory of Cognitive Dissonance. This theory contends that cognitive dissonance arises when a person holds two beliefs that have opposing implications for behavior. Most individuals find dissonance to be an aversive emotional state and, thus, are motivated to reduce it. Research has shown that choice and commitment are necessary preconditions for the arousal of dissonance (Brehm & Cohen, 1962). Moreover, dissonance increases with the number and importance of the dissonant beliefs and can be reduced by increasing the number or importance of consonant beliefs or decreasing the number or importance of dissonant beliefs. Either a cognitive or a behavioral strategy can be used to change the structure of existing beliefs. The cognitive strategy involves selective reevaluation of one's existing beliefs, whereas the behavioral strategy involves selective search for new information to add to one's existing beliefs.

An important feature of the Theory of Cognitive Dissonance is that individuals are not only motivated to reduce dissonance with existing beliefs, but they also are motivated to increase the accuracy of their judgments and decisions. The conflict between the two goals of dissonance reduction (which decreases as losses increase) and accuracy enhancement (which increases as losses increase) is resolved by defending existing beliefs up to a certain point, followed by accommodating external information beyond that point. Thus, dissonant information may be preferred under certain circumstances, such as when it is perceived as relevant to a later decision or when the initial decision is reversible. The search for information also is affected by the subsequent circumstances in which the information is likely to be used. Dissonant information is more likely to be sought by those who expect to use it to defend in person why they made their decision, while consonant information is more likely to be sought by those who expect to use it to explain in writing the reason for their decision (Canon, 1964).

A person may seek out and obtain information without accepting it; in some cases information is sought out because it is perceived as easily refutable. Similarly, information from a low credibility source may be sought out so that the initial opinion can be bolstered through source derogation. Thus, findings on the reversibility of decisions suggest, although they have not been explicitly addressed in this line of research, that dissonant information is likely to be sought for a decision whose negative consequences can be minimized rather than completely eliminated. This situation would be of particular significance to the adoption of hazard adjustments because a strong personal commitment to a hazardous location that was freely chosen would be quite likely to elicit dissonance in the face of information indicating the degree of hazard at that location.

Research on information seeking can be summarized by the following propositions that are relevant to risk communication.

1. Conflicts in the available information about risk can be resolved by selectively re-revaluating the available information or by seeking new information.
2. Whether or not decision makers seek information about risk is determined by the relative importance of two goals, accuracy (problem-focused coping) and reassurance (emotion-focused coping), with conflicts between these goals resolved by defending existing beliefs up to a point and then accommodating external information after that point.
3. Dissonant (conflicting) information about risk is more likely to be sought if people expect to defend their decisions in person, but consonant information is more likely to be sought if people expect to defend their decisions in writing.
4. Additional information about risk is sometimes sought out so it can be refuted or its source can be derogated.

❖ THEORIES THAT INTEGRATE SOCIAL AND COGNITIVE PROCESSES

There are two theoretical perspectives that integrate the social and cognitive processes addressed in the previous sections. These perspectives address theories of protective action and the adoption of innovations. The first of these has explicitly examined people's responses to situations involving environmental threats, whereas the second has focused on situations in more benign environments. Both of these theoretical perspectives are important because they have identified specific attributes of behavioral responses that influence their selection.

Theories of Protective Action

One line of research that seems particularly relevant to risk communication involves the perception of personal risk as embodied in theories of protective action. Early research in this area assumed that increasing fear would increase the level of compliance with a recommended protective action, but a number of studies produced inconsistent results; increasing the level of fear could result in an increase, a decrease, or no change in attitudes and behavior. Leventhal (1970) proposed that messages about dangerous situations elicited two parallel processes: danger control and fear control. *Danger control*, a behavioral strategy for reducing actual hazard vulnerability by taking protective action, is equivalent to what Lazarus has called problem-focused coping (Lazarus, 1966; Lazarus & Folkman, 1984). *Fear control*, which is a cognitive strategy for regulating emotional reactions to the threatening situation and reducing perceived hazard vulnerability by ignoring or denying the danger, is equivalent to Lazarus's concept of emotion-focused coping. Leventhal (1970) concluded that compliance with protective action recommendations was positively related to warning recipients' perceptions of the efficacy of the recommended protective actions and their perceptions of their ability to implement those actions. He also reported that fear is lower and protective action recommendations are more readily accepted when they follow the danger warning.

Janis and Mann's (1977) Conflict Model addresses the distinction between the adaptive and defensive functions of information processing. Specifically, they have noted that awareness of hazard vulnerability can be emotionally distressing. Thus, while such hazard awareness sometimes motivates adaptive responses to reduce potential physical consequences (problem-focused coping), it also can motivate defensive responses to reduce the emotional distress (emotion-focused coping). Further, unlike the Theory of Reasoned Action, the Conflict Model has identified specific perceived characteristics of the threat and of the adaptive response that are likely to affect action. Moreover, Janis and Mann also proposed a detailed process model of emergency decision making in which the response to a credible warning is determined by the recipients' perceptions of the severity and immediacy of the threat, the perceived efficacy of available protective actions, and expectations of obtaining more information and other response resources. The Conflict Model identifies five patterns of coping with the warning: unconflicted inertia, unconflicted change, defensive avoidance (denial), hypervigilance (panic), and vigilance (rational information seeking). The two emotional reactions, denial and panic, result from appraisals of the situation as hopeless, with hopelessness about the efficacy of the protective response leading to denial and with hopelessness about the time available to implement the protective response leading to panic. Both of these coping patterns are identified as defective strategies. By contrast, the two instrumental reactions result from appraisals of the situation as hopeful, with hopefulness about the time available to implement the protective response leading to vigilance and with hopefulness about the efficacy of the protective response leading to unconflicted change.

Other models also specify the situational attributes (i.e., the characteristics of an environmental threat) and the characteristics of the alternative actions that people consider when deciding whether or not to respond to an environmental threat.

Rogers proposed Protection Motivation Theory (Maddox & Rogers, 1983; Rogers, 1975, 1983; Rogers & Mewborn, 1976). Research based on Protection Motivation Theory has confirmed that two characteristics of the event (probability of occurrence and severity of damage), a characteristic of the person (self-efficacy), and a characteristic of the response action (outcome efficacy) affect the initiation of protective actions.

Protection Motivation Theory has been applied with some success to a variety of different threats, but it has been difficult to determine how the key theoretical variables combine to produce attitude and behavioral change (Neuwirth, Dunwoody, & Griffin, 2000). This problem has been addressed by a more recent theory, the Person-relative-to-Event Model (Duval & Mulilis, 1999a, 1999b; Mulilis & Lippa, 1990), which asserts that people's decisions about protective behavior are determined by the level of threat in relation to their personal resources. This formulation, which draws from Lazarus's (1966; Lazarus & Folkman, 1984) theory of coping, has been supported by research on the adoption of adjustments for earthquake (Mulilis & Duval, 1995) and tornado (Mulilis & Duval, 1997) hazards. These studies found that the model's predictions were consistent with the outcome measures but significantly improved by including a measure of felt responsibility for preparing for the threatening event.

Theories of protective action can be summarized by the following propositions that are relevant to risk communication.

1. Adaptive response to warnings (also known as danger response or problem-focused coping) is determined by people's perceptions of a threat, the available protective actions, and their own abilities.
2. Adaptive response to warnings is affected by expectations of receiving more information and other response resources.
3. Maladaptive response to warnings (also known as fear response or emotion-focused coping) results from appraisals of hopelessness about the efficacy of a protective action or of success in implementing it within the time available.
4. Fear is lower and warning compliance is higher when protective action recommendations follow a danger warning.
5. The likelihood of engaging in a protective action increases with three characteristics of an event—probability, severity, and immediacy—as well as with one characteristic of the person, self-efficacy, and one characteristic of the response action, outcome efficacy.

6. The level of threat from an environmental hazard is judged in comparison to an individual's personal resources.

7. The adoption of hazard adjustments is affected by individual's felt responsibility to act.

Innovation Processes

Individuals can generate innovations—novel behaviors or technologies—for a variety of reasons, not all of which have to do with their adaptiveness to the physical environment. The degree to which such innovations are adopted by others has been the subject of many studies on innovation diffusion that have pointed to a number of factors influencing this process (Perry, 2000). Perhaps the most comprehensive catalogue of innovation characteristics was presented by Rogers (1984, 1987), who summarized the attributes of successful innovations as consisting of relative advantage, compatibility, simplicity, trialability, and observability. *Relative advantage* is the perceived improvement of an innovation over the idea it supersedes. Components of relative advantage include lower initial cost, higher profitability, lower risk, decreased discomfort, reduced time and effort, and more immediate reward. *Compatibility* is the consistency between an innovation and the needs, values, and past experiences of the receivers, while *simplicity* is the degree to which an innovation is perceived as easy to understand and use. *Trialability* is the extent to which an innovation can be experimented with on a limited basis, and *observability* is the degree that the results of an innovation are visible to others.

In contrast to persuasion, innovation processes need not necessarily be driven by an explicit motivation of one person to change the beliefs, values, attitudes, or behaviors of another. Innovation can take place through *social modeling,* which involves the observation and imitation of others' behavior. From the standpoint of behavioral decision theory, observation of others' behavior can enlarge one's awareness of available alternative actions.

Research on innovation processes can be summarized by the following propositions that are relevant to risk communication.

1. The adoption of innovations is determined by prospective users' beliefs about a number of characteristics of the new product or service.

2. Adoption is more likely when an innovation is perceived to be an improvement over previous ideas, is compatible with the needs of the receivers, and can be tested on a trial basis—and when its results are observable to others.

3. Innovation can be stimulated by social modeling (i.e., observation), as well as through social communication.

❖ THE PROTECTIVE ACTION DECISION MODEL

The review of research on social influence, behavioral choice, protective action, and innovation processes shows that a wide variety of theoretical perspectives provide useful accounts of the ways in which risk communication influences the processes of disaster response and hazard adjustment. We have seen that social influence models emphasize the effects that other people have on an individual's protective action decisions. The Classical Persuasion Model provides a basic framework within which to understand risk communication, identifying the ways in which characteristics of Sources, Messages, Channels, and Receivers achieve changes in beliefs and attitudes and, ultimately, behavior.

By contrast, behavioral decision theory focuses on the cognitive processes by which people judge probabilities and consequences when evaluating a threat. The term *behavioral decision theory* is somewhat misleading because most of the research in this area has been directed toward the differences among social groups in their risk perceptions or, at most, the prediction of behavioral intentions rather than actual behavior. This limitation is compensated for by attitude-behavior theory, which calls attention to the other factors that influence behavior, such as habits, social norms, and external conditions that facilitate or impede action. Of course, people sometimes postpone protective action because they do not believe that they have adequate information; this necessitates an examination of the conditions under which people initiate information seeking.

In addition, there are theories that link cognitive and behavioral processes. Theories of protective action specifically examine the attributes of threats that motivate people's choices to respond to a threat or avoid thinking about it. This research also has revealed some of the attributes of response actions that affect people's decisions to seek additional information or to take protective action. Similarly, research on innovation processes has confirmed that people take action on the basis of communicated information and personal observation, and it also has identified the attributes of innovative products and services that influence their adoption.

Each of these theoretical perspectives overlaps to some extent with disaster response and hazard adjustment processes, but all of them provide valuable insights that can extend our understanding of ways in which people adjust to the threat of environmental hazards. If the relevant elements of these complementary approaches can be integrated with the findings of disaster research, they will provide a more complete understanding of the process by which individuals decide to adopt protective actions. Thus, the objective of following discussion is to draw on all of these conceptual models and assemble a model of the factors that influence individual's adoption of protective actions against natural and technological hazards and disasters. This integrated model is labeled the Protective Action Decision Model (PADM).

The PADM is most directly based on a long history of research on disasters that has been summarized by many authors (Barton, 1969; Drabek, 1986; Fritz, 1961a; Lindell & Perry, 1992; Mileti et al., 1975; Mileti & Sorensen, 1987; Perry et al., 1981; Tierney et al., 2001). This research has found that sensory cues from the physical environment (especially sights and sounds) or socially transmitted information (e.g., disaster warnings) can each elicit a perception of threat that diverts the recipient's attention from normal activities. Depending on the perceived characteristics of the threat, those at risk will either resume normal activities, seek additional information, pursue problem-focused actions to protect people and property, or engage in emotion-focused actions to reduce their immediate psychological distress. Which way an individual chooses to respond to the threat depends on evaluations of both the threat and the available protective actions.

The long-established view that social norms influence people's actions under normal conditions gave rise to the *emergent norm* perspective (Turner & Killian, 1972), which emphasizes the social context of emergency response and the situational norms that arise when some change in the social or physical environment renders traditional norms inappropriate as guides for behavior (Gillespie & Perry, 1976; Perry et al., 1981; Tierney, 1978; Turner & Killian, 1972; Weller & Quarantelli, 1973). Drabek (1968) has summarized the emergent norm orientation to disaster behavior as indicating that

> Societies are composed of individuals interacting in accordance with an immense multitude of norms, i.e., ideas about how individuals ought to behave. Our position is that activities of individuals . . . are guided by a normative structure in disaster just as in any other situation. In disaster, these actions are governed by emergent rather established norms, but norms nevertheless. (p. 143)

Thus, human behavior in disaster can be conceptualized as a process of adapting conventional behavior in an effort to respond to the novel (and imperfectly understood) demands of a changing environment. An actual or impending change in the environment that is diagnosed as threatening stimulates individuals to reexamine their activities in a process referred to as arriving at a new or different "definition of the situation." Broadly speaking, the purpose of most disaster warnings and hazard communications is to prompt people to redefine the situation from one in which the environment is primarily positive to one in which the environment is threatening. The process of redefining the situation leads to the identification of possible actions that could be taken and concludes with decisions about appropriate responses to the threat.

The findings of previous disaster research can be combined with the propositions drawn from the theories reviewed earlier in this chapter to express the PADM

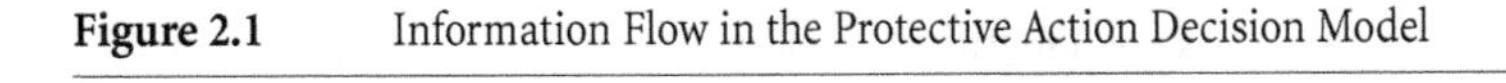

Figure 2.1 Information Flow in the Protective Action Decision Model

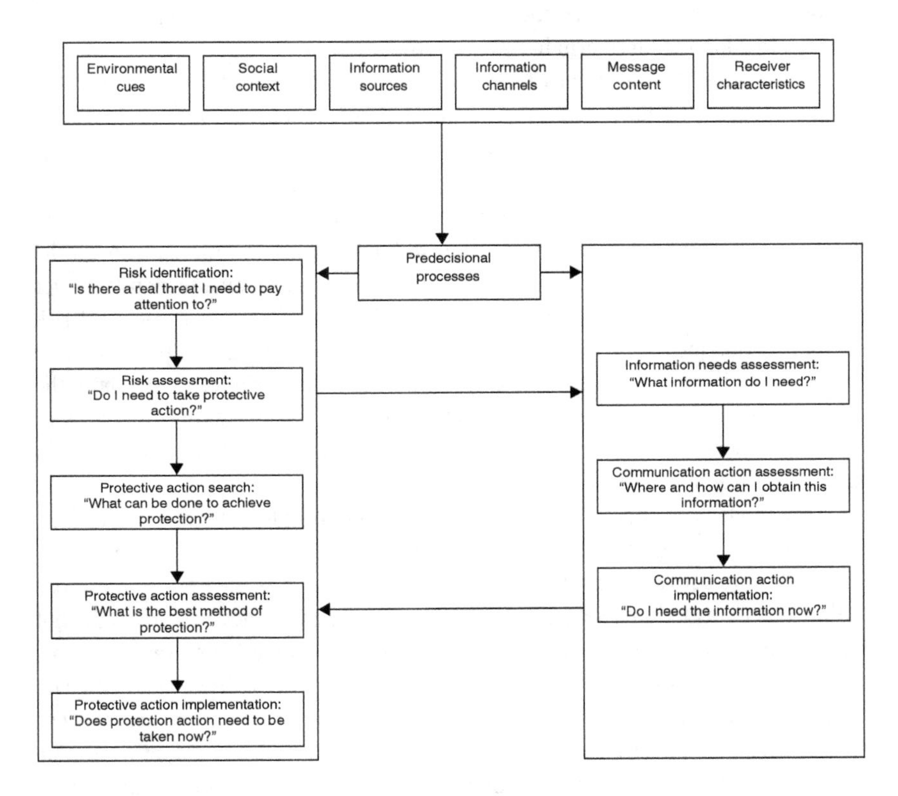

in terms of a flow chart that provides a graphic representation of the model (see Figure 2.1). This figure takes the form of what is called a *block model* in the causal modeling literature; each box contains a collection of variables that represent the possible mechanisms of action for that block (Blalock, 1982). The purpose of the block approach is to specify broader mechanisms that influence decisions. Variables listed within each block serve to identify specific aspects of the broader concept that come into play at different times in the decision process. This derives from empirical observations cited earlier that suggest that many of the variables in a single block can exert influence on multiple decision stages. For example, source credibility can affect the perception of the threat as real, the assessment of the risk, the alternative protective actions considered, and the perceived characteristics of those actions. The utility of the model lies in its function as a generalized framework for understanding protective action decision making, which can subsequently be used to create specific causal models of adoption intentions under specific conditions. In Chapter 3 the

PADM is used as the basis for creating a conceptual model of disaster warning response, and Chapter 4 uses the PADM to build a conceptual model of factors involved in adopting long-term hazard adjustments.

The process of decision making is represented as boxes connected by arrows that capture the proposed flow of information and action, which begins with environmental cues or risk communication messages and is constrained by the social context. As will be discussed below, the environmental cues or risk communication messages initiate a series of predecisional processes that stimulate either a protective action decision-making process or an information seeking process. To proceed through the successive stages of either process, the individual must arrive at an affirmative answer to the questions posed. The dominant tendency is for environmental cues and risk communication messages to prompt protective action decision making process rather than information seeking. The latter only occurs when there is uncertainty about the critical question at a given stage in the protective action decision making process. Once information seeking has resolved the question, processing proceeds to the next stage in the protective action decision-making process.

The model attempts to characterize the way that people "typically" make decisions about adopting actions to protect against environmental hazards. The stages within the protective action decision-making process are sequential, as are those within the information-seeking process, but we recognize that people might not always follow every step. For example, an extremely credible (or powerful) source might obtain immediate and unquestioning compliance with a directive to evacuate an area at risk—even if there were no explanation why evacuation was necessary or what alternative protective actions were feasible. Such an order would, of course, be quite improbable in contemporary American society, but compliance with such an order would bypass all of the intermediate stages in the PADM. Other situations can be imagined in which some, but not all, stages would be bypassed. The important lesson is that—unless risk communicators have an extreme amount of credibility or power to compel compliance—the more stages in the PADM that they neglect, the more ambiguity there is likely to be for message recipients. In turn, greater ambiguity is likely to lower compliance and cause warning recipients to spend more time in seeking and processing information rather than preparing for and implementing protective action.

Predecisional Processes

The primary focus of the PADM is on decision-making processes that take place in conscious awareness, but people must obtain information about the occurrence of an environmental hazard before the decision-making process is initiated. There are two sources of information that can initiate the decision-making process, environmental cues and risk communications from other people. Both information sources prompt three predecisional processes that must occur to bring information to conscious awareness. These are exposure to, attention to, and interpretation of environmental cues or, alternatively, reception of, attention to, and comprehension of socially transmitted information (see Fiske & Taylor, 1991). Environmental cues and risk communication are independent of each other, so one household might only observe environmental cues, whereas another might act only on the basis of warnings. Still other households might have access to both environmental cues and warnings or neither. Whether information comes from environmental cues or warnings, however, all three predecisional processes are necessary. That is, information from the physical environment will not lead to the initiation of protective action decision making unless people are exposed to, heed, and accurately interpret the environmental cues. Similarly, information from the social environment will not lead to the initiation of protective action decision making unless people receive, heed, and comprehend the socially transmitted information.

These predecisional processes are critical because some of those at risk who are exposed to environmental cues will heed this information, but others will not. Whether or not people heed the available information is determined by their expectations, competing attention demands, and the intrusiveness of the information. Specifically, expectations of threat are established when people have advance information that leads them to believe that there is the potential for a significant environmental threat. For example, many people in tornado-prone areas know the months of the year in which there is a peak level of activity and, therefore, check weather forecasts frequently and attend to environmental cues such as cloud formations. Competing demands are important because attention is limited and, thus, absorption in one task will tend to prevent the processing of information associated with other tasks. Continuing with the example of tornadoes, people who are engaged in tasks that require intense concentration are less likely to notice gathering storm clouds and might not notice a warning even if they have a radio turned on. Of course, the intrusiveness of hazard information affects attention because it disrupts cognitive processing of the primary task at hand. Those who did not notice the gathering storm clouds, or even an approaching funnel cloud, are certain to notice the roar of the wind or will notice a warning if it is preceded by a loud signal from a radio or a nearby siren. Finally, the interpretation of environmental cues is critical because this requires an understanding of the hazard. For example, some coastal residents have lost their lives because they did not understand that a sudden recession of water is the trough phase of a tsunami. The naive reaction to receding water has typically been to confuse it with a sudden low tide and to take advantage of an unexpected opportunity to collect stranded fish. Of course, those who have been properly trained would recognize this as a sign of danger and immediately evacuate to high ground.

The predecisional processes for warnings are similar to those for environmental cues. First, people must receive information from another person through a warning channel and attend to this information. As will be discussed in Chapter 3, the characteristics of the warning channel itself can have a significant impact on people's reception and attention to warning message content. Once a warning has been received and heeded, some people will comprehend the available information, whereas others will not (what Turner, Nigg, & Heller-Paz, 1986, call "hearing and understanding"). The comprehension of warning messages will depend on whether the message is conveyed in words that the message recipients understand. Quite obviously, warnings disseminated in English are unlikely to be understood by those who only speak Spanish. In addition, however, there are more subtle factors that affect comprehension. A warning source cannot achieve comprehension of a warning message if it uses technical terms that have no meaning for those at risk. For example, specialized terms such as "hypocenter," "Saffir-Simpson Category 4," "oxidizer," and "15 millirem" will not be understood by all who hear them. Specialized terms cause confusion and distract people from processing the information in the rest of the message. If such terms must be used in warning messages, they should be explained—ideally before any emergencies arise.

Once these three predecisional processes have been successfully completed, cognitive processing turns to the five stages in the core of the model, which are derived from a framework that Lindell and Perry (1992) proposed as an extension of a Rowe's (1977) three-stage model of decision making under uncertainty. According to Rowe, any social unit—individuals, households, or larger organizations—must address the three stages of risk identification, risk assessment, and risk reduction when undertaking protective actions. As will be seen below, the first two of these stages provide an adequate understanding of the protective action decision process, but it is important to distinguish among the three distinct components of risk reduction. In addition, Rowe's formulation overlooks the important role of information seeking in disaster response and hazard adjustment. Each of the stages in the PADM is discussed in detail below.

Decision Stages

Risk Identification

According to the PADM, people's decisions about how to respond to a hazard or disaster begin with risk identification, which can be interpreted as the initial step in what Lazarus and Folkman (1984) have called "primary appraisal." As noted earlier, this process can be initiated by the detection of environmental cues, but the most important sources of risk identification usually are warning messages from authorities, the news media, and peers (e.g., friends, relatives, neighbors, and coworkers). Similarly, the first step that risk communicators must take when promoting the adoption of hazard adjustments is to disseminate their message widely to attract the attention of those at risk and inform them that there is a potential for environmental extremes that could threaten their health, safety, and property.

In both disaster response and hazard adjustment, those at risk must answer the basic question of risk identification, "Is there a real threat that I need to pay attention to?" (Anderson, 1969; Janis, 1962; Janis & Mann, 1977; Mileti, 1975; Perry, 1979a; 1985; Williams, 1964). In past studies of warning response, researchers have described the outcome of this stage of the protective action decision process as the establishment of a "warning belief" (Drabek, 1986; Mileti, 1974), but this term unnecessarily excludes people's reactions to environmental cues so the term *threat belief* is generally more appropriate. The importance of a threat belief is supported by research showing that individuals routinely try to maintain their definition of the environment as "normal" in the face of evidence that it is not. Indeed, Drabek (1986) has pointed out that the most common reaction to a disaster warning is disbelief. According to emergent norm theory, a positive answer to the basic question of risk identification concludes the initial phase by defining the situation as requiring the discontinuation of normal activities in favor of considering protective action. Researchers have found a positive relationship between the level of threat belief and disaster response across a wide range of disaster agents, including floods (Mileti, 1975; Perry et al., 1981), volcanic eruptions (Perry & Greene, 1982; Perry & Hirose, 1991), hazardous materials emergencies (Lindell & Perry, 1992), hurricanes (Baker, 1991), earthquakes (Blanchard-Boehm, 1998), and nuclear power plant emergencies (Houts, Cleary, & Hu, 1988; Perry, 1985).

Risk Assessment

The next step in the protective action decision-making process, *risk assessment*, refers to the process of determining the likely personal consequences that the disaster or hazard could cause (Otway, 1973; Perry, 1979a). Decades of research have indicated that the perception of personal risk—the individual's expectation of personal exposure to death, injury, or property damage—is a critical variable in explaining disaster response (Mileti & Sorensen, 1987). This process of assessing personal relevance, which Mileti and Sorensen (1987) refer to as the "personalization of risk," has been recognized as an important factor by persuasion theorists as well as disaster researchers (Eagly & Chaiken, 1993). In the risk assessment stage, those at risk turn to the question "Do I need to take protective action?" Their perceptions of personal risk, and thus their *protection motivation,* are determined by their assessments of the personal consequences of disaster impact. This is the case whether the risk involves a disaster response or long-term hazard adjustment (Danzig, Thayer, & Galanter, 1958; Diggory, 1956; Fritz & Marks, 1954; Perry, 1983a; Tyhurst, 1957). Some of the factors associated with people's personalization of risk are illustrated by Withey's (1962) research, which emphasized the importance of people's perception of "the probability of the impending event occurring [and] the severity, to the individual, of such a development" (p. 106). Glass (1970), in discussing contingency responses to threat, pointed out that people are generally reluctant to cooperate with emergency plans unless they are convinced that impact is certain and that they are within the danger area. Menninger (1952), in reporting evacuation problems during the floods in Kansas during the summer of 1951 found that "an amazing number of people refused to believe that the flood would hit them . . . [and] would not move themselves or their belongings out of their homes" (p. 129). Finally, Kunreuther and colleagues (1978) reported that proximity, certainty, and severity were important threat characteristics influencing the purchase of hazard insurance.

The importance of certainty (probability) and severity (consequences) have been recognized by many researchers (see Neuwirth and colleagues, 2000, for such evidence in a review of research on Protection Motivation Theory and Lindell and Perry, 2000 in a review of research on seismic hazard adjustment), but the immediacy of a threat is also important because warning recipients must understand that the message describes a threat whose likely consequences will occur in the very near future. Thus, immediacy is related to the amount of *forewarning*, which is the amount of time between the arrival of the warning and the arrival of disaster impact. For environmental hazard managers, the amount of forewarning received from hazard detection agencies such as the National Weather Service and U.S. Geological Survey affects their choice of message content, the channels feasible for delivery, and the number of times the warning can be repeated. For those at risk, the amount of forewarning received from environmental hazard managers affects their sense of urgency to act. Other factors being equal, the likelihood of immediate disaster response increases as the amount of time until impact decreases. When people believe that there is more time before impact than the minimum necessary to implement protective action, however, they tend to devote this time to other activities, such as information seeking and expedient property protection. Information seeking can ultimately increase compliance with recommended protective actions but does, inherently, delay it. Similarly, the time that risk area residents devote to expedient property protection also delays their initiation of personal protective action. In both cases, the delay in protective action can be dangerous because the time of disaster impact cannot be predicted with perfect accuracy. For most of the events studied in previous disaster research, warnings were issued when impact was imminent, thereby reducing the extent of these other activities. Ultimately, increasing the amount of forewarning changes the risk communication from a disaster warning to a hazard awareness message (Nelson & Perry, 1991; Perry et al., 1981).

Previous research also has addressed people's beliefs about other temporal dimensions of hazard impact, as well. The duration of impact, which refers to the length of time that the hazard impacts will persist, has been addressed principally in connection with studies of technological risk perception (Lindell & Barnes, 1986; Lindell & Earle, 1983; Slovic, Fischhoff, & Lichtenstein, 1980). For radiological and toxic chemical hazards, it appears that many people are concerned that long-term contamination could prevent them from returning to their homes for over a year after a disaster (Lindell, 1994a).

In general, research has shown that simple measures of risk perception are positively correlated with disaster response (Drabek, 1999), but there have been inconsistencies in the research because the magnitude of the correlation between perceived risk and disaster response varies across studies. Two issues appear to be important in understanding these inconsistencies. The first issue concerns the type of protective action that has been recommended. Most of the empirical record has focused on evacuation—leaving an endangered area—as the recommended protective action, and high correlations between perceived risk and warning compliance have been reported (Vogt & Sorenson, 1987). In part, this might be due to the fact that evacuation is the only effective response known to those at risk in most disasters. When there is only one appropriate behavioral response to an attitude object, contemporary theories of attitude-behavior relations would predict that there would be a high correlation between an individual's attitude toward a hazard object and behavior related to that object (Eagly & Chaiken, 1993). Thus, the empirical finding is not only replicable across hazard studies, but it is also consistent with theoretical predictions from other domains. However, it also is important to qualify this finding in light of one further consideration. Specifically, the hazards most frequently studied by disaster researchers are ones whose principal physical impacts are property damage and traumatic injuries. In such cases, the exposure paths from the hazard agent to those at risk are relatively simple and well understood by the general public. Physical proximity to the hazard increases risk, so safety increases with distance from the point of impact. The correlations between attitude toward an environmental object (risk perception) and behavioral responses to that object might not be so high in cases where the exposure paths are more complex, such as for food contamination or exposure to chemical contamination or infectious diseases.

Similar issues must be considered in examining hazards that have different types of impacts. For example, some data suggest that the ways in which individuals perceive risk depends on whether the danger from an environmental hazard is to their person or their property. Perry and Montiel (1997) reported that the magnitude of perceived risk was higher for threats that affected life safety and property than for those that affected property alone. Thus, in this case also, the nature of the protective response alternatives could significantly affect the magnitude of the correlation between people's attitudes toward the hazard, as measured by their risk perceptions, and their choice among mutually exclusive behavioral responses to that hazard.

Another issue deals with the definition and measurement of perceived risk. Some studies have used very global measures of risk, whereas others have used more specific measures. Early studies of evacuation compliance that defined risk in terms of three components—certainty, severity, and immediacy—of the threat have reported high positive correlations between risk perception and disaster response (Perry et al., 1981). However, some researchers have applied these characteristics to the occurrence of a disaster impact, whereas others have applied them to hazard exposure, and still others have applied them to the consequences of that exposure. In some cases, there are essentially no differences among disaster impact, hazard exposure, and personal consequences. For example, people living close to a volcano might think that the occurrence of a major eruption is highly likely to occur within the next year, that their chances of severe exposure are high because they live so close to the volcano, and that their chances of experiencing severe adverse health consequences within that time interval are high because the effects of blast and ash will be felt immediately.

In other cases, the differences among disaster impact, hazard exposure, and personal consequences could be profound. For example, people living in the vicinity of a toxic chemical facility might think that the occurrence of a major release to groundwater is highly likely to occur within the next year but that their chances of severe exposure within that time interval are low because they live upstream from the plume. Even if they thought the chances of exposure were high, they might believe that their chances of experiencing severe adverse health consequences within that time interval are low because it would take many years to develop cancerous tumors.

The differences among disaster impact, hazard exposure, and personal consequences are important because a number of investigators have found that many people have an unrealistic sense of optimism about their ability to avoid danger—in extreme cases resulting in a sense of total invulnerability. For example, data from Lindell and Prater (2000) indicate that people's perceptions that there is a significant probability of an earthquake in their community do not necessarily imply that they believe that there is a high probability of being personally affected by that earthquake. Moreover, some studies have indicated that perceptions of severity also can be quite complex. Research on earthquake hazard has revealed that perceptions of severity are multidimensional because people are concerned about death, injury, property damage, and disruption to work and daily activities (Lindell & Perry, 2000). Other research on risk perceptions regarding radiological and toxic chemical hazards indicates that people are concerned about delayed health effects such as cancers and genetic effects (Lindell, 1994a; Lindell & Barnes, 1986; Perry & Montiel, 1997).

Protective Action Search

If the threat is judged to be real and some unacceptable level of personal risk exists, people turn to Rowe's third stage—risk reduction—which corresponds roughly to what Lazarus and Folkman (1984) refer to as secondary appraisal. Lindell and Perry (1992) noted that it is more useful to think of risk reduction as consisting of three distinct stages—identifying actions that can reduce or eliminate the risk, assessing their merits, and implementing the chosen action. The first of these steps, *protective action search,* involves retrieving one or more feasible protective actions from memory or obtaining information about them from others. The relevant question in protective action search is "What can be done to achieve protection?" and its outcome is a *decision set* that identifies possible protective actions. The results of some studies suggest that risk area residents' first answer to this question often involves a search for what can be done *by someone else* to provide them with protection against the hazard. When there is insufficient time to find someone else to provide protection—as is usually the case during disasters—or when such a search is unsuccessful, households must rely on their own resources to achieve protection. In many instances, an individual's own knowledge of the hazard will suggest what type of protection to seek (e.g., sheltering in the basement following a tornado warning). People are especially likely to recall actions they have taken on previous occasions if they have had personal experience with the hazard. Alternatively, they might consider actions that they have taken in the course of their experience with similar hazards—recognizing, for example, that the impact of a volcanic mudflow is similar to that of a flood and, thus, protective responses to flood are likely to be effective for a mudflow as well.

Information about protective actions also can be received from a variety of external sources. Specifically, those in the risk area are likely to become aware of alternative protective actions by observing the behavior of others. This occurs, for example, when neighbors are seen packing cars prior to flood evacuation or employing contractors to reinforce their homes against earthquake shaking. People also are likely to consider actions with which they have had vicarious experience in reading or hearing about others' actions in response to a hazard. Such vicarious experience is frequently transmitted by the news media, and often it is passed on by friends, relatives, neighbors, and coworkers. Finally, people also are made aware of appropriate protective actions by means of disaster warnings and hazard awareness programs that carry protective action recommendations from authorities. Specifically, a well-designed warning message will assist recipients in constructing a decision set by including one or more protective action recommendations. Nonetheless, authorities should not assume that warning recipients will implement their protective action recommendation, even if they mention only one in the warning message. As noted earlier, people will always be aware that continuing normal activities is an option, and they might think of other alternatives by recalling such actions from memory or observing the actions of others.

Protective Action Assessment

After people have established that at least one protective action is available, they pass from the protective action search stage to *protective action assessment,* which involves examining alternative actions, evaluating them in comparison to the consequences of continuing normal activities, and determining which of them is the most suitable response to the situation. At this point, the primary question is "What is the best method of protection?" and its outcome is an *adaptive plan.*

As noted earlier, choice is an inherent aspect of emergencies because those at risk generally have at least two options—taking protective action or continuing normal activities. The comparison of alternatives with respect to their attributes leads, in turn, to a balancing or trade-off of these attributes with respect to their relative importance to the decision maker. There is considerable debate about the specific nature of the decision process as the research review in Chapter 2 indicates. Contingent Decision Theory (Beach, 1990) suggests that decisions about disaster response and hazard adjustment will differ from each other because the decision problem and decision environment differ for these two situations. Specifically, protective action decisions during disaster response usually involve unfamiliarity due to lack of experience, few alternatives but more constraints, conflicting criteria (protecting personal safety, protecting property, and minimizing disruption of normal activities), irreversible decisions having high significance, high personal accountability to the rest of the household, and motivation to maximize decision accuracy. By contrast, protective action decisions during hazard adjustment usually involve more familiar situations (hazard mitigation and emergency preparedness actions), more alternatives, reversible decisions having moderate significance, high accountability, and motivation to minimize decision time, effort, and resources. In addition, there is evidence that decision processes vary from one individual to another and can vary from one situation to another for a given individual (Feldman & Lindell, 1990).

Under some conditions, those at risk can only take one action and therefore must make a choice among the alternatives. Evacuation maximizes the protection of personal safety but abandons property to the action of the hazard agent or, as some evacuees have feared, to potential looters (Lindell & Perry, 1990; Perry et al., 1981). On the other hand, emergency measures to protect property (e.g., sandbagging during floods) require that the property owner remain in a hazardous location. This problem also exists in the context of long-term hazard adjustment but is significantly reduced because households have time before a disaster occurs to carefully consider trade-offs among alternative protective actions and plan to implement multiple actions. Even when there is only a moderate amount of forewarning, households might be able to engage in a combination of actions. For example, if a flood has been forecast to arrive within a few hours, people could perform emergency floodproofing and elevate contents to higher floors, to provide as much property protection as possible, and still evacuate family members before the floodwater reaches a dangerous level.

When households assess the salient characteristics of alternative protective actions, they are likely to consider a set of characteristics that have been identified by previous research on disaster response and hazard adjustment. In reviews of disaster studies conducted since the 1940s, Fritz (1961a), Sorensen and White (1980), Sims and Bauman, (1983), Drabek (1986), and Tierney and colleagues (2001) have noted that unless the alternative protective actions are likely to be effective in reducing the negative consequences associated with disaster impact, they will not receive further consideration. Thus, *efficacy,* which is measured by the degree of reduction in vulnerability to the hazard, refers to success in protecting both people and property. Efficacy was found to be important by Cross (1980), who reported that residents of the Florida Keys stated that "safety in a severe storm" was one reason for choosing the type of structure in which they lived. Similarly, Kunreuther and colleagues (1978) found that lack of efficacy ("it won't help anyway") emerged as a significant criterion in hazard insurance purchases.

In some cases, such as sandbagging during floods, property protection is the specific objective of the protective action. In other cases, however, people consider the implications for property protection of actions whose principal goal is to protect people. For example, many researchers have found that those who fail to comply with an evacuation recommendation do so because of concerns about looting. That is, people are concerned about the loss of their property to other people, not to disaster impact. As is the case with safety, people's perceptions are often at variance with historical data indicating that looting rarely occurs in American disasters. Consequently, local authorities who want to increase compliance with evacuation recommendations must ensure that people are aware that their property will be safe if they leave the area.

Research also suggests that people sometimes evaluate a protective action in terms of its *safety*—that is, the risks that might be created by taking that protective action. For example, some research has reported that those who have not complied with recommendations to evacuate did so because they were concerned about the traffic accident risks involved. As a general rule, the traffic accident risks of evacuation appear to be no greater than those of normal driving (Lindell & Perry, 1992). However, warning recipients' behavior is determined by their *beliefs* about traffic accident risks, not the historical data about those risks, so it is important for local authorities who want to increase compliance with evacuation recommendations to ensure that people are aware that evacuation accident rates are low.

Alternative protective actions also can be assessed in terms of their perceived *time requirements* for implementation, which are a function of the number and duration of the steps required to complete a given action. Evacuation is typically time consuming, requiring unification of the family, preparation for departure, selection of a safe destination and route of travel, and transit out of the risk area (Lindell & Perry, 1987; Lindell, Prater, Perry, & Wu, 2002). By contrast, time requirements for in-place protection are small—requiring only that occupants shut off sources of outside air, such as doors, windows, chimney dampers, and forced air circulation systems for heating and cooling. Thus, successful implementation of a protective action requires that the amount of forewarning be greater than the time required for the risk area population to complete their protective actions (Perry, 1979b). In connection with floods, for example, if a warning is received only seconds prior to impact or simultaneously with impact, evacuation is effectively precluded.

The *perceived implementation barriers* that affect protective action decisions arise from resource constraints that preclude the selection of a preferred protective action, as well as obstacles that are expected to arise between the decision to take a protective action and the achievement of protection. In the former category, resource constraints include the lack of knowledge or skill, equipment, or social cooperation required to achieve protection (Lindell & Prater, 2002). In the case of evacuation, this may include the lack of knowledge of a safe place to go and a safe route to travel (Perry, Lindell, & Greene, 1980; Windham, Posey, Ross, & Spencer, 1977). Related barriers include the lack of access to a personal vehicle (e.g., those who are routinely transit dependent or families in which one spouse has the only car during the workday), lack of personal mobility due to physical handicaps, or lack of security in the evacuation area (for those who are concerned about their property being looted in their absence). In some instances, the separation of family members may be considered to be a barrier to evacuation. Until family members have been reunited, or separated family members can establish communication contact and agree on a place to meet, evacuation is unlikely to occur (Drabek & Boggs, 1968; Drabek & Key, 1976; Haas, Cochrane, & Eddy, 1977; Killian, 1952). Once again, it is important to recognize the distinction between people's perceptions of the implementation barriers to protective action and the actual implementation barriers to those actions. The perceived barriers inhibit behavioral intentions by making the attitude toward the act more negative, whereas actual implementation barriers intervene between behavioral intentions and behavior.

Finally, the *perceived costs* of actions to protect personal safety include out-of-pocket expenses (gasoline, food, and lodging), as well as opportunity costs such as lost pay from workdays missed during evacuation. Disaster response costs also include any additional property damage resulting from the action of the hazard agent or looters that is suffered as a result of being unable to engage in property protection actions. When choosing to adopt hazard adjustments, some costs can be incurred gradually (monthly payments for insurance or on a loan for earthquake proofing), but others (relocating to a different town to escape volcanic hazards) can involve large initial monetary and social costs. Perceived cost of protective action was cited by Fritz (1961a) and Sorensen and White (1980), who documented the importance of time, effort, personal sacrifice, and money in the adjustment decision. Similarly, Kunreuther and colleagues (1978) reported that cost ("too expensive") was mentioned by a majority of floodplain residents who failed to take protective actions of whose existence they were aware, while Cross (1980) found evidence for a multiattributed meaning of "cost," since residents of the Florida Keys used this term to refer to the daily effort of climbing stairs (behavioral effort), property sale price (economic cost), and unattractive appearance (aesthetic cost).

A significant impediment to the assessment of protective actions is that none of the available alternatives is likely to dominate the others (i.e., be superior to the others on all of the evaluation attributes). For example, Lindell and Perry (1992) reported that evacuation was rated higher than sheltering in-place and expedient respiratory protection in personal protection (a positive consequence). However, evacuation also was judged to be higher in its resource requirements for time, effort, skill, cost, and barriers to implementation (all negative consequences). This suggests that, in some cases, people must make the difficult choice between the higher effectiveness of evacuation (and its higher resource demands) and the lower effectiveness of the alternative protective actions such as sheltering in-place and expedient respiratory protection (and their lower resource demands). In such cases, there are likely to be lower correlations between people's attitudes toward the hazard (i.e., their risk perceptions) and their adoption of any individual protective action such as evacuation. As noted earlier, this is because a high level of risk perception implies a high motivation to take some protective action, but this does not predict which protective action will be taken.

The importance of *perceived* attributes in the protective action assessment stage should alert risk communicators to the potential for differences between the judgments of experts and the public, especially in connection with protective actions that are not well known. Sheltering in-place, sometimes known as in-place protection (Wilson, 1987, 1989), can substantially reduce toxic gas exposure to safe levels, but its effectiveness does not seem to be recognized outside a relatively narrow circle of experts. Moreover, attempts to evacuate immediately prior to tornado impact, which are contrary to scientific recommendations, are probably due to the observation that sheltering in-place during the tornado does not guarantee survival (Glass et al., 1980). A similar observation also has been made by many victims of fires in high-rise buildings who have attempted unsuccessfully to evacuate when sheltering in their rooms would likely have saved their lives.

Perceptions of the protective action alternatives can be inaccurate with respect to attributes other than efficacy. Indeed, this has proved to be a significant problem in hurricane evacuations because people usually pick a familiar location (such as a relative's home) as their evacuation destination and the time required for them to travel there under evacuation conditions is much greater than they are accustomed to because a high volume of traffic can significantly reduce the average speed of evacuating vehicles (for an analysis of hurricane evacuation times, see Lindell and colleagues, 2002; for empirical data on hurricane evacuation traffic problems, see Baker, 1979, 1980, 1993; Dow & Cutter, 2002; Perry & colleagues, 1981; Prater, Wenger, & Grady, 2000). Alternatively, it is possible that people could overestimate, rather than underestimate, evacuation time requirements. For example, the majority of the residents in the area around Three Mile Island reported that one of the reasons for their evacuating in response to the governor's limited evacuation advisory was to avoid a later forced evacuation (Lindell & Perry, 1992).

The end result of protective action assessment is an adaptive plan, but people's adaptive plans vary widely in their specificity, with some being only vague goals (e.g., "we'll stay with my sister's family") and others begin extremely detailed. At minimum, a specific evacuation plan includes a destination, a route of travel, and a means of transportation. More detailed plans include a procedure for reuniting families if members are separated, advance contact to confirm that the destination is available, consideration of alternative routes if the primary route is unsafe or too crowded, and alternative methods of transportation is the primary one is not available.

Research has documented that those who lack a ready adaptive plan tend to experience more negative disaster outcomes (Drabek, 1986; Perry, 1979b; Quarantelli, 1960; Windham et al., 1977). A classic example in the literature on floods lies in the Hamilton, Taylor, and Rice (1955) interview with the recipient of an evacuation warning that contained no information on safe evacuation routes or safe destinations: "We couldn't decide where to go . . . So we grabbed our children and were just starting to move outside . . . if it had just been ourselves, we might have taken out. But we didn't want to risk it with the children" (p. 120).

Protective Action Implementation

The fifth step, *protective action implementation,* occurs when all of the previous questions about risk reduction have been answered satisfactorily. Specifically, those at risk have determined that action should be taken, at least one available option is likely to be effective in achieving protection, and that option is logistically feasible with the available resources. In general, the implementation of protective actions consumes resources that those at risk would prefer to allocate to other activities, so they frequently delay implementation until they have determined that the immediacy of the threat justifies the disruption of normal activities. Thus, people often ask the question "Does protective action need to be taken now?" The answer to this question, whose outcome is the *threat response,* is crucial because people sometimes postpone the implementation of protective action even when there is imminent danger. As noted earlier, recipients of hurricane warnings have often been found to endanger their safety because too many of them wait until the last minute to begin their evacuations. Unfortunately, they fail to recognize that adverse weather conditions and a high volume of traffic can significantly reduce the average speed of evacuating vehicles, thus preventing the evacuation from being completed before the arrival of storm conditions (Baker, 1979, 1980, 1993; Dow & Cutter, 2002; Perry et al., 1981; Prater et al., 2000). The problem of procrastination is even more severe in connection with long-term hazard adjustment than it is in disasters with ample forewarning, because hazard awareness programs cannot specify even an approximate deadline by which action must be taken.

Information Needs Assessment

At all stages of the protective action decision process, people who are responding to the threat of imminent disaster must act on the basis of the available information, even if it is insufficient for a confident appraisal of the threat or the available protective actions. However when time is available, they can cope with the lack of information by implementing three additional stages involving information search. Information seeking in its broadest sense involves the "reduction of descriptive uncertainty" through such activities as active information screening and passive information monitoring (Kates, 1976). The process of information search begins with an *information needs assessment* that arises from an individual's recognition that the available information is insufficient to justify proceeding further in the protective action decision process. The research literature indicates that ambiguity at any point in the protective action decision process will lead to information seeking, especially when the probability of disaster impact reaches a critical threshold. Thus, if any of the questions cannot be answered with an unequivocal yes or no, this will lead people to ask "What information do I need to answer my question?" This results in an *identified information need.* As is the case with lack of information about the threat, it is also possible to resolve conflicts or uncertainties about appropriate protective actions by seeking further information about the situation. In particular, additional information about the hazard and about alternative protective actions could make it clearer which action would be most appropriate for that situation. Such information is frequently needed because, as we have noted earlier, those at risk are rarely aware of all of the alternatives available to them.

Communication Action Assessment

Identification of a need for information does not necessarily suggest where the needed information can be obtained. Thus, the next question in the information seeking process is "Where and how can I obtain this information?" Addressing this question leads to information source selection and information channel selection, which constitute an *information search plan.* The sources from which information is sought are likely to differ depending on the stage of the protective action decision process that has generated the need for information. For example, uncertainty about risk identification can stimulate questions directed to officials and, more likely, the news media (see Lindell & Perry, 1992). The high level of reliance on the news media appears to be due to a desire to confirm the information initially received by contacting a different source from the one that delivered a warning message (Drabek, 1969). By contrast, uncertainties abou protective action search, about protective action assessment, and—especially—about protective action implementation are likely to prompt questions directed to peers.

The sources sought are likely to be affected by the channels that are available, which in many disasters precludes the use of the telephone because circuits are so overloaded that it is impossible to obtain a dial tone for many hours or days. Further, attempts to reach authorities sometimes prove futile because the telephone numbers for emergency-relevant agencies are busy handling other calls. Thus, people may be forced to rely on the mass media and peers even when they would prefer to contact authorities. This distinction between risk area residents' preferred and actual channels of information receipt also can be seen in connection with long-term hazard adjustment. For example, Lindell and Perry (1992) reported that residents of communities downstream from the Mt. St. Helens volcano revealed some significant disparities between their preferred and actual channels of information receipt in the years after the 1980 eruptions. However, there also were significant differences between the two communities of Toutle and Lexington in both their preferred and actual channels of information receipt. Thus, it does not appear that there are any principles of source and channel preference that generalize across communities.

Communication Action Implementation

The final step in the information search process is communication action implementation, which provides *decision information* by answering the question "Do I need the information now?" If the answer to this question is positive, that is, they are threatened by an imminent disaster, people will actively seek the needed information from the most appropriate source through the most appropriate channel.

However, if the answer to this question is negative, for example when there seems to be an adequate amount of time before disaster impact, people will most likely engage in passive monitoring. Drabek's research indicated that people will go to great lengths, contacting many people over a period of minutes to hours, if the prospect of an imminent disaster needs to be confirmed (Drabek, 1969; Drabek & Stephenson, 1971). However, information seeking will be less frequent and less active if the location is specific but the time of impact is ambiguous. Perry, Lindell, and Greene (1982b) reported that many residents of the area around Mt. St. Helens monitored the radio four times a day or more after the initial ash and steam eruptions led authorities to believe that increased activity could occur that would indicate an increased probability of a larger eruption. By contrast, the absence of locational specificity and time pressure inherent in a hazard awareness program provides little need for those at risk to obtain immediate answers, so they are likely to forego active information seeking in favor of passive monitoring of the situation. Unfortunately, the absence of a deadline for action means that this passive monitoring is likely to continue until an imminent threat arises (as in the case of hurricanes and floods) or until a disaster strikes (as in the case of earthquakes or tornadoes).

Communication action implementation can have one of three outcomes. If the query elicits a message that meets the information needs that initiated the search, then information seeking has been successful and the decision maker can return to the point in the protective action decision process that generated the information search. However, if the source is unavailable, the query produces no additional information but does identify an alternative source, or the query produces no useful information at all, then information seeking is unsuccessful. The response to unsuccessful information seeking is likely to depend on the individual's expectations for success in obtaining the information from another source or through another channel. Optimism regarding either of these is likely to motivate further information seeking. Pessimism regarding the success of obtaining the needed information is likely to force the decision maker to attempt a protective action decision on the basis of the information available.

❖ SUMMARY

The PADM provides a framework that identifies the critical stages relevant to household adoption of protective actions and, for each stage, the activities performed, the typical question asked, and the outcome (see Table 2.1). If an individual cannot determine a satisfactory answer to the question posed at one of the decision stages, then progress toward implementation of a protective action is

Table 2.1 Warning Stages and Actions

Stage	*Activity*	*Question*	*Outcome*
1	Risk identification	Is there a real threat that I need to pay attention to?	Threat belief
2	Risk assessment	Do I need to take protective action?	Protection motivation
3	Protective action search	What can be done to achieve protection?	Decision set (alternative actions)
4	Protective action assessment and selection	What is the best method of protection?	Adaptive plan
5	Protective action implementation	Does protective action need to be taken now?	Threat response
6	Information needs assessment	What (additional) information do I need to answer my question?	Identified information need
7	Communication action assessment and selection	Where and how can I obtain this information?	Information search plan
8	Communication action implementation	Do I need the information now?	Decision information

likely to be terminated. If the process terminates due to a negative answer about risk identification, then the decision maker is likely to return to normal activities. If the process terminates due to a negative answer about risk assessment, then the decision maker is likely to monitor the situation. If the process terminates due to a negative answer about the availability or acceptability of protective actions, then the decision maker is likely to enter a state of either denial or panic. Which of these emotion-focused coping strategies is used depends on a person's susceptibility to distraction, with the most distractible being inclined to denial and the least distractible being inclined to panic.

The PADM derives conceptual strength by integrating theories of social influence and behavioral choice with research on disaster response and long-term hazard adjustment. Another important feature of the model lies in its utility for explaining the adoption of protective actions in response to two distinctly different situations—warnings of the need for disaster response and hazard awareness programs to promote the adoption of hazard adjustments. Finally, the model avoids the frequently made distinction between natural and technological hazards; it is appropriate for household response to both categories of events.

3

Disaster Warnings as Risk Communication

In this chapter we will address the implications of the PADM for disaster warnings, examine the degree to which the model fits the empirical literature on human response to warnings, and discuss the implications of this model for the practice of warning multiethnic populations about environmental threats. As noted earlier, two features of disaster warnings set them apart from other kinds of risk communication. First, there is the issue of urgency. Disaster warnings are used when a threat is imminent, so there are only minutes or possibly hours before disaster impact. The amount of time available is a function of the state of forecast technology for a given hazard, and this varies from one hazard agent to another (Sorensen, 2000). For example, it is possible to detect and track hurricanes quite accurately, so the amount of forewarning before impact can be measured in days. Conversely, the geophysical theory and monitoring technology to support seismic prediction is considerably more limited, so there usually is no forewarning for earthquakes. The limited amount of forewarning leads to the second feature of disaster warnings, which is that the protective action recommendations must focus on behaviors that can be quickly and easily implemented with whatever resources are available to those at risk. Often, the protective action recommendation is simply to evacuate—put distance between oneself and the threat—or to shelter in-place (see Lindell and Perry, 1992, for a detailed discussion of these protective actions). Moreover, the protective action recommendations specified in a warning message usually focus on minimizing risks to personal safety rather than on reducing property damage.

This chapter extends the discussion in the previous chapter by examining the ways in which the stages of the protective action decision process are affected by four types of situational influences. These are (1) environmental cues; (2) social context; (3) warning characteristics, including source, channel, and message characteristics; and (4) receiver characteristics. Next, this chapter remedies a pervasive limitation in the risk communication literature—a narrow focus on warning *compliance*—by examining the spontaneous response of those for whom authorities are not recommending the protective action be taken. This section also addresses another neglected issue, the timing of disaster response. Finally, the closing section of the chapter addresses the problem of issuing warnings in multiethnic communities.

❖ PROTECTIVE ACTION DECISIONS

As noted in the previous chapter, the PADM emphasizes that people's response to disasters is characterized by three predecisional stages that involve either the exposure, attention, and interpretation of physical cues or the reception, attention, and comprehension of warning content. They then pass through the five stages of the protective action decision process, marked by risk identification, risk assessment, protective action search, protective action assessment, and protective action implementation. In addition, since the immediately available information is almost never sufficient, people usually engage in the information-seeking activities of information needs assessment, communication action assessment, and communication action implementation. The process of protective action decision making is affected by four categories of variables—environmental cues, social context, warning components (source, message, and channel), and receiver characteristics. The following discussion identifies specific variables within each class in terms of their *direct* impact on disaster response and also their *indirect* impact on disaster response via other variables.

❖ SITUATIONAL INFLUENCES ON DISASTER RESPONSE

Environmental Cues

Environmental cues have been shown to have a direct impact on disaster response because physical cues such as sights, sounds, and smells can serve as evidence that a real threat exists and that it should be assessed as a danger demanding protective action. Indeed, physical cues are sometimes the only source advance information about disaster impact. The sight of funnel clouds or the roaring of the wind has given a number of tornado victims indisputable evidence that protective actions should be initiated (Moore, 1958). Similarly, in connection with the eruption of Mt. St. Helens volcano, risk area residents reported that seeing the ash plume and hearing the eruption removed all doubt that a dangerous eruption was under way (Perry & Lindell, 1990a; Saarinen & Sell, 1985). Such findings also have been reported in hazardous materials incidents associated with train derailments, where evacuees reported that seeing the derailed cars or a plume convinced them that immediate response was needed (Lindell & Perry, 1992).

Conversely, the apparent absence of physical cues that would be expected during hazard impact can hamper protective action decision making. Gruntfest, Downing, and White (1978) described a flood in Colorado's Big Thompson Canyon that was caused by heavy, but localized, nighttime rains far up in the mountains. Shortly after daybreak, people in a restaurant at the mouth of the canyon were warned of imminent flooding but refused to evacuate, observing that the skies were clear and it had not rained where they were located. Shortly afterward, they received an *erroneous* warning that an upstream dam had collapsed and evacuated immediately. Warning recipients acted as they did because the accurate warning was in apparent conflict with the available environmental cues, but the incorrect warning was not.

It should be obvious that environmental cues provided by the hazard agent itself promote predecisional processes and facilitate the decision stages of the protective action decision process. These conditions occur when those at risk are exposed to observable cues that attract attention and are readily interpretable as indicating that the risk is certain, severe, and immediate. However, cues from the physical environment do not directly facilitate protective action search, protective action assessment, protective action implementation, or any of the three information-seeking stages of information needs assessment, communication action assessment, and communication action implementation.

Another set of environmental cues is defined by the behavioral responses of others. For example, the sight of neighbors filling sandbags is likely to stimulate others to take floodproofing actions, whereas seeing others packing their cars will tend to prompt observers to evacuate (Flynn, 1979; Mileti, 1975; Zeigler, Brunn, & Johnson, 1981; Zeigler & Johnson, 1984). More generally, behavioral observations can reinforce the advisability of complying with protective action recommendations, inform observers of protective actions previously unknown to them, or remind them about relevant protective information that was communicated to them previously (Cutter & Barnes, 1982; Dynes & Quarantelli, 1976; Sorenson, 1991; Tierney, 1988).

The environmental cues provided by the behavioral responses of others promote predecisional processes and facilitate the decision stages of the protective action decision process more completely than do those of the hazard agent itself. Specifically, protective action is more likely when those at risk are exposed to social behaviors that attract attention and are readily interpretable as indicating that the risk is certain, severe, and immediate. In some cases (e.g., widespread evacuation), it is not only obvious that others are responding to a threat, but it is also obvious what protective action they are taking. Thus, the behavioral cues facilitate protective action search, protective action assessment, and protective action implementation. When it is obvious only that there is an elevated level of activity, but the purpose of the activity is unclear, the behavioral cues are likely to stimulate the information-seeking stages of information needs assessment, communication action assessment, and communication action implementation.

Social Context

The social context of the warning includes kin network integration, community involvement, and family obligations. According to the PADM, immersion in kin and friendship networks is a very important aspect of the effects of social relationships on the protective action decision process. Although these variables have received little attention from disaster researchers, there is some evidence that these variables have significant relationships with more direct determinants of disaster response. In particular, people's interaction and exchange patterns with their kin can play an important role in the warning dissemination process and, consequently, in the promotion of successful adaptation to disaster warning (Clifford, 1958). Similarly, the availability of many peers—such as friends, relatives, neighbors, and coworkers—can also facilitate many aspects of people's disaster response. When officials deliver warning messages in a community, these tend to be propagated by informal social networks, thus increasing the potential number of sources for initial warnings (Drabek, 1969; Drabek & Boggs, 1968). People's interaction patterns with their peers have an impact on the number of warnings received and the speed with which they receive those warnings. In addition, community integration influences the amount and specificity of information about the hazard and suitable protective actions and the opportunities for warning confirmation. For example, Drabek and Stephenson (1971) report that "extended family relationships were crucial as warning message and confirmation sources . . . telephone conversations with relatives during the warning period were usually a key factor" (p. 199). Kin networks also serve as reservoirs of contacts with whom warning recipients can confirm and evaluate messages (Bates, Fogelman, Parenton, Pittman, & Tracy, 1963; Blanchard-Boehm, 1998; Lindell & Perry, 1992; Mileti & Beck, 1975; Perry et al., 1981).

These considerations are not an unmixed blessing because immersion in kin networks, in particular, can influence the structure of the household and, consequently, the family context in which warnings are received (Gruntfest, 1977; Liverman & Wilson, 1981; Mileti & Sorenson, 1988; Quarantelli, 1980; Sorenson, 1986; Worth & McLuckie, 1977). For example, high levels of kin involvement often indicate the presence of multigenerational households or at least extended family households. Consequently, the larger the household, the greater the number of people whose safety must be accounted for when a warning is received (Drabek & Boggs, 1968; Hill & Hansen, 1962; Lansing & Kish, 1957). Friendship networks serve a function that is similar to that of kin networks. Informal dyadic relationships are often based on geographic proximity (neighbors), but they also can be based on professional association (coworkers).

By contrast to immersion in kin and friendship networks, community involvement refers to people's membership in voluntary associations and other community organizations. When a disaster threatens, community participation operates much like kin and friendship networks, enhancing the individual's social contacts and access to information. Research suggests that this aspect of people's integration into the community affects the source, content, and number of warnings received, as well as the opportunities for warning confirmation (Aguirre, 1991; Baker, 1979; Barton, 1969; Perry et al., 1981). It has also been argued that community contacts are less important sources of evacuation information than are kin relationships (Drabek & Boggs, 1968), but community ties can substitute for kin relations when the latter are weak or absent. Thus, they also affect the likelihood and speed of warning receipt and the number of warnings, as well as the amount and specificity of information about the hazard and suitable protective actions and the opportunities for warning confirmation.

There also is some evidence that community participation is related to demographic variables, but the empirical record on these relationships is not consistent. Watson and Maxwell (1977) argued that the elderly have higher levels of social isolation (such as shrinking friendship networks and decreased affiliations with organizations), but other studies have found only weak relationships between age and social participation (Cottrell, 1974; Kent, 1971). As discussed below, ethnic group membership also appears to be related to the nature, but not necessarily the level, of community involvement.

Knowledge of the safety or condition of family members as a contingency for warning response behavior was systematically addressed by Killian (1952) in his early work on primary groups in disasters. As disaster studies dating back to the bombing of London during World War II have indicated, the study of human behavior in disaster must take into account the network of family roles in which the individual is immersed (Bernert & Ikle, 1952; Titmuss, 1950). In particular, families faced with disaster seek to protect members (Quarantelli, 1960) and generally perform as units when undertaking any protective behavior. Drabek and Boggs (1968) summarized similar findings as indicating that "when they did evacuate, families left as units . . . these data [therefore] provide additional support for the hypothesis that families move as units and remain together, even at the cost of overriding dissenting opinions" (p. 446).

It is important to recognize that evacuation compliance does sometimes occur when family members are separated, as long as there is knowledge that other family members are safe (Perry et al., 1981). Although there are no data for the effect of family context on compliance with other types of protective action recommendations, it is likely that the conditions for compliance would be similar to those for evacuation. For example, sheltering in-place involves remaining indoors and minimizing the exchange of air to the outside. If family members were separated when a warning was received to shelter in-place, a high level of compliance would be expected from them as long as other family members were believed to be safe. In addition, however, evacuation creates uncertainty about where those who have evacuated have gone, so reunification of the family following evacuation is problematic because family members do not know how to find each other. By contrast, family members would know how to contact each other after sheltering in-place, because this protective action—unlike evacuation—does not require movement to a location that is unknown to the family members who are away from home. Currently, an increasing number of households have multiple cellular phones, so communication among separated family members is becoming less problematic. However, if a major disaster affects a large number of people, even these cellular telephone connections could become so overloaded that separated family members would remain out of contact with each other for extended periods of time. In the absence of empirical data, it is unclear how people will respond to protective action recommendations if they expect to be able to contact each other eventually by cell phone to make arrangements for reunification but are prevented from doing so immediately because of telephone convergence. The most cautious assumption is that lack of knowledge about the safety of family members would slow any protective action (Lindell & Perry, 1983, 1990). In extreme cases, people might not only ignore protective action recommendations but also engage in actions that they perceive to be protective of separated family members (for example, by delivering a warning themselves or attempting to reunite the family), even if they actually would increase danger to themselves.

In terms of the PADM, these research findings indicate that family context does not serve as direct information for the protective action decision process so much as it forms a constraint on the implementation of any protective action that has been selected. That is, it principally affects the last stage in the protective action decision process, protective action implementation activities, by providing a negative answer to the question "Does protective action need to be taken now?" It generally seems to be the case that family members have identified the risk and concluded that the danger demands some response before the family context comes into play. At that point, implementing a protective action such as evacuation requires that households not only attempt to protect those who are present but also consider the safety of separated family members.

Warning Components

Research indicates that three components of a warning affect people's disaster response: warning sources, warning channels, and message content. These factors are especially important in rapid onset disasters that do not provide environmental cues to their onset. Well-constructed warnings stimulate recipients' protection motivation and compliance with a protective action recommendation by providing information that establishes a threat belief, protection motivation, a protective action decision set, an adaptive plan, and—ultimately—an adaptive disaster response.

Warning Sources

Warning sources vary in terms of their type (authorities, media, peers), and each of these types of sources is judged in terms of its credibility. In turn, credibility is comprised of two primary characteristics, expertise and trustworthiness. For example, McGuire (1969, 1985) characterizes expertise as access to special skills and information and trustworthiness as the willingness and ability to communicate information without bias. McGuire's definition of expertise appears to be similar to French and Raven's conception of information power—in this context, specialized knowledge about the state of the physical environment—and expert power—in this context, specialized knowledge about cause and effect relationships in the physical environment. Perceptions of trustworthiness are most likely when the source is an authority and, therefore, has what French and Raven would define as legitimate power. Whether or not a source has credibility, its use of reward or coercive power can increase compliance with protective action recommendations, but these bases of power are rarely used in American emergencies. Finally, sources also differ in their accessibility to warning recipients, which is not a basis of power but a characteristic that can significantly influence the ease with which recipients receive any decision information that they seek.

Perceptions of source credibility have an impact on many stages of the protective action decision process. First, a warning from a credible source is more likely to attract attention and be accepted as accurately representing the nature of the threat. Thus, source credibility affects the stages of risk identification and risk assessment, producing positive correlations with threat belief and perceived risk (Lindell, Perry, & Greene, 1983; Mileti et al., 1975; Perry & Greene, 1982; Perry et al., 1981). Second, a protective action recommendation from a credible source is likely to be seen as an effective and feasible means of protection. Although much of the research that has examined the effects of source characteristics is based on laboratory experiments, the findings of these studies are consistent with the results found in research on disasters. Using field data collected from residents of areas exposed to volcanic hazards, Perry and Lindell (1990a) found that people used assessments of expertise and trustworthiness in evaluating sources, but that they also considered these sources' past reliability in communicating information as a means of judging their credibility.

The credibility of different warning sources varies by disaster agent; friends and relatives are often rated as highly credible in flood settings, but governmental authorities tend to receive the highest ratings in radiological emergencies (Lindell & Perry, 1992). Such attributions also appear to vary by ethnic group membership (Perry, 1987) and by the individual's level of experience with a given threat (Tierney et al., 2001). The empirical literature is somewhat equivocal regarding patterns of credibility attributions to different classes of warning sources. In general, it appears that authorities are commonly considered credible (Carter, Clark, Leik, & Fine, 1977; Christenson & Ruch, 1980; Greene, Perry, & Lindell, 1981; Mileti & Sorenson, 1988), but mass media and peer contacts have also been identified as sources that are perceived to be credible. Source credibility is a perception that can be developed over time, so we will address it further in Chapter 5 where we address risk communication programs.

Because source credibility is positively related to threat belief and protection motivation, it is negatively related to warning confirmation and other information-seeking activities (Perry et al., 1981). Drabek (1999) has emphasized that a consistent research finding is that the most common response to any disaster warning is disbelief, reflecting a normalcy bias in disaster response. Particularly when risk area residents receive a warning from a source of questionable credibility, they attempt to confirm the message by contacting a different source to verify that disaster is threatening and that they are at risk. Warning confirmation is a logical solution to the dilemma of minimizing disruption to normal activities and maximizing personal safety. Obtaining additional information about the threat can enable the warning recipient to disconfirm the warning (supporting the continuation of normal activities), to find that an imminent personal threat exists (supporting the protective action search, protective action assessment, and protective action implementation), or to find that the threat to self and property is uncertain, remote, or modest in severity (supporting continued active information seeking or passive information monitoring).

Warning confirmation and other information-seeking behaviors have been documented in the case of floods (Drabek, 1969; Drabek & Stephenson, 1971; Perry et al., 1981), as well as in the cases of volcanic eruptions (Perry & Greene, 1982), hurricanes (Nelson et al., 1989), and hazardous materials emergencies (Lindell & Perry, 1983). Lindell and Perry (1992), describing data from two hazardous materials emergencies and one flood, reported that more than 60% of all warning recipients in each community attempted to confirm the warnings they received, about 25% contacted more than three different confirmation sources, and the range of sources contacted included different government offices, mass media, and peers such as friends, relatives, neighbors, and coworkers.

Warning Channels

Warnings can be disseminated through a number of different channels, including face-to-face contact, telephone, siren, mobile loudspeaker (route alerting), radio (normal and tone alert), television (broadcast and cable), and newspaper. As noted earlier, each of these warning channels has different characteristics (Lindell & Perry, 1987, 1992). The first of these is precision of dissemination, which refers to a channel's ability to warn all of those at risk (sensitivity) and only those at risk (specificity). At one extreme, face-to-face warnings can be targeted quite precisely because those delivering the warning can be given very detailed instructions about who is at risk. At the other extreme, the broadcast media (radio and television) are very imprecise because a warning message can be received by anyone in their reception area and the latter is likely to be much different from (usually much larger than) the risk area. This problem can be avoided if broadcasters provide specific information about who is and is not at risk, but this is sometimes neglected.

Although it seems obvious that the failure to deliver a message to those who are at risk is a problem, disaster response problems also are created when messages designed for one group of recipients who are at risk also are received by other groups who are not at risk. This situation most commonly arises in connection with warnings disseminated over the broadcast media in large scope threats such as hurricanes, volcanic eruptions, major riverine flooding, or tsunamis. Radio and television stations broadcast messages intended for reception in the communities where they are located, but the messages are also received in other communities in these stations' broadcast area. If the warning messages fail to identify the geographic area in which the hazard impact is expected and the protective actions are recommended, the potential arises for those in unaffected areas to initiate protective response. The most obvious consequence of this is social and economic disruption for those who respond unnecessarily, but there also is the potential for loss of warning system credibility. More significantly, response by those not at risk could endanger those who are at risk if the former fill evacuation routes that are needed by the latter. This consideration underscores the need to be aware of the broadcast area for each channel and to carefully specify the risk area in each warning message.

Another important characteristic of warning systems is the degree to which they can penetrate normal activities. A warning message is useless unless the method of delivery can seize the attention of those at risk. In many instances, the affected population is unaware of the pending disaster and will be engaged in routine activities. Rogers and Sorensen (1988) have identified seven fundamental activities of interest to emergency planners because they differ in the ease to which they provide ready access to warning messages. These are (1) home asleep, (2) indoor activities, (3) outdoor activities, (4) in transit, (5) working or shopping, (6) watching television, and (7) listening to radio. These activities differ in the ease with which they can be interrupted by different warning mechanisms. Clearly, warnings transmitted over the broadcast media are more likely to be received and attended to when the population at risk is watching the television or listening to the radio. Conversely, such warnings transmitted over this channel are least likely to be effective when those in the impact area are home asleep; in such cases, telephone alerts or face-to-face warnings are more likely to penetrate. Lindell and Perry (1992) have argued that risk communicators who wish to provide immediate warnings should carefully select the warning channels that are most likely to penetrate the dominant activities that are taking place at that time of the day and day of the week. For example, if a threat is detected in the middle of the night with a short time until impact, the channel selected must have the capacity to wake the majority of the population from their sleep. Tone alert radios such as NOAA Weather Radio can do this, whereas normal radio and television receivers cannot.

Warning channels also vary in the specificity of the messages they can transmit. At one extreme, most sirens can only provide an *alert*, which indicates only that there is an emergency but not what it is or what should be done. By contrast, radio or television can be used to obtain a *specific warning* that describes the threat and recommended protective actions in detail.

Susceptibility to message distortion exists when information is communicated through a chain. For example, telephone trees structure warnings so that each person in the tree calls a designated list of (for example, five) people. Although this procedure is much faster than having a single individual call all members of the total list, the message is likely to be distorted as it is passed from one person to the next. Distortion in telephone trees can be minimized if there is a standard warning message and people have been trained it its use.

However, there also is the potential for susceptibility to warning message distortion even if telephone trees are not used. This is because official warnings will be relayed and possibly elaborated by unofficial intermediates. That is, those at risk might hear unofficial warnings from radio announcers, television reporters, friends, relatives, neighbors, and coworkers, as well as official warnings from public safety authorities. To the extent that unofficial sources relay official warnings, there is potential for omission from, as well as embellishment and distortion of, the original messages. This creates the potential for multiple messages to appear to be or to actually be inconsistent and contradictory. The resulting ambiguity is likely to be seized on by some warning recipients as an excuse for downplaying the threat.

Rate of dissemination over time is important because short forewarning usually demands reliance on channels that reach the largest number of those at risk as soon as possible. In many cases, this is the important characteristic considered in deciding how to warn those at risk. The electronic media are very high on this characteristic, whereas newspapers are low.

Sender and receiver resource requirements consist of the capital (equipment) and personnel training resources required for warning dissemination. Some warning channels, such as telephones, require no new equipment or personnel training, but others might require major investments in new communication technology. Sirens require major investments by the sender, whereas tone alert radios require investments by the receivers.

Finally, it is helpful if risk communicators can obtain feedback that indicates whether those at risk received, attended to, and understood the warning message; personalized the risk; and complied with the recommended protective actions. This information can, to a significant extent, be provided by face-to-face warnings.

Overall, radio has poor precision of dissemination and penetration of normal activities (unless it is provided with a tone alert capacity), and it can transmit much specific verbal information, some numeric information, but no graphic information unless it is described verbally. Radio's message distortion is relatively low (if announcers are provided with scripted warning messages), the rate of dissemination is extremely high, and there are no incremental sender and receiver resource requirements, but there is no feedback from warning recipients.

Because they broadcast information in a similar way, television has limitations that are similar to those of radio. The major differences are that television currently has no enhanced capability for penetrating normal activities that is equivalent to tone alert radio and that television is inherently able to transmit substantial amounts of information in all three categories—verbal, numeric, and graphic. Indeed, the limitations of televised warnings probably are dictated mainly by the limitations of the warning recipients' ability to attend to and comprehend the information provided.

Route alert systems (mobile loudspeakers on public safety vehicles) have limitations that are similar to those of radio. However, they have greater precision of dissemination and penetration of normal activities than does radio. Like radio, their message distortion is relatively low (if announcers are provided with scripted warning messages). Although the rate of dissemination is only moderate, there are essentially no incremental sender and receiver resource requirements, and there is a modest degree of feedback from warning recipients.

Current automated telephone alert systems have high precision of dissemination and penetration of normal activities, and their message distortion is relatively low (a recorded message is played to each warning recipient). The rate of dissemination is quite high and there are essentially no incremental receiver resource requirements, but there are significant sender resource requirements. There is a modest degree of feedback from warning recipients (automated telephone alert systems provide an indication of warning receipt but not of the subsequent stages of the warning response process). However, the telephones can be used to seek additional information from other sources—if circuits are not overloaded as, unfortunately, is often the case in disasters. As with radio, telephone alert systems can provide much specific verbal information, some numeric information, but no graphic information. However, this is changing as advanced cellular telephone technology is overcoming these limitations by providing greater transmission of numeric and graphic information, depending on the characteristics of the video screen.

Face-to-face warnings also have limitations that are similar to those of route alert systems. They have a high degree of precision in dissemination and penetration of normal activities, and their message distortion is relatively low (if those disseminating the warnings are provided with scripted warning messages). Although the rate of dissemination is very low, there are essentially no incremental sender and receiver resource requirements, and there is a high degree of feedback from warning recipients. Indeed, direct contact with the warning source allows the recipient to request repetition and elaboration of the warning message. Moreover, face-to-face warnings can be supplemented by brochures or flyers that provide large amounts of information in all three categories—verbal, numeric, and graphic.

Finally, sirens have high precision of dissemination and penetration of normal activities, but they generally cannot transmit anything other than categorical information unless they are equipped as loudspeaker systems (in which case they have many of the same characteristics as route alert systems). Sirens' rate of dissemination is extremely high, and there are no incremental receiver resource requirements, but sender resource requirements are high and there is no feedback from warning recipients.

Although few studies address this point explicitly, the literature suggests that warning coverage is increased when authorities send warning messages over multiple channels, because the probability of receiving at least one warning increases with the number of warning channels and the number of warnings disseminated over each channel. Moreover, the reception of warnings via multiple channels (e.g., television, radio, and route alerting) increases the likelihood that all of the elements of the warning message will be attended to and comprehended, that warning recipients will believe that the threat is real and that there is an imminent likelihood of serious consequences (Mileti, 1975). Furthermore, the use of multiple official channels is likely to increase warning relay through unofficial sources such as friends, relatives, neighbors, and coworkers. This provides additional reinforcement for threat belief and assessment of the risk as highly probable, serious, and imminent consequences (Drabek & Boggs, 1968).

The channels through which warning messages are transmitted affect the disaster response process in a variety of ways. First, channels vary in the ways in which they affect the predecisional processes of disaster response. For example, channels that are high in speed and precision of dissemination, penetration of normal activities, sender and receiver resource requirements, can ensure that there is rapid and complete reception of the warning message by the population at risk. Those that are high in penetration of normal activities can ensure that the message is attended to, whereas those that are high in specificity, low in message distortion, and high in feedback from warning recipients can ensure that the message is comprehended.

Warning channels also can vary in the degree to which they affect the decision stages of risk identification, risk assessment, protective action search, protective action assessment and selection, and protective action implementation. Specifically, the conditions that promote message comprehension (high specificity, low distortion, and high feedback from warning recipient) are likely to promote the protective action decision process.

Finally, warning channels differ in the degree to which they support the information seeking stages of information needs assessment, communication action assessment, and communication action implementation. Specifically, face-to-face warnings and telephones support information seeking by warning recipients, but the other channels do not. The rise of the Internet has brought this channel increasing prominence as an information source that could be used for incidents with ample forewarning (e.g., hurricanes), but it suffers the same problems as radio and television as a warning channel. Moreover, the number of homes with Internet access and the proportion of those online when a warning is disseminated is likely to be even lower than with these more conventional electronic media.

Warning Content

Warning message content describes sources' assessments of the existence of a threat, its seriousness, and what should be done in response to it. Research indicates that protective action decision making is most adaptive when warning messages that convey specific information about the likely location, time, and magnitude of disaster impact (Lindell & Perry, 1992; Makosky, 1977; Mileti & Harvey, 1977; Mileti & Sorenson, 1987). When message content is specific regarding these factors, warning recipients are more likely to believe that there is a real threat and to personalize the risk and, thus, establish protection motivation (Drabek & Stephenson, 1971; Fritz & Marks, 1954; Fritz & Williams, 1957; Moore, Bates, Lyman, & Parenton, 1963). It is important to recognize that information about the likely location, time, and magnitude of disaster impact will only create an appropriate level of protection motivation if warning recipients can accurately estimate their level of risk from the information about location and magnitude. If they cannot accurately estimate their distance from the impact point or if they incorrectly estimate the risk gradient (the decrease in risk as a function of distance from the impact point), then warning recipients will respond inappropriately. Specifically, people will underrespond if they overestimate their distance from the impact point or the slope of the risk gradient, but they will overrespond if they underestimate their distance from the impact point or the slope of the risk gradient. Indeed, Houts and colleagues (1984) found that residents' evacuation of the area near the Three Mile Island nuclear power plant could be predicted by their proximity to the damaged reactor (see also Lindell, 1994a, and Lindell and Earle, 1983, for further discussion of perceived risk gradients).

Furthermore, as indicated above, messages that contain a specific protective action recommendation are more likely to generate an appropriate disaster response than are warnings that lack such guidance (Drabek, 1986; Fitzpatrick & Mileti, 1991; Mileti & Beck, 1975; Perry et al., 1981). There are at least two possible explanations for this effect. First, protective action recommendations contribute to the development of a decision set—warning recipients are given an alternative to continuing normal activities. Second, an official protective action recommendation implies that authorities consider the recommended action to be effective and feasible, which facilitates protective action assessment.

Although there has been some conflicting evidence in the empirical literature, it appears probable that repetition of a warning message (even without adding new information) increases threat belief (the outcome of the risk identification stage) and enhances people's perceptions of personal risk (the outcome of the risk assessment stage). Lachman, Tatsuoka, and Bonk (1961) called attention to this effect in a study of tsunami warnings in Hawaii, which showed that after a siren signal was disseminated, further warnings via other channels increased evacuation compliance. Mileti and Beck (1975) replicated these findings for flood evacuation warning recipients in Rapid City, South Dakota, although they found that the magnitude of the increases in disaster response declined with each successive warning. Perry and colleagues' (1981) study of flood evacuation in four communities suggested a further qualification to the apparent relationship between number of warnings, threat belief, and disaster response. These researchers found that warning repetition was positively (though modestly) correlated with threat belief, but the correlation with disaster response was not statistically significant. This latter finding is consistent with the PADM, according to which threat belief is a single element that takes place early in the protective action decision process. The later steps in the disaster response process introduce additional information that determines whether there will be compliance with a protective action recommendation. Furthermore, message repetition is confounded with other variables (content specificity and warning confirmation processes) whose impacts have not been empirically partialled out in the research conducted to date. Regardless of the effect of repeated receipt of warning messages, it is clear that repeated transmission across a variety of channels is most likely to enhance warning penetration of normal activities and, thus, the probability that each person in the risk area will receive at least one warning (Mileti, Fitzpatrick, & Farhar, 1992; Rogers & Sorenson, 1988).

Other message characteristics have been addressed by Mileti and Peek (2000) and Mileti and Sorensen (1987), who contend that warnings should be specific, consistent, certain, clear, accurate, and sufficient. Many of these propositions have been supported by research on persuasive communications, which has demonstrated that receivers are affected by factors such as the use of figurative language, which is consistent with findings from research on social cognition that vivid images are more readily understood and remembered. Similarly, the inclusion of explicit conclusions—which sometimes is counterproductive in other contexts—is always recommended in disaster warnings. Research on disasters indicates that warnings should begin with a description of the threat (the ordering of message content) and use this as the basis for recommendations about the protective actions that authorities think should be taken (explicit conclusions). It also is clear that warnings should be delivered forcefully; many jurisdictions have found that emphasizing the high likelihood of death from remaining in a risk area substantially increases evacuation rates. Moreover, disaster research confirms the need to address any counterarguments resulting from disbelief by emphasizing the certainty, severity, and immediacy of the threat (which establishes a threat belief and protection motivation), as well as the efficacy and feasibility of the recommended protective action (which facilitates the production of an adaptive plan). Disaster research also indicates that risk communicators should include uncertain information (the equivalent of "weak information" in the context of persuasive communication) and explicitly discuss the reasons for the uncertainty. In the case of many natural hazards, this uncertainty arises from the inherent unpredictability of physical systems such as hurricanes and volcanoes. It can be difficult to apply some of the other principles of persuasion because the optimal level of factors such as message clarity and speed of message delivery will depend on the characteristics of the warning recipients, especially their preexisting level of knowledge about the hazard and protective actions.

The discussion to this point has referred to "the warning message" as if there were only one warning message, but, as we have indicated at many points, it often is the case that those at risk receive multiple warning messages from a variety of sources. The multiplicity of sources is frequently associated with conflicting risk assessments or differences in protective action recommendations. Even when there is a single source or when warning sources agree, the warning message might conflict with environmental cues, as when risk area residents are advised to evacuate 36 hours before an approaching hurricane makes landfall, even though the sky is currently clear. Alternatively, those who receive a recommendation to evacuate might observe that no one else in the community is making visible preparations to leave. In all of these cases, conflicts cause delays while the conflicts are resolved cognitively or while additional information is either actively sought or passively awaited.

Receiver Characteristics

A variety of receiver characteristics have been shown to be related to disaster response and four categories of these are discussed here: previous experience, pre-existing beliefs, personality traits, and demographic characteristics (including ethnicity).

Previous Experience

Previous experience (either direct or vicarious) with disasters, especially people's knowledge about the hazard and protective actions, has been posited to be related to the protective action decision process in a variety of ways. Unfortunately, empirical studies of the effects of previous experience on people's assessment of the hazard and alternative protective actions have produced conflicting results. In support of a positive effect, Anderson (1969) found that individuals who had recently experienced a natural disaster were more likely to believe warnings and more likely to attempt some adaptive response. Moreover, a study of people who left their homes in response to what turned out to be a false warning reported that "few of the evacuees complained about being misled by the false alarm: the vast majority said that they would evacuate again under the same circumstances" (Janis, 1962, p. 85). Thus, assuming that a warning has been confirmed, these studies indicate that previous experience with disaster (even with false alarms) enhances threat belief and the probability of an adaptive response. Moreover, Nelson and colleagues (1989) studied 2,820 residents of the Tampa Bay area following Hurricane Elena and found a statistically significant correlation between the number of years people had lived in the area (a surrogate for experience) and their evacuation compliance.

On the other hand, some studies of evacuation in response to hurricanes on the Gulf coast report that a large proportion of people who failed to evacuate were long-time residents of an area that previously had experienced hurricane impact (Windham et al., 1977). In a review of four hurricane studies, Baker (1979) could find no evidence for a direct effect of experience on warning response; those who had previously experienced hurricanes were no more or less likely to evacuate than those who had no experience with hurricanes.

The apparent conflict among these results can be resolved through careful reexamination of some of the conclusions drawn by previous researchers. Fritz (1961a) concluded that "the most highly organized preparation exists in communities and societies that have *repeatedly* and *recently* experienced the *same* kind of disaster" (p. 659; emphasis added). This community experience can affect individual households in a number of ways. First, community experience can result in the development of community-level mechanisms such as an emergency management system that is capable of responding to disaster onset. However, the community's experience with a hazard might have little effect on individual households if the occurrence of disaster impact is so infrequent and, especially, remote in time that many residents were not alive (or were living elsewhere) during previous impacts. In such cases, community members who had not personally experienced disasters within the community could only learn about them vicariously.

In summary, there are no consistent effects of direct hazard experience on the predecisional processes of reception/exposure, attention, or comprehension/interpretation. Nor do there appear to be any systematic effects on the decision stages of risk identification, risk assessment, protective action search, protective action assessment, and protective action implementation. Finally, there appears to be no research addressing the effects of direct hazard experience on the information-seeking activities of information needs assessment, communication action assessment, and communication action implementation. It appears that personal experience affects very general beliefs about hazards, but it does not necessarily determine people's situational assessments. Thus, experience can produce erroneous conclusions that sometimes enhance disaster response but other times detract from it.

Prior Beliefs

The failure to find a consistent effect of experience can be explained by variations in people's interpretations of their experience. Burton and Kates (1964) described people as "prisoners of their experience" who find it difficult to conceive of situations that are more extreme than their previous experience. Similarly, Mileti and colleagues (1975) observed, "Many people apparently couldn't conceive of the magnitude of the event because their prior flood experience gave them a less than adequate view of what a 'flood' could produce" (p. 20). That is, the effect of experience depends on *what is learned* from that experience.

A slightly different issue concerns the perceived relevance of previous experience. Researchers have found that many people think that the occurrence of one event will somehow affect the occurrence of a subsequent event (Burton et al., 1993; Slovic et al., 1974). For example, some people erroneously believe that disasters cannot be repeated ("lightning doesn't strike twice in the same place"), while others think that once a catastrophic event does occur, it will not occur again for a long time ("we had a 100-year flood last year, so we're safe for the next 99 years"). This appears to be a slightly different phenomenon from people's sense of invulnerability to the negative personal consequences of such events. That is, frequently even those who believe that two 100-year floods can occur in successive years believe that such events will not affect them significantly.

What people have learned from their prior direct or vicarious experience is contained in their prior beliefs about the hazard and protective actions—what can be called *salient beliefs* (Fishbein & Ajzen, 1975) or *schemas* (Fiske & Taylor, 1991). There has been a significant amount of research on beliefs about environmental hazards, much of which has been conducted under the rubric of risk perception and has focused on identifying the attributes that differentiate acceptable from unacceptable technological risks (e.g., Slovic, 1987). This research has found that perceptions of the risks of a broad range of technologies and societal activities can be defined by characteristics such as whether the risks are dreaded and whether they are known to those people who are exposed to them. In particular, these risk perception studies have shown that nuclear facilities are viewed very negatively because they are high on both dimensions (Flynn, Peters, Mertz, & Slovic, 1998). Other work on risk perception has focused more narrowly on people's perceptions of the characteristics of three environmental hazards: a volcanic eruption, a release of chlorine from a railroad tankcar, and a release of radioactive materials from a nuclear power plant (Lindell, 1994a). The four categories of hazard characteristics identified included characteristics of the hazard agent (likelihood of a major event, ease of reducing risks, and likelihood of release prevention), impact characteristics (existence of environmental cues, speed of onset, scope of impact, and duration of impact), personal consequences (immediate death, delayed cancer, genetic effects, and property damage), and affective reactions (dread, frequency of thought about the hazard, and frequency of discussion about the hazard). Comparing the profiles of the three hazard agents across the different perceived risk characteristics confirmed previous risk perception results in showing that a nuclear power plant accident was rated extremely high in the perceived scope and duration of impact, as well as in delayed cancer and genetic effects. A nuclear power plant accident was rated as higher in dread, but the possibility of a volcanic eruption generated greater frequency of thought and discussion about the hazard. Although a chlorine release was perceived to be more similar to a nuclear power plant accident in some respects, it was judged to be more similar to a volcanic eruption in others.

Curiously, there appears to have been relatively little research on beliefs about protective actions in response to environmental hazards. Data on perceptions of three protective actions for a toxic chemical emergency showed that evacuation was perceived to have a higher level of efficacy than sheltering in-place or expedient respiratory protection, but it was also perceived as higher in time, effort, skill, money, and barriers to implementation (Lindell & Perry, 1992). Comparison of the perceived characteristics of 12 different seismic hazard adjustments indicates that a diverse set of seismic hazard adjustments can be differentiated by means of their perceived efficacy and resource requirements (Lindell & Prater, 2002; Lindell & Whitney, 2000). Moreover, the efficacy attributes—efficacy in protecting people, efficacy in protecting property, and utility for other purposes—are the strongest correlates of seismic hazard adjustment adoption.

Unfortunately, there does not appear to be any research that has specifically addressed the ways in which prior beliefs about environmental hazards or protective actions affect predecisional processing, the decision stages of protective action decision making, or information search activities. There appears to be no obvious reason to assume that prior beliefs would affect the predecisional process of reception/exposure, but they are likely to affect people's attention to and interpretation of environmental cues, as well as their attention to and comprehension of warning messages. It also is likely that there are systematic effects of personal beliefs about the hazard and protective actions on the decision stages of risk identification, risk assessment, protective action search, protective action assessment, and protective action implementation. Finally, there appears to be no research addressing the effects of prior beliefs on the information-seeking activities of information needs assessment, communication action assessment, and communication action implementation. It seems likely that prior beliefs about hazards and protective actions provide schemas that organize people's expectations and interpretations of the information they receive during emergencies, thus significantly affecting their situational assessments. However, further research is needed to examine the ways in which these effects are caused.

Personality Characteristics

Researchers have speculated about a variety of personality characteristics relevant to warning response (e.g., Lifton & Olson, 1976), but comparatively few of these variables have been subjected to empirical testing (Perry, 1983a). Sims and Bauman (1972) reported that individuals who believe they control what happens to them (internal locus of control) are more likely to undertake protective actions in response to tornado warnings. However, those with an external locus of control "place less trust in man's communal knowledge and control systems; they await the fated onslaughts, watchful but passive" (Sims & Bauman, 1972, p. 1391). These studies suggest that those who have an external locus of control, described as "fatalistic" by Turner and colleagues (1986), believe that it is not possible to achieve protection regardless what action they take and, therefore, are less likely to act on a disaster warning.

In examining this issue, it is very important to distinguish between fatalism and low self-efficacy (Bandura, 1977). The personality trait of *fatalism* is a generalized belief about all of an individual's activities, whereas *self-efficacy* refers to a belief that is specific to an individual's level of achievement on a given task. Thus, individuals might have a generally high level of internal fate control, yet have a low sense of self-efficacy in successfully implementing an unfamiliar protective action. Moreover, it also is important to distinguish between an individual's sense of self-efficacy in performing a protective action and the efficacy of that protective action, as we described it previously. *Self-efficacy* therefore refers to people's expectations as to whether they have the personal resources—such as knowledge, skill, and energy—to make successful efforts to perform a specific task (for example, develop a family emergency plan), whereas *response efficacy* refers to an individual's expectation that successful completion of this task will ensure protection from the hazard. Thus, it is possible for an individual to have a high level of self-efficacy about implementing a protective action (e.g., that one can shelter in-place by closing doors and windows and shutting off heating, ventilation, and air conditioning systems) but to believe that the protective action is low in efficacy for providing protection against the hazard (e.g., that sheltering in-place will prevent chemical or radiological exposure).

It is also important to recognize that when we find some people who believe they have a low level of personal control (and thus think they do not control their own fate), this does not tell us who or what they think *does* control their fate. Some people believe that their safety in an emergency can be affected by forces such as luck or God's will, yet others believe that the external sources of control are human agents such as their peers (friends, relatives, neighbors, and coworkers) and government at the local, state, and federal levels. It is important to make this distinction among different sources of external control because individuals' belief in control by other human sources could provide optimism that protection will occur, whereas their belief in luck or fate would not. This distinction can be illustrated by data from Perry and Lindell (1990a), who asked residents near an active volcano to judge the degree to which their safety in an emergency would be affected by different forces or agents. Their data revealed that those in the risk area felt that their safety would be most significantly influenced by their actions and those of their immediate family. Although the importance of luck or chance was judged to be relatively small, the importance of God's will was considered to be greater than any human agent other than the respondent personally.

In summary, the PADM makes no predictions regarding the effects of personal control on predecisional processes (warning reception/exposure to environmental cues, attention to such information, and message comprehension/environmental cue interpretation). Nor is there any expectation that beliefs about personal control would affect the formation of a threat belief or protection motivation. The PADM does predict that self-efficacy affects protective action assessment and, to a lesser degree, information search. Fatalism is expected to be correlated with disaster response to the extent that people who are high in fatalism would, by their very nature, be low in self-efficacy for any protective actions. By contrast, those who are low in fatalism might be high in self-efficacy for one protective action and low in self-efficacy for another. Thus, the correlation of fatalism with the adoption of protective action would be expected to be lower than the correlation of self-efficacy with the adoption of that protective action.

Demographic Characteristics

Demographic characteristics of warning recipients have been identified by a variety of researchers as influencing different aspects of warning response behavior (Mileti, 1974). In some cases, it has been argued that income and education (combined as socioeconomic status), age, gender, and ethnicity directly affect the predecisional stages of disaster response, as well as the five stages of the protective action decision process (risk identification, risk assessment, protective action search, protective action assessment, and protective action implementation). These demographic variables also appear to affect the social context variables that themselves affect the protective action decision process (participation in kin, friendship, and community networks and family context) and information-seeking behaviors such as warning confirmation. For example, it has been reported that women are more likely to believe warning messages than are men (Mack & Baker, 1961; Turner, Nigg, Paz, & Young, 1981) and that older people are less likely than those in other age groups to believe warnings (Friedsam, 1962; Windham et al., 1977) or to adopt protective measures (Mileti, 1975). Research also has reported that there is a curvilinear relationship between socioeconomic status and threat belief (Mack and Baker, 1961) and that ethnic minorities are less likely to consider messages from authorities as credible (Perry & Mushcatel, 1986).

For the most part, the utility of demographic variables in warning response models has been limited (Drabek, 1986; Zeigler et al., 1981). After an exhaustive review of research, Quarantelli (1980) concluded that "studies dealing with demographic characteristics and evacuation are simply not conclusive" (p. 43). An important theoretical qualification should be made any time demographic variables are argued to be causes of disaster response. In particular, variables like age, gender, and ethnicity are set at (or counted from) birth—long before the occurrence of a given disaster requires a response. That is, these variables are temporally antecedent to all of the other variables that are used to explain warning response. Because they precede environmental cues, social context, warning components (source, channel, content), and other receiver variables, demographic variables are unlikely to appear as proximal causes in multistage models of disaster response. When differences in disaster response do appear for people in different categories of a given demographic variable, it is advisable to identify the variables that intervene between demographic variables and disaster response. Many early studies in particular used very simple models (often bivariate) to document the covariation of demographic characteristics with disaster responses. Modern multivariate, multistage statistical models have revealed that when intervening variables are introduced into analyses, some apparent direct relationships between demographic variables and warning response behaviors disappear (Perry & Lindell, 1991). Consistent with this argument, Aguirre's (1991) multivariate analysis of hurricane evacuation compliance found that socioeconomic status, gender, age, and marital status were not statistically significantly related to disaster response.

Two other complications arise in interpreting the importance of demographic variables. First, there is little meaningful data on some demographic variables in warning settings. Studies indicating gender differences in the disaster response are probably important, for example, but more needs to be learned about the relationship of gender to environmental cues, social context, warning components, and other receiver characteristics, as well as its effects on predecisional processes and the stages of the protective action decision making. It is possible that family roles account for gender differences, but virtually all of the data on gender in disaster response uses the individual, not the family, as the unit of analysis. Second, some demographic variables are intercorrelated, and their effects are difficult to separate in most of the disaster response literature. Thus, unless age, ethnicity, income, and education are all included in an analysis, it is difficult to determine which one (or combination) of these is responsible for a particular pattern of cognitive and behavioral response, and little of the available data has been analyzed or reported in a way that permits specific conclusions to be drawn. In light of these concerns regarding the use of demographic variables in disaster response models, we will focus our attention here on two demographic variables that have received some empirical attention: age and socioeconomic status.

The age of warning recipients has been recognized for decades as a limitation on response behaviors. Research indicates that the elderly are more likely than those in other age groups to experience serious outcomes such as death (Perry & Lindell, 1997a), monetary loss (Bolin & Klenow, 1983), and negative emotional and physical health consequences (Logue, Melick, & Struening, 1981). However, the data that might explain these outcome differentials are sparser and less consistent than data on the general population. One potential explanation for differences in death rates is differences in disaster response (e.g., differential evacuation rates) and, consistent with this hypothesis, a number of early studies reported that the propensity to comply with an evacuation warning decreases as age increases (Friedsam, 1962; Mileti et al., 1975; Moore et al., 1963; Sorenson & Richardson, 1984; Steele, Lyons, & Smith, 1979; Windham et al., 1977). Difficulties in interpretation arise, however, because these studies tended to confound factors such as physical health and social participation with age. Failure to include intervening variables probably accounts for competing findings that elderly are no less likely to engage in protective action than other age groups (Drabek, 1983; Drabek & Boggs, 1968; Quarantelli, 1980). Perry and Lindell (1997a) conducted a review of age and evacuation compliance in nine disasters, including floods, volcanic eruptions, and hazardous materials emergencies. These data revealed that for all events there was no statistically significant relationship between age and evacuation compliance; when dealing with healthy people who live independently, compliance with an evacuation warning does not appear to be solely a function of age.

Perry and Lindell (1997a) did emphasize that age is important in warning response to the extent that it is related to other factors such as social context, which itself appears to influence still other factors more closely related to the protective action decision process. Specifically, age has an impact on two social context variables. As age increases, there are decreases in the levels of both community participation (involvement in voluntary associations) and immersion in kin and friendship networks (Perry, 1985; Perry et al., 1981). Thus, differentials in disaster death rates might be due to lower rates of warning receipt from peers.

Like age and other demographic variables, the influence of socioeconomic status on disaster response is equivocal. For example, Lachman and colleagues (1961) found that education was unrelated to evacuation, whereas Flynn and Chalmers (1980) reported a positive relationship between formal education and evacuation. Moore (1958) found that income (confounded with ethnicity in his data) was inversely related to threat belief, but Mileti (1974) found a nonsignificant correlation between these variables. Mack and Baker (1961) reported that a combination of education and income had a curvilinear relationship with threat belief; those with moderate levels of education and income were more likely than those at the extremes to develop a threat belief. Two points are important in interpreting these data. First, among studies that did show relationships of income and education with any warning variable, the magnitude of the correlation was low. Second, a compelling theoretical rationale has not yet been presented for why either education or income should be *directly* related to any of the stages of the protective action decision process. One possible explanation for effects of income and education is that they decrease evacuation feasibility due to restricted material resources, knowledge, and skill. For example, low income could decrease the likelihood of having a personal vehicle and both of these variables could be related to low locational mobility. In particular, those who remain in the same area where they grew up have a high likelihood that all their friends and relatives live in the same risk area. This would limit them to sheltering only in public facilities for mass congregate care.

Another possible role for socioeconomic status in disaster response might lie in its influence on social context variables. For example, there is evidence that socioeconomic status is positively correlated with participation in voluntary associations and other community organizations (Alvirez & Bean, 1976; Tomeh, 1973). This finding was replicated by Cohen and Kapsis (1978) who determined that lower socioeconomic status is associated with lower rates of participation even when ethnicity is controlled.

In summary, age is predicted to have a significant effect on the predecisional process of warning reception but not on exposure to environmental cues, attention to warnings and environmental cues, or message comprehension and environmental cue interpretation. Socioeconomic status is not predicted to have effects on any of the predecisional processes and neither of these demographic variables is predicted to affect the formation of a threat belief, protection motivation, protective action search, or protective action assessment. The research reviewed here suggests that there could be a modest effect of age on information search, but only via the correlation of age and social integration.

Ethnicity

As noted above, some studies cite evidence of ethnic differences in disasters, but most of these studies have been descriptive in nature or have used very simple bivariate models linking ethnicity directly to disaster response (Drabek, 1986). Moreover, research on disaster response to date has addressed ethnic identity at only a superficial (respondent self-report) level and only sporadic studies since the mid-1980s have measured ethnicity at even this level (Perry, 1987). This scanty empirical record would seem to preclude any definitive statements about the role of ethnicity in disaster response, because it is not possible to determine the extent to which self-reported ethnicity adequately measures adherence to ethnic subcultural activities and, in turn, accounts for ethnic differences in disaster response. However, research on ethnic minorities indicates that they are more deeply immersed than the majority in kin and friendship networks and community participation (Bianchi & Farley, 1979). In turn, this suggests that ethnicity could influence disaster response via its effects on family context, community participation, and warning characteristics. This proposition is supported by a study of a Mexican community during a flood of the Rio Grande in which Clifford (1958) observed that "people were oriented so strongly toward the extended family that they almost completely neglected neighbors and friends" (p. 116). Further, Staples (1976) reported that "the Black kinship network is more extensive and cohesive . . . a larger proportion of Black families take relatives into their households" (p. 123). Similar observations have been made regarding Mexican Americans and Asian Americans (Wilkson, 1999). Hence, family structure and role responsibilities are different in minority and majority groups (Bianchi & Farley, 1979; Staples & Mirande, 1980), with minority households being more likely to be extended families, to involve multigenerational depth, and to have more than a single family in the same household. For disaster warnings, one result of a propensity toward such households is an expansion of the number of warning sources. However, it also implies an increase in the number of individuals whose safety must be accounted for at the time of warning receipt. Consequently, there is a greater probability among minority families that some family members may not be present or accounted for, thereby slowing or stopping family disaster response at the stage of protective action implementation. Indeed, it may be this difficulty in the family context, rather than any inherent issues in personal risk assessment, that has been detected by researchers who report that minorities fail to comply with disaster warnings (Moore, 1958; Sims & Baumann, 1972).

More recent research has tested a multivariate model of disaster response that included three American ethnic groups—Whites (non-Hispanic Caucasians, primarily of European ancestry), African Americans, and Mexican Americans—reacting to a flood and a hazardous materials accident (Perry & Lindell, 1991). A key finding of this study was that ethnic group membership was associated with small partial regression coefficients that were not statistically significant. Instead, evacuation was more a function of perceived risk (measured in terms of certainty and severity), possession of an adaptive plan, and warning characteristics (including source credibility, warning confirmation, and warning content). These findings indicate that, *without regard to ethnicity,* people are likely to comply with a protective action recommendation if they are convinced that the warning is accurate, risk is high, and they have an adaptive plan. Thus, the disaster response process is similar across all three ethnic groups, implying that separate versions of the PADM are not needed for Whites, African Americans, and Mexican Americans.

It is important to recognize that this does not mean that ethnicity is not an issue for disaster response. Instead, these data reveal that ethnicity is strongly related to source credibility and warning confirmation behavior, an observation that was made in a more general way by McLuckie (1970). However, there appears to be no simple relationship between ethnicity and source credibility because there are variations from one community to another. Specifically, Perry and Lindell (1991) found that in Abilene, Texas—a community affected by a major flood—Mexican Americans cited social network contacts (friends, relatives, neighbors) as the most credible sources, followed by mass media and then uniformed authorities (firefighters and police officers). By contrast, Mexican Americans in Mt. Vernon, Washington, who were warned of a hazardous materials emergency most often identified authorities as the most credible source, followed by mass media and then social networks. Further complicating the findings, African Americans in the Abilene flood had the highest confidence in authorities, followed by social networks, whereas Whites in that community had the most confidence in the mass media, followed by authorities. The important point here is that attributions of source credibility can vary not only between ethnic groups but also, for a particular ethnic group, between communities (or hazard agents, since communities and hazard agents were confounded in this study).

We have already seen that the most common response to a disaster warning is disbelief and a search for further information. The data reported by Perry and Lindell (1991) indicate that there are ethnic variations in both the level of warning confirmation behavior and the types of sources contacted by warning recipients. It was found that slightly smaller proportions of Whites attempted to confirm warning messages than did either African Americans or Mexican Americans. Data on the first additional information source contacted by the ethnic groups is also informative. In both the flood and hazardous materials emergencies, Whites were most likely to contact the mass media (radio or television station) and somewhat more likely to contact social networks. Mexican Americans confronted with a flood threat followed the same pattern as Whites, but when faced with a hazardous materials emergency, Mexican Americans were most likely to use a social network contact first, followed by mass media. African Americans, on the other hand, were most likely to use a social network contact, followed by contacting an authority. Again, the important conclusion is that, left to their own devices, members of different ethnic groups contact different categories of sources for warning confirmation. There is also variation within the same ethnic group and across types of disaster agent.

In summary, ethnicity is predicted to have a significant effect on the predecisional process of warning reception, but not on exposure to environmental cues or attention to warnings and environmental cues. Ethnicity also is predicted to affect message comprehension and environmental cue interpretation. Based on the available data, there is no expectation that ethnicity would affect the formation of a threat belief or protection motivation. However, there is a possibility that it could affect protective action search and protective action assessment indirectly via a correlation with perceptions of personal control. The research reviewed here suggests that there are no consistent effects of ethnicity on information search.

❖ WARNING COMPLIANCE AND SPONTANEOUS RESPONSE

The discussion to this point has focused on the factors that affect disaster response, but it is important to recognize some important distinctions among different forms of disaster response. When people receive a warning that contains a protective action recommendation—the guidance offered by authorities—they can choose whether or not to comply with the protective action recommendation. A failure to comply with the guidance can result from deficiencies in the warning message or from additional information obtained from environmental cues or other social sources. In fact, the level of noncompliance with official recommendations is quite high in many disasters. For example, Dow and Cutter (2002) reported an evacuation rate of 65% during Hurricane Floyd in South Carolina but Riad, Norris, and Ruback (1999) found only a 42% rate of compliance with evacuation warnings in their samples of victims from Hurricanes Hugo and Andrew. Similarly, Prater, Wenger, and Grady's (2000) data showed that only 34% of their respondents evacuated from the Texas counties most severely threatened by Hurricane Bret. Indeed, Baker (1991) reported that evacuation rates have varied significantly from one location to another in a given storm and from one storm to another at a given location. The observed variation in compliance rates is presumably due to variation in the availability of environmental cues, situational variables, warning components, and receiver characteristics, but further research is needed to confirm that this is the case.

One additional issue that concerns warning compliance relates to people's use of recommended evacuation routes and destinations, but this also is a neglected area of research. Data from recent hurricane evacuations (Dow & Cutter, 2002; Prater et al., 2000) show that evacuees do not distribute themselves evenly over the available evacuation routes. Instead, they take the most familiar routes inland (especially interstate highways), thus overloading those routes and creating traffic jams that take many hours to clear. The data from actual evacuations are replicated in evacuation expectations data (Lindell et al., 2001), which suggest that the problem of unbalanced evacuation route loading arises from beliefs that coastal residents have formed long before a hurricane threatens.

In addition to noncompliance, people can be said to engage in spontaneous protective response when they choose to take action that has not been recommended by authorities. Spontaneous protective response is a potential problem for environmental hazard managers if protective response by those who are not at risk impedes protective response by those who are. This problem can arise in the evacuation of risk areas where there is a high population density and limited evacuation route capacity, as would be the case for some hurricane, chemical facility, and nuclear power plant emergencies. Spontaneous evacuation has received increasing attention since Zeigler and colleagues (1981) called attention to the occurrence of this phenomenon during the Three Mile Island nuclear power plant incident. They noted that there was an extremely high level of spontaneous evacuation during the emergency, with estimates ranging to up to ten times as many people evacuating as would have been appropriate given the governor's limited evacuation advisory (Lindell & Perry, 1983).

Spontaneous protective response appears to occur for a number of specific reasons, but the underlying cause is that those who think they are at risk lack confidence in the credibility of the authorities to provide either timely or accurate information about the situation. In some cases, this is because authorities are suspected to be withholding information or, worse yet, actually have been found to be withholding information. When the latter situation occurs, the usual reason is that the authorities were concerned that people would panic if accurate information were released or that the available information was extremely uncertain and they were awaiting further data before making an official statement. Even though withholding information does not actually cause panic (which is extremely rare in disasters), it does cause outrage and a loss of credibility that becomes manifest in people seeking other sources of information on which to base their protective action decisions.

Another reason for spontaneous protective response is that the protection actions recommended by authorities are inconsistent with other information that people have (such as environmental cues) or with their evaluation of the available information. The latter case can be illustrated by the finding of Houts and colleagues (1984) that the high level of spontaneous evacuation at Three Mile Island appeared to be defined by a gradient of perceived risk that differed from the one identified in the governor's limited evacuation advisory. The official warning advised evacuation for pregnant women and preschool children within 5 miles of the plant. Houts and his colleagues found that the probability of evacuation was inversely related to geographic distance from the plant and positively related to demographic similarity to those described in the warning (see also Lindell & Earle, 1983). That is, the likelihood of household evacuation increased as households were located closer to the plant, women were closer to childbearing age, and children were younger. Although some have attributed the high level of spontaneous evacuation during the Three Mile Island incident to the public's unique fear of radiation hazard, there also was evidence of spontaneous evacuation during the Mississauga Ontario train derailment (Burton et al., 1981) and the May 18, 1980 eruption of Mt. St. Helens (Perry & Greene, 1982).

Gladwin and Peacock (1997) recently confirmed the occurrence of spontaneous evacuation in hurricanes, which Baker (1991) reported to range from 20% to 50% of residents in areas of low risk. Lindell and colleagues (2001) found that rates of expected spontaneous evacuation decayed exponentially as a function of hurricane risk area (topographical elevation and distance from the coast) and that expectations of spontaneous evacuation had a significant inverse relation to respondents'

Table 3.1 Smoothed Percentages of Households Expecting to Evacuate as a Function of Hurricane Category and Risk Area

Risk Area	*Category One*	*Category Two*	*Category Three*	*Category Four*	*Category Five*
1	45.9	63.7	87.8	98.2	100.0
2	35.9	53.7	77.8	88.2	91.4
3	31.1	48.9	73.0	83.4	86.6
4	28.2	46.0	70.1	80.5	83.7
5	26.5	44.3	68.4	78.8	82.0

confidence in the accuracy of evacuation warnings. In a hurricane emergency, it would be ideal if residents evacuated only for hurricanes that were expected to affect their risk area, where Risk Area 1 is the geographic area that is expected to be affected by a Category One hurricane, and so on. Under these conditions, each category or storm would elicit 100% evacuation by the population of the corresponding risk area and all risk areas closer to the coast (perfect compliance). Conversely, none of the population in risk areas farther inland would evacuate (no spontaneous evacuation). In contrast to this idealized pattern, Lindell and colleagues (2001) found that there is a substantial percentage of the population that does not expect to evacuate when authorities consider it appropriate for them to do so (i.e., the noncompliant) and also a substantial percentage that expect to evacuate before authorities consider it appropriate (i.e., spontaneous evacuees).

Table 3.1 shows smoothed data on risk area residents' expectations about their evacuation behavior that differ significantly from the idealized pattern of 100% evacuation in areas where this is recommended and 0% evacuation farther inland. Substantially less than 100% expect to evacuate the risk area corresponding to each hurricane category (e.g., Risk Area 1 for a Category One Hurricane) and significantly more than 0% expect to evacuate from risk areas that are inland from the risk area corresponding to each hurricane category (e.g., Risk Areas 2–5 for a Category One Hurricane).

This continuous gradient of expected protective response is quite consistent with the perceived risk gradient reported by Houts and colleagues (1984). In contrast with the situation involving the Three Mile Island nuclear power plant accident, where the definition of the risk area was entirely ad hoc, the situation studied by Lindell and colleagues (2001) is defined by a long-established state policy on hurricane evacuation. Thus, there is a similarity in the results despite differences in the hazard and the scientific basis for the policy. Indeed, the problem is compounded by a recent research finding that as many as one third of the evacuees from Hurricane Bret could not accurately identify their risk area on a map (Zhang, Prater, & Lindell,

2003). Thus, warnings that specifically mentioned the recipient's risk area would not necessarily improve compliance.

Response Timing

Environmental hazard managers need to understand the timeliness of disaster response because tardy implementation can sometimes put people as much at risk as can noncompliance. Unfortunately, researchers have given this problem only limited attention. Urbanik, Desrosiers, Lindell, and Schuller (1980) proposed that the evacuation process consists of four time components. These are (1) the time required by authorities to make an evacuation decision, (2) the time required for a household to receive a warning, (3) the time that a household devotes to preparation for evacuation, and (4) the response time required to travel to safety. Lindell and colleagues (Lindell & Perry, 1987, 1992; Lindell et al., 1985) reported warning and preparation times from four floods and the eruption of Mt. St. Helens, Rogers and Sorensen (1989) reported warning and response time data from two hazardous materials spills, and Sorensen (1991) analyzed factors that accounted for household differences in warning and preparation times. In addition, Lindell and colleagues (2001) collected data on Texas coastal residents' expectations about the time it would take them to perform six preparation activities for evacuation from hurricanes.

Local residents are not the only people located in risk areas who need to receive warnings, but there has been little research on the evacuation of tourists and other transients. Unfortunately, this topic has been neglected until very recently (Drabek, 1996) and even that study did not address components of evacuation time estimates (ETEs) for this population segment. Drabek's data suggest that transients will have high levels of warning compliance and spontaneous evacuation, use only a single vehicle per room, be warned more rapidly than local residents, and prepare to evacuate much more rapidly than residents. However, there are only limited qualitative data to support these hypotheses.

Decision Time

Decision time, as defined by Urbanik and colleagues (1980), is primarily a concern in events such as hazardous materials facility accidents where public officials have little forewarning of disaster onset in their communities. In such situations, the time required for public officials to make a decision about evacuation can be a significant fraction of the interval between initiation of the incident and impact on the community (Lindell & Perry, 1992). Indeed, incidents involving airborne release of hazardous materials can evolve so rapidly that even a single hour's delay could result in significant hazard exposures for a large proportion of the risk area population

(McKenna, 2000). In a hurricane, by contrast, public officials often have days of forewarning and the problem is to determine whether the strike probability is high enough to justify an evacuation. Consequently, the problem in such incidents is how much time will be required to complete an evacuation after a decision is made, not after the hazard has been detected. Thus, the importance of the decision time component depends on the amount of forewarning associated with the hazard.

Empirically Based Warning Times

There are limited data on the amount of time that it takes each household to receive a warning, but one source consists of data on the elapsed time to first warning in two communities impacted by the eruption of Mt. St. Helens (Lindell & Perry, 1992). Toutle is located close to the volcano on its north side (the side toward which the blast from the May 18, 1980 eruption was directed) and Woodland is equally close to the volcano, but it is on the south side and was less vulnerable to the effects of the May 18 eruption.

At the time of the May 18 eruption, both communities were in a high state of alert and had been so since the first ash and steam eruptions began in late March of that year. Greene and colleagues (1981) reported that 34% of all respondents to a survey conducted in early April checked the news media for information about the volcano 2 to 3 times per day and another 56% checked more than 4 times per day. Lindell and Perry (1992) reported the warning data from Toutle and Woodland only in terms of the percent of households having received a warning at 15, 30, 60, and 120 minutes. These values, together with interpolated values that form a continuous series with equal intervals among data points, are displayed in Figure 3.1. These data can be approximated by the following function:

$$p_t = 1 - exp\ (-at^b), \qquad [1]$$

where p_t is the proportion of the households that have been warned at time t and *exp* denotes the base of the natural logarithm (e), which is multiplied by the coefficient a and raised to the b power. The warning time curve for Toutle rises very steeply because warnings were disseminated by multiple sources including face-to-face (24% of all warnings received) and route alert (16% of all warnings received) warnings from public safety officials. Warnings also were disseminated via radio and television (10% of all warnings received) and informal social networks (37% of all warnings received). As Figure 3.1 indicates, the speed of warning described by the Toutle data can be approximated by the "rapid" warning curve generated by substituting the constants $a = 2.00$ and $b = 0.50$ into Equation 1. A curve approximating a "moderately rapid" warning can be generated by inserting the constants $a = 1.30$ and

Figure 3.1 Warning Time Distributions

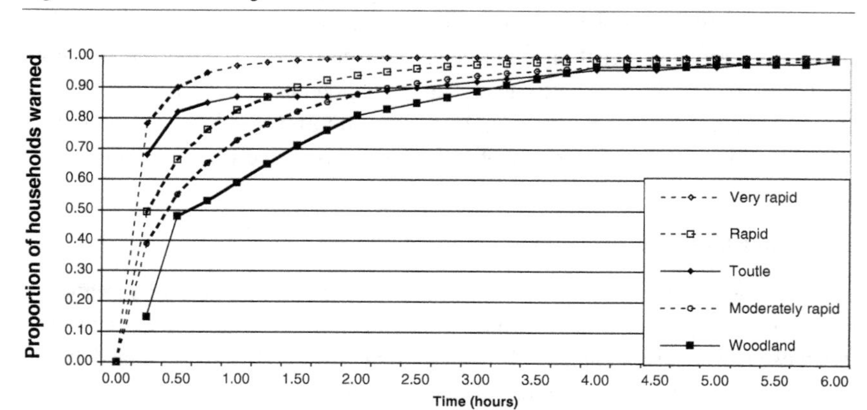

$b = 0.70$ in to Equation 1. The resulting curve falls (approximately) midway between the data from Toutle and Woodland.

As noted above, there is a limited amount of research on the evacuation of tourists, and what little research is available does not provide data on evacuation time components. However, Drabek's (1996) research suggests that tourists are warned at a faster rate than permanent residents, so the "very rapid" warning curve in Figure 3.1 seems appropriate for this population segment. This curve is generated by substituting parameters $a = 3.50$ and $b = 0.60$ in Equation 1.

Empirically Based Preparation Times

Evacuation preparation times can be estimated from data collected by Lindell and colleagues (2001), who asked residents of the five study areas along the Texas Gulf coast to report the length of time they estimated that it would take them to prepare to leave work, travel from work to home, gather household members, pack travel items, install storm shutters, and secure their home before evacuating from a hurricane. The cumulative distribution of times required for residents to prepare for evacuation if they must complete all of these tasks, beginning with return from work, is indicated by the curve labeled "residents/work" in Figure 3.2. The curve labeled "RW*" shows that the plot of the function in Equation 1 with the constants $a = 0.015$ and $b = 2.90$ provides a good approximation to the empirical data.

The curve labeled "residents/home" indicates the cumulative distribution of times required to complete only the last four of the tasks (i.e., assuming that the entire household was at home when a warning was received). The curve labeled "RH*" shows that the plot of the function in Equation 1 with the constants $a = 0.085$

Figure 3.2 Preparation Time Distributions

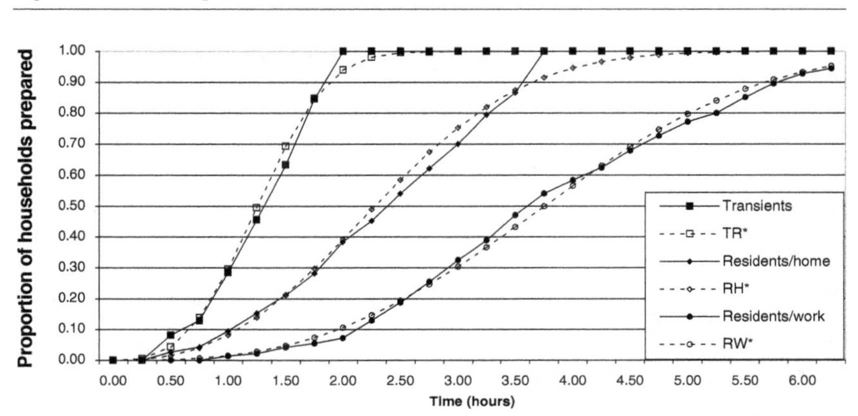

and $b = 2.55$ provides a good fit to the empirical data. Data from Drabek (1996) suggest that tourists evacuate more rapidly than residents, but there are no quantitative data on the size of this difference. Data from Lindell and colleagues (2001) indicate that the evacuation preparation times for permanent residents at home are expected to take place at the rates indicated by the center curve in Figure 3.2. A plausible assumption is that tourists would be three times as fast as permanent residents at home (the left-hand curve of Figure 3.2). The rationale for this assumption is that transients would only need to pack and check out, so three times as many transients as residents at home would be able to prepare to leave in a given period of time. The curve labeled "TR*" shows that the plot of the function in Equation 1 with the constants $a = 0.35$ and $b = 3.00$ fits the "transients" data well.

It is important to recognize that these ETE distributions are most likely to be accurate for hurricanes and other hazards in which there is some degree of forewarning. Sudden onset hazards, including many incidents involving releases of toxic materials, are likely to have different ETE distributions because the impact area for such hazards will be smaller (leading to a shorter warning time distribution). In addition, the threat to property for such hazards often is small compared to the threat to personal safety and the duration of impact could be shorter (especially for irritant gases such as chlorine and ammonia). As a result, the preparation time distribution also would be shorter (see Burton et al., 1981).

Empirically Based Trip Generation Times

The cumulative distributions of warning times and preparation times must be combined to produce a cumulative distribution of trip generation times (TGTs)—the

Figure 3.3 Trip Generation Times for Households

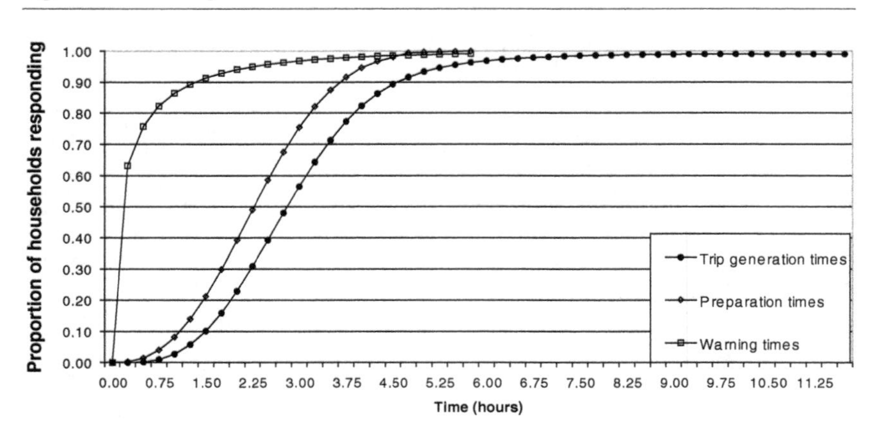

total time required for risk area residents to receive a warning *and* prepare to evacuate. Assuming statistical independence between warning time and preparation times, the TGT distribution is calculated by multiplying the probability of warning receipt within each time interval by the probability of preparing within each time interval (Urbanik, 2000). This operation generates a p (warning time periods) by q (preparation time periods) matrix. Once values are computed for all cells in the matrix, any cells that yield the same TGT are summed. For example, the cell for a warning time of 15 minutes and a preparation time of 30 minutes yields a TGT of 45 minutes, just as the cell for a warning time of 30 minutes and a preparation time of 15 minutes does. Consequently, the probabilities for these two cells are summed to produce the probability of a household taking 45 minutes to enter the ERS. The resulting distribution of TGTs describes the loading (i.e., the rate of vehicle entry) of households into the ERS. Figure 3.3 shows (from left to right) the distributions of "warning times," "preparation times," and "trip generation times" for households. A similar procedure is used to develop the loading function for transients.

A notable limitation in the present analysis is that household preparation and evacuation are assumed to begin only after an official warning is received. This is contrary to anecdotal data suggesting that some households evacuate early. To overcome this limitation, future evacuation studies should collect data on the time at which household evacuation preparations were initiated and also the time at which departure occurred. It is especially important that researchers establish when these activities occurred in relation to official evacuation warnings. Once these data have been collected, revised TGT distributions can be computed that have non-zero fractions of the risk area population evacuated at $t = 0$.

Finally, as noted earlier, there is uncertainty about the estimates for many input variables about which empirical data are available. This is especially true for the distributions of warning times and preparation times, but there also is uncertainty about spontaneous evacuation, evacuee route choice, and even the rate of warning compliance and the number of evacuating vehicles per household. Consequently, sensitivity analyses should be conducted to determine the extent to which any ETEs will be significantly affected by changes in the values of these parameters.

Surveys of evacuees' reports of their actual behavior and of risk area residents' reports of the behavior in which they expect to engage can obtain information about evacuation time components, although few studies conducted to date have collected such data. One reservation about collecting survey data arises from concerns that evacuees' reports of their actual behavior might be inaccurate if the data are collected long after the event. Conversely, risk area residents' reports of the behavior in which they expect to engage are, to some extent, speculative. In particular, respondents could provide distorted data about their future behavior unless they are asked specific questions that reproduce the context in which they will have to make their evacuation decisions during an actual incident.

Nonetheless, disaggregated data on evacuation time components are important because each time component could be the controlling factor in determining the time required to evacuate a given risk area under a particular set of conditions. For example, clearance time could be largely determined by warning time if the population is dispersed and has poor communications access, by preparation time if separated families must return home from work and school, by queue time if the risk area is densely populated with limited evacuation route capacity, or by travel time if evacuees must travel long distances to reach safety or if traffic jams decrease evacuation travel speeds. Consequently, generalizability of evacuation time data from one situation to another and one location to another requires data on each of the evacuation time components and a knowledge of the factors that influence the data that were obtained from a given situation and location.

❖ WARNING MULTIETHNIC COMMUNITIES

Given local authorities' concerns about reducing casualties and property loss—not to mention avoiding the likelihood of being held legally liable for failures to adequately protect public safety (Mileti, 1999), it is extremely important to communicate an adequately informative message that minimizes assumed knowledge about the hazard and protective actions. Drabek (1999) points out that poorly functioning warning systems and vague warning messages during Hurricane Mitch produced a death toll in excess of 10,000 throughout Central America. Such problems can be avoided by conceptualizing warnings from a social systems perspective, wherein warnings are

Figure 3.4 Disaster Warning System

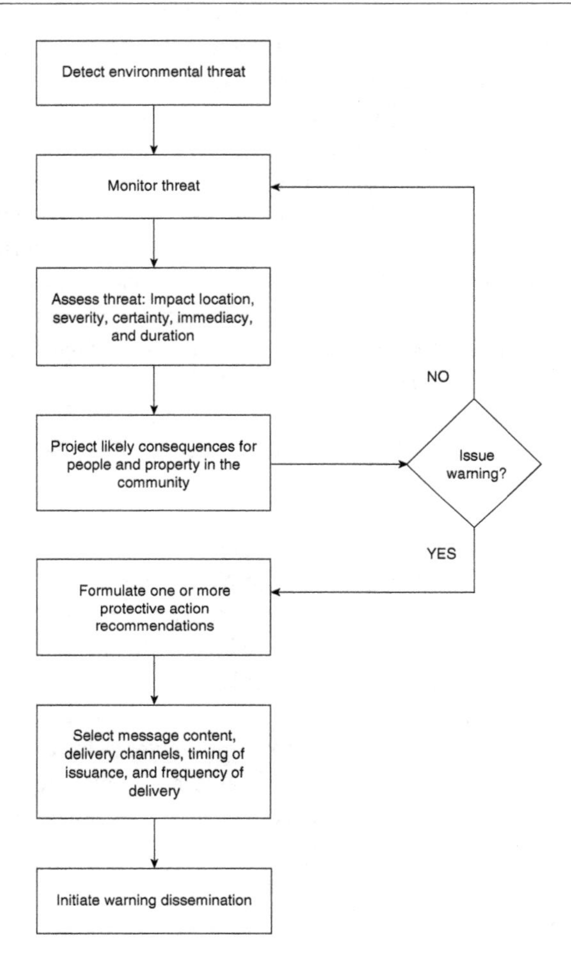

the products of social organization (McLuckie, 1970; Mileti, 1974; Quarantelli & Taylor, 1977). Figure 3.4 shows, from the perspective of community officials, a flow diagram of the steps involved in issuing most disaster warnings. The operation of a warning system begins with detection of an environmental threat and a prediction (sometimes probabilistic) of its location, time, and magnitude of impact. Threat detection and prediction may be managed by a variety of organizations, usually external to local governments, and the organizations involved in such hazard monitoring differ from one type of hazard to another. For example, the National Weather Service addresses most meteorological threats, whereas the U.S. Geological Survey monitors earthquake and volcano threats. Technological facilities such as chemical plants, nuclear power stations, and dams monitor their own operating status and some of these are monitored by regulatory agencies such as the U.S. Nuclear Regulatory Commission. Thus, a community warning agency must be able to receive information about environmental threats from a variety of sources, and this, in turn, requires a commitment to disaster preparedness that ensures that the essential information is received in time for protective action to be implemented.

Once an environmental threat has been detected, community officials begin the process of monitoring the threat and assessing its potential impacts, many times supported by expert advice external to the community. Information from these sources allows environmental hazard managers to identify the geographic areas in which protective action will be needed and the amount of time available to implement such action. It is important to note that monitoring and assessment are continuing activities; with some threats—such as floods, hurricanes, and tornadoes—the estimated location, time, and magnitude of impact can change very rapidly. Based on this information about the threat, environmental hazard managers can judge the urgency of actions to protect people and property in the community.

Projections of impact consequences are the primary data on which community officials base their decision whether to warn those at risk. The level of projected negative consequences needed to justify a warning is specific to the affected communities; local standards of acceptable risk are interpreted by elected officials and environmental hazard managers (Lowrance, 1976). Until an action threshold is reached, environmental hazard managers will continue to monitor the threat. Once the action threshold is reached, local officials must formulate one or more protective action recommendations, the choice of which is influenced by the level of emergency preparedness of households, businesses, and government agencies, as well as the amount of forewarning and likely severity of impact. When forewarning is short and severity is high, protective action recommendations are likely to focus on personal safety measures. With greater amounts of forewarning, lower estimated severity, or higher levels of community preparedness, protective action recommendations might include suggestions about property protection.

Once the protective action recommendation has been formulated, attention turns to message construction. A *general* warning is a message that indicates the onset of a hazardous event. Examples include "the river is flooding" and "a tornado is coming." A *specific* warning describes the nature of the threat in terms of the magnitude and time of impact and the people and places at risk. A specific warning also provides a protective action recommendation, details about implementation (e.g., evacuation routes and destinations), and instructions on how to seek assistance. Warnings can be sent by anyone (including the news media and peers such as friends, relatives, neighbors, and coworkers), but *official* warnings are issued by community authorities.

Message content should be formulated to identify the threat (and perhaps its origins) and to describe the expected location, timing, and magnitude of impact. The message should recommend the appropriate protective action and also should discourage any actions that might seem reasonable but are actually dangerous (such as driving through running water during storms). Message content should be clear, specific, and internally consistent so that people will pay attention to the message and understand it. In addition, the message should be repeated as many times as is feasible because repetition enhances the three predecisional processes, as well as the decision stages. Specifically, repetition is needed to maximize the probability that all of those at risk will receive at least one warning. Second, repetition is needed to overcome any inattention to the early portions of the warning message. Third, repetition is needed to ensure comprehension and retention of the information in the warning. This is especially important when people are unfamiliar with the hazard or when the message is complex. When people are unfamiliar with the hazard, they need repetition to ensure that the warning message will contain all of the information that is needed to produce a high level of protection motivation. In addition, they need all of the information that is required to implement the recommended protective action. When the message is complex, people need repetition to ensure that they have attended to and comprehended all parts of the message that are relevant to them. Message complexity often is low when warnings are delivered face-to-face because message content can be tailored to the needs of each individual household. However, message complexity tends to be higher when warnings are broadcast over radio or television because the message content must contain all of the information about the hazard and protective action recommendations that will be needed by *all* the households at risk. This means that the warning message must address the varying needs of recipients who differ in their level of risk (e.g., who differ in their proximity to the impact area), as well as of those who differ in their capability to respond (e.g., those who need medical support or public transportation when evacuating). In addition, there also must be parts of the message directed to those listeners who are not at risk that explain why they are not at risk and, thus, do not need to take protective action. Eventually, authorities also will need to prepare messages that facilitate reentry into the risk area once the emergency is over (Stallings, 1991).

Authorities also need to decide what channels, or physical mechanisms, will be used to deliver the warnings, because these information channels differ significantly in their delivery characteristics (Lindell & Perry, 1987, 1992). As noted earlier, warning channels include the Emergency Alert System (which provides digital interruption of radio and television), local emergency management agency relay of warning to broadcast media (radio and television), NOAA Weather Radio, telephone ring-down systems, route alert systems (mobile loudspeakers driven through risk areas), and face-to-face delivery to homes by emergency authorities. In addition, sirens—which provide alerts rather than warnings—can be used to indicate the presence of a threat if previous contacts by environmental hazard managers have taught people to interpret the alert as a signal to seek information by turning to a specific radio or television station for a warning message or to initiate a specific protective action.

The warning channels vary with respect to a number of attributes that are significant for warning dissemination. Local authorities need to choose among these channels on the basis of their precision of dissemination, rate of dissemination, penetration of normal activities, message specificity, susceptibility to message distortion, sender and receiver resource requirements, and feedback from recipients.

Applying PADM to Multiethnic Communities

The PADM has a variety of implications for the issuance of warnings to communities threatened by disasters, especially the warning plans and procedures that community officials develop as part of the emergency operations plan. This means that the support functions for implementing the decisions described as a community warning system in Figure 3.4 must be executed before a disaster threatens. Consequently, local officials must be aware of the hazards to which their communities are vulnerable, establish arrangements for receiving and monitoring threat information, install computer software or other decision support systems for threat assessment, and develop warning mechanisms before they must actually issue such warnings (see Lindell and Perry, 1992, for details of such arrangements). In addition, local officials should be prepared to control official message content and channels; influence warning confirmation and information search; and anticipate the effects of critical contingencies such as environmental cues, social context, and receiver characteristics. Finally, authorities should disseminate information about their plans and procedures for population warning in their communities as part of routine risk communication, which is usually embodied in hazard awareness programs (Dynes, Quarantelli, & Kreps, 1972; Fowlkes & Miller, 1987; Greene & Gori, 1982; McLuckie, 1970; White, 1972). Through such programs, environmental hazard managers can inform risk area residents in advance about what communication channels to monitor, what protective action recommendations to expect, what logistical preparations to make, and how to confirm warnings (Kartez & Lindell, 1987). If this information is communicated effectively, the warning message will be less surprising, more consistent with people's knowledge of the hazard agent, easier to confirm, and more strongly suggestive of protection actions that have been previously identified by authorities.

The following discussion links the tenets of the PADM with empirical data on household disaster response and derives measures based on these linkages that environmental hazard managers can use to enhance the effectiveness of warnings issued to ethnically diverse communities. Such multiethnic communities are composed of people with differing experiences, beliefs, values, and norms, so the challenge for risk communicators is to determine how to gain timely and complete compliance with protective action recommendations from this diverse population when disaster strikes.

Vulnerability Assessments and the Community

Communities are advised to base the management of their environmental hazards on hazard and vulnerability assessments (Federal Emergency Management Agency, 1997). At the most general level, these hazard analyses identify the environmental extremes to which the community is exposed and map the geographical areas that are likely to be affected by these hazards. The process of hazard and vulnerability assessment enables local authorities and community members to set priorities for hazard management and sets the stage for the implementation of that management strategy. Vulnerability assessments identify what types of structures are located in these hazardous areas and the demographic characteristics of those who live and work in those structures. An assessment of structural vulnerability systematically inventories residential, commercial, and industrial structures. In particular, structural vulnerability assessment emphasizes critical facilities such as schools, hospitals, and public safety facilities, as well as infrastructure such as electric power, fuel, water, sewer, transportation, and telecommunications (e.g., see Texas Governor's Division of Emergency Management, 2002).

It also is important to conduct capability assessments that provide a systematic accounting of the emergency-relevant resources of the jurisdiction's households, businesses, and government agencies. When these capability assessments identify shortfalls, strategic plans should be developed to acquire preparedness resources at that level or at the community level (Federal Emergency Management Agency, 1996). For example, assessments of warning system capability should include identification of access points for hazard relevant organizations such as the National Weather Service and U.S. Geological Survey. It also should include inventories of local news media (e.g., newspapers, radio and television stations), Emergency Alert System stations, NOAA Weather Radio broadcast stations, siren systems, route alert systems, and telephone trees.

Managing Source Credibility

An important principle in building warning source credibility is that authorities generally achieve this through repeated contacts with risk area residents during normal conditions and in the early stages of an emergency (if there is a significant amount of forewarning, as with a hurricane). In particular, hazard awareness programs form an important opportunity for local officials to enhance their credibility before they must disseminate warnings. Hazard awareness programs can engage local residents in a wide range of hazard-relevant issues, explain disaster warning processes, demonstrate officials' expertise and access to specialized information, and confirm their commitment to community safety. To the extent that these objectives are achieved, it is likely that authorities will resolve any questions about their expertise and trustworthiness before disaster warnings must be delivered.

As noted earlier, source credibility attributions (and the perceived seriousness of the threat) can vary across communities and ethnic groups. The appropriate strategy for addressing such variation is not to attempt to determine which source is best for each group and match each group with a different source. Instead, local officials should observe three general principles. First, they should build credibility for environmental hazard management organizations by working with local groups before emergencies occur. A continuing outreach program that explains the results of hazard/vulnerability analyses and describes agencies' emergency management programs can build confidence in local agencies' expertise and trustworthiness.

Second, local officials should use multiple sources and multiple channels to maximize the coverage of the warning network. If multiple sources agree on the warning, this will provide evidence of consensus, which is one of the determinants of people's attributional processes (Eagly & Chaiken, 1993). Of course, care should be taken when using mass media to ensure either that the warning is direct from authorities (using the Emergency Alert System) or that the message relayed by media is in fact the message prepared by authorities. This will assure that message distortion is minimized.

Third, when delivering warnings, local officials should emphasize the seriousness with which they take the threat by ensuring that those who deliver face-to-face warnings wear emergency response gear. The Phoenix, Arizona Fire Department has implemented this principle by using firefighters, who generally enjoy a high level of credibility in American communities (across the demographic spectrum), to disseminate face-to-face warnings. In addition, this agency's Standard Operating Procedure for hazardous materials incidents requires that firefighters wear bunker gear (response uniforms), helmets, and self-contained breathing apparatus whenever they deliver warnings to risk area residents.

Finally, environmental hazard managers should emphasize the official sources of the hazard assessment (e.g., the U.S. Geological Survey and National Weather Service). Such identification allows recipients to appreciate the credentials and authority of the source and its access to specialized knowledge, skills, and equipment that make the message meaningful. Warning recipients respect such credentials, especially in technological disasters or natural events with which they are unfamiliar. The impact of distortion and conflicting messages also can be reduced by disseminating official warnings through multiple channels and repeating them frequently.

This approach has the effect of increasing the "availability" of official messages for intended recipients, while the repetition also emphasizes the seriousness with which officials view the threat. The use of "warning confirmation centers," discussed below, also serves as a means of reducing message distortion.

Constructing Warning Messages

A warning message is a vehicle for conveying the results of a risk assessment from one person to another. An official warning is based on scientific risk assessments and is transmitted by community authorities to those who are in danger. Disaster researchers have found repeatedly that people rarely comply unquestioningly with the recommendations of authorities, especially when these warnings conflict with environmental cues, information from the mass media, or the observed behavior of friends, relatives, neighbors, or coworkers. In particular, environmental hazard managers should expect that people will disbelieve messages describing an unexpected danger and will distort ambiguous messages to support a conclusion that no major deviation from normal activities is necessary. Thus, ambiguous or conflicting messages will delay disaster response or stop it altogether. If there is sufficient time before impact, warning messages will be relayed by multiple intermediates in the mass media and among peers. Consequently, risk communicators must carefully construct messages to minimize the likelihood of distortion as information is transmitted from one person to another. One way of ensuring that people will comply with official warnings is to construct clear, concise messages. Specifically, the warning message should contain information that addresses personal risk assessment and protective action selection. There is much agreement among disaster researchers that warning content needs to include at least seven elements that arouse protection motivation and direct disaster response (Drabek, 1999). These elements can be expressed as questions that the message should answer:

1. Who is issuing the warning? The warning message should identify the governmental organization that collected and evaluated the risk information. This should be an agency that is recognized by warning recipients as one that has a legal responsibility and a special competence to protect the public.

2. What type of event is threatening? The warning message should identify the environmental event (e.g., the hurricane, tornado, or toxic chemical) that poses a threat. If environmental cues (or their absence) might conflict with the message, this should be explained briefly.

3. Who is being threatened? The warning message should clearly indicate which people and property are at risk. For most environmental hazards, this

can be expressed as a geographical impact area that is defined in terms of recognizable landmarks such as transportation routes, political boundaries, or geographical features (e.g., rivers). In cases where specific demographic groups are at risk, these should be defined specifically.

4. When is the anticipated impact expected to occur at the warning recipient's location? If time allows and the information is available, the warning message should project progressive impact times over large impact areas (e.g., flood cresting at different locations along the river).

5. How intense is the event expected to be at the warning recipient's location? The warning message should clarify the severity of the physical impact. It is important to distinguish between the physical magnitude of the event and the physical and social consequences for the warning recipient. In the case of a hurricane, physical magnitude can be described in terms of its Saffir-Simpson category or its wind speed and surge height, but these are likely to have relatively little meaning for most people unless these physical impacts are linked to the likelihood of death or injury, property destruction, and disruption of work and daily activities.

6. How probable is it that the event will strike the warning recipient's location? The warning message should clarify the likelihood that the warning recipient will be affected. Even when impact is uncertain, authorities should make it clear that the uncertainty is determined by the probabilistic nature of the event, not incompetence on the part of the warning source. Since responsible "false alarms" do have some impact on people's later disaster responses, it is difficult to overemphasize the need for taking protective action even when there is uncertainty about the location, time, and magnitude of impact.

7. What specific protective actions should be taken? Protective action recommendations in the warning message should provide specific guidance about what to do, as well as when and how to do it. For example, an evacuation recommendation should indicate when to leave, what to take, where to go, and how to get there. Those who need assistance (i.e., those who have a physical mobility limitation or who do not have their own means of transportation) should be told how to obtain it.

8. Are there high-risk groups that require special actions? The warning message should identify population segments and activities that are at especially high risk. In the case of hurricanes or tornadoes, this would include those who live in mobile homes; in the case of floods, this would include those who might attempt to drive automobiles through moving water.

Although this might seem to be a large amount of information to transmit in a warning message, each element has a theoretical basis in the PADM and has been empirically demonstrated in decades of research. Emergency planning guidance advises environmental hazard managers to develop "fill in the blank" warning messages that contain open spaces where event-specific information can be inserted (Daines, 1991). Such message formats allow environmental hazard managers to ensure that all relevant information is included, yet eliminate extraneous information to keep the message as brief as possible.

The need for the information addressed in these recommendations can be seen by contrasting the recommended information with a simple message like "the river is flooding—residents of low lying areas should evacuate" that might be broadcast by a local radio station. This general warning does indicate the threatening event and provides guidance about what protective action to take, but it is inadequate in many respects. First, it fails to indicate the authority for issuing the warning, so listeners cannot tell if the warning has been issued by a competent source. Second, the message does not specifically describe the impact area. The term *low lying area* is especially vague, but even telling listeners that the flood will crest 10 feet above flood stage fails to help people personalize the risk because many floodplain residents will not know the elevation of their homes. Moreover, as noted earlier, a significant proportion of those in the risk area will not be able to correctly identify their risk area on a large-scale map (Zhang et al., 2003).

Third, the message indicates that flooding is in progress, so there is certainty about the event, but warning recipients need information about the likelihood that *their* locations will be flooded, not that *any* locations will be flooded. Fourth, the message fails to indicate the estimated time of impact, thereby failing to instill a sense of urgency. Even if the message indicates the time at which the flood is expected to crest, this does not indicate when the warning recipient's location will be inundated. Fifth, the guidance to evacuate fails to indicate a safe route of travel, a safe destination, or methods of obtaining assistance for those who lack transportation. Finally, it fails to caution people against driving through fast moving water (a significant cause of death during floods).

The principal problems with a general warning are that it fails to personalize the risk and that its guidance for protective action is vague. Assuming that this warning is received by all of those who are at risk (which, of course, would be a highly dubious assumption if the warning were only being disseminated via radio), few listeners would be able to determine if it applied to them (what is a "low lying" area?), and even those who did conclude that they were at risk would be unlikely to feel a sense of severe threat or a sense of urgency. Local authorities have found it difficult to significantly get people to personalize the risk in many types of environmental emergencies, ranging from hurricanes to hazardous materials releases. In some cases, this is because people fail to understand the potential safety and health consequences that can occur, but more often it is because people think that death, injury, or disease simply will not happen to them. A number of public agencies, including Phoenix, Arizona, have established a policy for responding to refusals to evacuate when advised to do so. In such cases, those who are delivering the warning are instructed to ask for and write down the name and contact phone number for the individual's next of kin. The evacuation compliance rate for hazardous materials emergencies in Phoenix has remained extremely high over the years. Conveying a sense of urgency is especially important during flooding because people tend to rely on environmental cues such as rising water to determine when to evacuate. Unfortunately, such cues often provide inadequate forewarning—resulting in people being trapped in their homes by the rising water.

As will be discussed further in Chapter 4, many of these problems can be avoided if communities establish hazard awareness programs that disseminate risk area maps and information about evacuation routes, evacuation reception centers, and telephone numbers to call for transportation assistance. Even if many of the risk area residents lose their brochures or forget about them, some will keep them and remember to use them. The latter group will not only be able to help themselves, but they also can pass on useful emergency information when their friends, relatives, neighbors, and coworkers contact them to relay warnings or seek information.

It might seem as if the deficiencies in the brief warning could be overcome simply by having uniformed public safety personnel supplement a radio warning by disseminating warnings face-to-face. In such a case, the officers could answer questions raised by warning recipients. However, this solution will be no more effective than the radio message if the warning disseminators have no additional information. The credibility of these sources will be higher and the location of the risk area will be clearer, but the other essential elements of a warning must be addressed. This suggests that public safety personnel distribute "fill in the blank" warning messages, which also would avoid the increase in warning dissemination time caused by repeatedly answering the same questions for each household. Of course, the best solution would be to combine a hazard awareness program, warnings disseminated by the mass media, and warnings disseminated door-to-door.

Finally, frequent repetition of warning messages by authorities tends to increase the probability that the recipients will receive, attend to, and comprehend the warnings, and it also creates opportunities for the authorities to update warning information.

Selecting Warning Channels

Disaster warnings are effective only to the extent that those at risk actually receive the message and, in turn, coverage of the risk area varies with the channels through which warnings are disseminated. In selecting channels for disseminating official warnings, three issues must be considered: precision of dissemination, penetration of normal activities, and susceptibility to distortion. Each of these issues is affected by ethnicity, so this section will conclude with some qualifications regarding that factor.

The presence of diverse ethnic groups within a community requires authorities to consider three issues when choosing channels for warning dissemination. The first issue is that ethnic groups differ in their access to and preferences for warning channels. The second issue is that differences in language mastery or literacy could affect message comprehension. In practice, the two issues are intertwined because the channels that target minority groups often do so in that group's native language. With regard to differential channel preference, it is well known that radio and some television stations select or serve highly specialized audiences, including some ethnic groups. Especially in the southern tier of states from California to Florida, Spanish language radio, television, and newspapers are common. Asian and non-English European language stations can also be found in other communities where there is an audience of adequate size. Such channels can be useful in simultaneously targeting specific audiences while addressing them in the language with which they are most proficient. Whether issuing official warnings via Emergency Alert System or less formally passing on a warning to mass media with a request that it be relayed to listeners, it is important that environmental hazard managers coordinate closely with those who are translating the warning message from English into another language. The likelihood of message distortion is high if an English message is simply passed on for extemporaneous translation by radio or television announcers. However, message distortion is much lower if "fill in the blank" messages have been translated in advance and then translated back into English to verify their accuracy. Identification of warning channels that are targeted to specific ethnic groups should take place as part of a community hazard awareness program. Channels should be listed in standard operating procedures for warning dissemination and reviewed annually to ensure that they remain current.

The third issue is that messages are routinely relayed through communities by means of peer contacts among friends, relatives, neighbors, and coworkers. These intermediaries will be used regardless of what channels authorities use to initiate the warning process. Like mass media commentators, informal channels can be expected to elaborate and comment on official warning messages rather than just repeat the message verbatim. This informal warning dissemination process can produce distortion, especially when intermediate sources or warning recipients must translate official messages from English into their preferred language. Consequently, official warnings should be translated by authorities to ensure that accurate information is readily accessible to those who are initially warned by informal communication networks. Furthermore, each repetition of the official warning message serves as confirmation that the warning is accurate and the situation warrants serious attention and action.

Managing Information Seeking

As noted earlier, the most common initial reaction to a warning is disbelief, and there appear to be differentials—by ethnicity and possibly socioeconomic status—in the level of credibility attributed to a specific type of information source. Research also has shown that people attempt to confirm warnings by consulting multiple sources and that warning confirmation by credible sources is important in determining whether to comply with official warnings. The previous sections have some ways in which the information-seeking process can be managed by avoiding source deficiencies (e.g., lack of credibility), content deficiencies (e.g., inadequate warning messages), information conflicts (e.g., warning information that appears to be inconsistent with environmental cues), and channel deficiencies (e.g., relying on channels not monitored by ethnic minorities). These tactics can reduce the amount of information-seeking behavior, but they will not eliminate it altogether. Consequently, there will continue to be a need for systematizing risk area residents' opportunities to obtain additional information.

The principal methods of achieving this objective are to create information centers and to adapt community "hotlines" to facilitate the dissemination of timely and accurate information about the hazard and protective actions. In addition, such systems can be used to detect rumors and identify common questions whose answers would be appropriate for widespread dissemination over the news media. There are, of course, cautions that must be considered when advising people to use the telephone as a mechanism for obtaining disaster relevant information. Researchers dating back to Fritz and Mathewson (1957) have documented that snarled communications can arise from telephone convergence in disasters. For many years, disaster planning handbooks (Healy, 1969; Leonard, 1973) have warned that authorities should advise citizens to avoid using telephones during emergencies. During the Northridge earthquake in the Los Angeles area, even cellular telephone traffic was overloaded, prompting some emergency management agencies to switch to satellite-based telephones. It is widely known, however, that people in disaster impact areas seek information about the event, and people outside the impact area seek information about loved ones who might need assistance (Lindell & Perry, 1996). Moreover, it is probable that the magnitude of telephone convergence increases with the disaster's speed of onset and scope and intensity of impact. Quarantelli and Taylor (1977) observed that citizens continue to use telephones during disasters despite repeated requests not to do so. However, innovations in telecommunications technology have significantly increased local jurisdictions' capacity for handling surges in telephone demand. Thus, Quarantelli and Taylor suggested that directing people to use hotlines would be a feasible method of channeling the information demand. At present, local authorities frequently continue to discourage telephone use during disasters, but it has become commonplace for authorities to operate confirmation centers as well.

Predisaster planning to design, equip, and staff confirmation centers is an important first step toward managing information seeking, but for such centers to be used, people must be aware of their existence. An official warning message provides one opportunity for publicizing the existence of such centers, but these messages should only reinforce information disseminated as part of hazard awareness programs. For example, the San Francisco Fire Department, as part of its earthquake preparedness website, reminds citizens to limit telephone use during earthquakes, but also includes information center telephone numbers. There also are other ways to encourage people to use warning confirmation centers. Many counties and large cities have established community hotlines for people to obtain information about community activities or express concerns about a variety of routine issues. Such systems can readily be converted to support information seeking by connecting incoming calls to prerecorded messages or human operators. Some smaller communities advertise the availability of several different numbers (e.g., emergency management, fire, police, public works, city management offices) in an effort to spread calls across multiple exchanges. In either case, adequate measures must be taken to insure that the system is responsive to the community. A system that overloads quickly is likely to create significant frustration among those attempting to use it. Of course, the demands on a warning confirmation line can be minimized by constructing warning messages that adhere to the eight essential elements addressed in the previous section on warning message construction, that are delivered across many channels, and that are repeated frequently by a credible source.

Creating Specific Protective Action Incentives

For many years, disaster researchers have advocated creating incentives for people to comply with protective action recommendations, where an incentive is any measure that removes implementation barriers to recommended protective actions (Perry, 1979b). Most of the available research has focused on the creation of incentives for evacuation from endangered areas (Lindell & Perry, 1992). The facilitation of transportation out of the risk area by authorities constitutes one type of incentive for compliance with a request to leave. One common transportation incentive addresses the problems of safety and response time that arise from the reliance of most evacuees on private vehicles. To facilitate compliance with evacuation warnings, many jurisdictions devise and disseminate evacuation traffic management plans, including route information and designation of safe destinations—often in the form of labeled maps. Such plans are routinely used in connection with nuclear power plants and hazardous chemical facilities, and they also have been developed for areas prone to floods and hurricanes.

Another incentive is the provision of evacuation transportation support in high occupancy vehicles for those households without access to cars. Most of these households meet their routine needs for transportation to work, shopping, and other daily activities by receiving rides with friends, relatives, neighbors, and coworkers. These same individuals are almost certain to offer transportation assistance in an emergency as well, so the need for public evacuation transportation support will be small but cannot be assumed to be zero. Consequently, local authorities should describe the locations, such as elementary schools, at which buses will stop to pick up those who need evacuation assistance. In any community, there also will be those who have personal mobility limitations that will prevent them from walking to bus pick-up locations, so they will need to be picked up at their homes. Authorities also can provide an incentive for evacuation by systematizing and publicizing the availability of transportation assistance for this category of risk area resident.

Facilitation of communication among family members can also be used as an evacuation incentive because families rarely evacuate if the welfare of any members is not accounted for. Although families prefer to be united at the time of evacuation, some studies have indicated that uniting families is less important than helping family members to locate one another and verify that all are safe (Haas et al., 1977; Lindell & Perry, 1992). Authorities can systematize this function by establishing centralized family message centers and enhancing human accountability capabilities in congregate care centers. For decades, congregate care facilities operated by the American Red Cross and the Salvation Army have accounted for those who are staying in a given shelter and the status of their health. The advent of personal computers in the 1990s greatly enhanced the speed of information retrieval. Both organizations typically aggregate their information for a given disaster, providing a relatively comprehensive accounting that can be accessed both by concerned citizens from outside the impact area and by evacuees seeking separated family members. The American Red Cross site on the World Wide Web also offers an innovative system for distant relatives to locate information on families. Some larger municipalities undertake the aggregation themselves as part of an emergency operations center. By publicizing the existence of this capability either during an emergency or—more desirably—during a hazard awareness program, local officials can enable risk area residents to either develop a family communication plan ("If the family is separated at the time of an emergency, we will reunite at the evacuation shelter") or locate family members after the fact.

The establishment of congregate care facilities where evacuees can stay during a period of absence from homes raises a significant issue regarding their use. For years, disaster researchers and environmental hazard managers have noted that evacuees prefer to stay with friends or relatives than in public shelters. In most cases, utilization of congregate care is likely to be in the range of 5% to 15% of evacuees, depending on the characteristics of the evacuees, the situation, and the community (Lindell et al., 1985; Mileti, Sorensen, & O'Brien, 1992). Specifically, evacuees are more likely to rely on public accommodations if they are less integrated into the community, have lower incomes, and rely on public transit. Situational factors that increase use of public facilities include night evacuations, bad weather, evacuation of an entire community, and the anticipation of a brief evacuation. Finally, characteristics of the community that promote shelter use include isolation from other communities and high levels of community emergency preparedness—both of which are factors suggesting that congregate care facilities will be better equipped and better known to evacuees.

As with other incentives, the availability of congregate care facilities should be mentioned in warning messages, but this should not be the time that evacuees first hear about their existence or location. Even if public facilities are used only by a small proportion of evacuees, they are critical for those with no other place to go. Furthermore, it is possible that use will increase somewhat if hazard awareness programs explicitly address such facilities and emphasize advantages of shelter use—not the least of which is the family accountability achieved through shelter management. An incentive for those who would not normally choose public care lies in the development of flexible plans for temporary lodging of evacuees. Such a plan could involve creating an evacuation reception center where families could check in to a database. At that point they could either stay at the shelter or depart for an alternate location such as the home of a friend or relative, a commercial facility like a motel or hotel, or some other location. Such a plan would incorporate more evacuees into family status databases, yet provide a choice of accommodations. Note that reception centers should be co-located with shelters in safe areas, not located along the side of evacuation routes where they could impede traffic.

Finally, the incentives mentioned here are only a few of the ways in which evacuation compliance could be enhanced. Different incentives could be developed for different situations, such as toxic chemical, radiological, or biological materials releases, in which the protective action recommendation is to shelter in-place. The nature of the incentives actually implemented would depend on the threat, citizen concerns and response proclivities, and the resources of the jurisdiction. The important point is that incentives are a means of enhancing compliance with protective action recommendations. An equally important point is that the successful use of incentives demands much emergency planning and community outreach before a disaster strikes. As we have noted previously, this should be done in the context of a broad program of environmental hazard management. The next chapter examines such programs and reviews strategies and tactics for risk communication about long-term threats from environmental hazards.

4

Hazard Awareness as Risk Communication

According to Burton and colleagues (1978, 1993), *hazard adjustments* are actions that either intentionally or incidentally reduce risk from extreme events in the natural environment. Thus, evacuation and sheltering in-place in response to disaster warnings can be thought of as hazard adjustments, but the term *hazard adjustments* is more frequently applied to long-term risk reduction actions such as hazard mitigation, emergency preparedness, or recovery preparedness. *Hazard mitigation* refers to actions taken previously that provide passive protection to people and property at the time of disaster impact. For example, as noted in Chapter 1, to avoid the impacts of floods, communities can restrict construction to areas outside the floodplain or elevate structures above projected high water marks. To avoid the impacts of earthquakes, households can strengthen structural connections among building components to reduce the likelihood of building collapse and anchor heavy furniture to walls to minimize the danger of furniture falling on occupants.

Emergency preparedness supports active response at the time of disaster impact. For example, stockpiling supplies of bottled water and packaged food before an earthquake allows households to survive disruptions to distribution systems for goods and services. Similarly, development of a specialized emergency medical capacity to treat chemical or radiation exposures is one method of preparing for releases of hazardous materials.

Recovery preparedness presumes that damage and casualties will occur, but it attempts to cope with these impacts by providing guidance and resources for the community's return to normal patterns of social and economic functioning. For example, communities can engage in pre-impact recovery planning to facilitate activities such as debris clearance and the location of temporary housing (Schwab, Topping, Eadie, Deyle, & Smith, 1998). Households can purchase hazard insurance to provide themselves with the financial resources to pay contractors to rebuild their homes.

Hazard adjustments can be undertaken at different levels of human organization, including households, businesses, communities, and societies (Perry & Lindell, 1997b). In most developed nations, governments undertake the most resource intensive hazard adjustments, particularly those that involve community protection works such as dams and levees. In some countries, governments provide insurance against hazards such as floods, earthquakes, and volcanic eruptions. Governments also undertake mitigation measures for government-owned facilities such as water treatment plants and critical infrastructure such as roads and bridges.

Households can implement some of the same types of adjustments as those undertaken by government, but they tend to have a wide range of reasons for taking action. In some cases, the impetus for household adjustments arises from subcultural identity (e.g., members of the Church of Jesus Christ of Latter Day Saints—Mormons—are urged to keep a year's supply of food), whereas in other cases it is prompted by individual awareness of local hazards (e.g., "the river is nearby, so we always make sure we identify high ground"). Government can play a role in promoting the voluntary adoption of hazard adjustments by disseminating information derived from official hazard and vulnerability analyses. In addition, government can induce households to adopt hazard adjustments by providing economic incentives or threaten them by requiring compliance with regulations.

Whatever the household's reason for adopting hazard adjustments, it is important to recognize that some protective actions are useful for a wide range of emergencies, whereas others are suitable only for specific hazards (Perry, 1985). For example, battery-powered radios are useful for receiving emergency information in many types of disasters that cause electric power to be lost. Similarly, reserves of food and water are appropriate for any disasters that disrupt distribution systems. These include floods, hurricanes, tsunamis, volcanic eruptions, and hazardous materials emergencies. Moreover, minor injuries are commonly encountered in disasters, so it is generally useful to maintain a first aid kit.

Other adjustments are hazard-specific. For example, household seismic adjustment in earthquake-prone regions should include structural modification of houses (foundation anchoring or structural reinforcement of masonry walls), providing latches for cabinets, securing furniture to walls, and installing automatic shut-off valves on natural gas lines. For hurricanes, household adjustments can encompass structural strengthening of homes, installing shutters on windows, and learning local evacuation routes and procedures. For hazardous chemical or radiation threats, household adjustments can include storing self-contained breathing masks, acquiring plastic sheets and duct tape for sealing doors and windows, and learning the elements of warning and evacuation systems.

The fact that many hazard adjustments are specific to particular hazards reinforces an unfortunate tendency by citizens, scientists, and government officials to fragment the process of risk communication. That is, risk communication is often presented and discussed exclusively in terms of a specific health threat (e.g., smoking, cancer, human immunodeficiency virus), a particular natural hazard (e.g., floods, hurricanes, earthquakes), or a particular technology (e.g., nuclear power plants, toxic chemical facilities). Such fragmentation often arises because the content of each risk communication program is developed and disseminated by those who are responsible for assessing the risks of a particular hazard. The U.S. Geological Survey, the National Weather Service, the U.S. Environmental Protection Agency, and the U.S. Nuclear Regulatory Commission, to name only a few agencies, are each charged by law with a responsibility for managing a specific type of environmental hazard. Each of these agencies must adapt its risk communication programs to the distinctive nature of the hazards it regulates. Nonetheless, most households are vulnerable to multiple hazards but lack the time and energy to sort through the mass of information produced by all of these agencies. Thus, these agencies have a special obligation to provide the population at risk with a concise explanation of the hazard, its potential impacts, and appropriate hazard adjustments. That is, government agencies need to communicate what mitigation, preparedness, response, and recovery actions households, businesses, and communities can take in response to these hazards. Meeting these obligations requires that governmental officials understand the most effective ways to communicate the risks of environmental hazards. The work of Burton and colleagues (1993) suggests that they will need to adopt a broad environmental hazards perspective that integrates hazard analysis, vulnerability assessment, and capability assessment to inform and empower communities. As the following sections indicate, the PADM provides a framework within which to organize such efforts to communicate the risks of environmental hazards to households in ways that promote their adoption of hazard adjustments.

❖ HOUSEHOLD HAZARD ADJUSTMENT DECISIONS

The basic factors that the PADM has identified as being important in disaster response also serve as the framework for understanding the adoption of long-term hazard adjustments. Specifically, this involves the predecisional processes of message reception, attention, and comprehension. Similarly, the adoption of long-term hazard adjustments involves the decision stages of risk identification, risk assessment, protective action search, protective action assessment, and protective action implementation. When questions arise about the hazard or protective actions, people conduct information needs assessment, communication action assessment, and communication action implementation.

Although the PADM provides a general theoretical framework that can account for disaster response and long-term hazard adjustment, there are distinct differences between these two situations. The most obvious distinction is the time frame for these two types of risk communications. Warnings urge people to take prompt action that will provide immediate protection for themselves and their families. Because disaster impact is imminent, there is little time to reflect on the danger, consult with others, reflect on alternative adjustments, or engage in any but the most expedient actions.

On the other hand, risk communications promoting long-term hazard adjustment are usually delivered long before a threat arises, largely eliminating time constraints. Unfortunately, this doesn't mean that a longer time perspective increases the chances that adjustments will be adopted. To the contrary, a recent review of research conducted since 1975 indicates that it is quite difficult to induce households to undertake any type of protective measure before an immediate environmental threat arises (Tierney et al., 2001). The greater time available for analysis and implementation allows the protective action decision process for long-term hazard adjustments to be less organized than is the case for disaster response. In particular, there is no penalty for suspending information processing to pursue other life activities such as work, shopping, and recreation. The problem that arises when the protective action decision process is interrupted is that some of the information could be forgotten (if stored in memory) or lost (if stored on paper).

The difference between acute and chronic threats means that some of the variables that explain long-term hazard adjustments differ from those that explain disaster warning compliance. In other cases, the same variables are important in both settings but operate in different ways. Both of these conditions require a careful examination, and sometimes a redefinition, of the relevant predictor variables. Thus, this chapter will review literature on the adoption of hazard adjustments that is related to (1) the predecisional processes and the decision stages in the protective action decision-making process, (2) the effects of environmental and social context variables, (3) the role of message characteristics, and (4) the nature of receiver characteristics.

It is important to underscore a few cautions before reviewing empirical studies of hazard adjustment processes. The first of these was discussed in the context of disaster response, namely, that few studies have multivariate theoretical models in their research designs and, consequently, multivariate statistical techniques in their data analyses. This means that hypothesized relationships among variables that are conceptually important in the PADM have not been adequately tested using statistical controls for the effects of other variables. Thus, there is a risk that some of the reported relationships are spurious. That is, a proposed causal variable is correlated with hazard adjustment but only affects it through one or more other variables that have not been included in the analysis.

The second caution regarding the empirical base is that there remain significant gaps in the research literature. Some aspects of hazard adjustment adoption have not been studied at all, and where findings have been reported, many have not been replicated. Consequently, the level of confidence that can be placed in many empirical conclusions is lower than is desirable. We have attempted to cope with this problem in part by including literature from related areas on hazard adjustments, such as diseases, food additives, drugs, and occupational safety hazards. Ultimately, however, the empirical record is only as strong as the studies that compose it, and we have attempted to qualify our review by pointing out neglected areas of study.

Our final qualification is that the discussion below will focus on households' voluntary adoption of hazard adjustments. We recognize that governments sometimes attempt to promote household adoption of hazard adjustments by providing economic incentives for adoption or threatening sanctions for noncompliance with regulations. Incentives and sanctions can easily be incorporated in the PADM by treating them as extrinsic benefits and costs that are added to the intrinsic benefits and costs of hazard adjustment adoption. That is, economic incentives for adoption make hazard adjustment more attractive by reducing their initial costs of adoption, whereas regulations attempt to motivate the adoption of hazard adjustments by attaching immediate penalties for failure to adopt them. Whether or not local government establishes a program of economic incentives and regulations to promote the adoption of hazard adjustments, risk communication will be needed to explain why the program is needed.

Of course, the establishment of the program of incentives and regulations is itself the result of a risk communication process, but one that is characterized by an upward flow of communication from citizens and hazard professionals to policy makers. This upward flow is somewhat different from the downward flow that characterizes the process by which environmental hazard managers and nongovernmental organizations such as the American Red Cross attempt to change the behavior of households (Birkland, 1997; Prater & Lindell, 2000; Stallings, 1995). It is the downward flow of information to households that will be addressed in this chapter.

Predecision Processes

In the case of hazard awareness programs for long-term threats, as was the case for disaster warnings, risk communication messages must be processed through the three predecisional stages of reception, attention, and comprehension. In addition, however, there is often another predecisional stage of information processing, the recall of previously processed information. Recall plays a significant role because there is often a significant time lag between the initial receipt of information about a hazard and the implementation of hazard adjustments. Consequently, people must either recall relevant information from memory or, if they have written information that has been filed for later reference (e.g., a newspaper article or brochure), they must locate the document and retrieve the information.

One major difference between warning response and the adoption of long-term hazard adjustments is that the latter is usually impeded by environmental cues that suggest safety rather than danger. For example, normal tides, gentle surf, and balmy breezes are more common than hurricane conditions and, therefore, tend to lull people into a false sense of security. Even those who recognize that hurricanes can occur are likely to gain little appreciation for the destructive potential of such events by observing the normal variation in wind and water conditions. Thus, there is likely to be little protection motivation and/or adoption of hazard adjustments.

As a consequence, the major source of information that most people are likely to have about environmental hazards comes from risk communication—from authorities, the mass media, or peers. Information received through risk communication about long-term hazards is likely to be limited because those who are most concerned about environmental hazards—local officials specializing in emergency management, environmental health, and public health—tend to have limited access to mass media channels of communication before disasters strike. In the absence of a severe threat, elected officials regard environmental hazards as a low priority, so they are unlikely to make major investments in hazard awareness programs (Rossi, Wright, Webber-Burdin, Pietras, & Diggins, 1982). Environmental hazards are also a low priority for the news media, who are inclined to cover such issues as public service announcements that are broadcast during the least-watched hours of the week. Consequently, the principal ways in which authorities can gain access to risk area residents are through public meetings (which tend to have low attendance) and brochures (which tend to have limited distribution).

A significant similarity between long-term hazard adjustment and disaster response is that in both cases people's attention to the available information is determined by their expectations, by competing attention demands, and by the intrusiveness of the information. Specifically, expectations of threat are established when people have advance information that leads them to believe that there is the potential for a significant environmental threat. For example, people who know that their area is prone to hurricanes and who believe that this is a significant threat are more likely to passively monitor and actively seek additional information about the threat and appropriate hazard adjustments. Unfortunately, competing demands tend to reduce attention to long-term environmental threats because the probability of disaster impact is remote, and so it is easy for people to persuade themselves that they can return to this issue at a later time. Continuing with the example of hurricanes, people who are preoccupied with getting their children to school and themselves to work on time will be less likely than those who are not so preoccupied to take the time to read a newspaper story about hurricane risk areas and structural retrofit for existing homes. The intrusiveness of hazard information is important because it disrupts the cognitive processing of other tasks. Unfortunately, as noted earlier, normal environmental cues are reassuring rather than threatening, so hazard intrusiveness during normal times is likely to arise from other sources. These include thoughts generated by the distinctive hazard-relevant associations that people have with everyday events, informal hazard-relevant discussions with peers, and hazard-relevant information received passively from the media (e.g., a television news segment about the training activities of a local Community Emergency Response Team).

In another similarity to emergency warnings, information about long-term hazard threats and hazard adjustments will also be comprehended to the degree that the risk communication messages are conveyed in language that risk area residents understand. Once again, the disseminated information will produce comprehension only if any technical terms are already understood by those at risk or are explained to them in the message. In any event, specialized terms must be explained in hazard awareness programs if these terms are likely to be used in warning messages. Similarly, risk communication messages disseminated during hazard awareness programs should provide information about the appropriate interpretation of the environmental cues that are likely to be encountered during an emergency. For example, this is the time to explain that a sudden recession of water is the trough phase of a tsunami and that this is a sign to immediately evacuate to high ground.

As is the case for the previous stages, recall only occurs if all of the stages before it have occurred. That is, hazard-relevant information must have been received, heeded, and comprehended. To the degree that any new information was successfully linked to existing schemas about hazards, the information is likely to be retained and successfully recalled at a later time. As noted earlier, brochures and newspaper articles can be especially useful because the receiver needs only to retain the "gist" or general idea conveyed in the written material and to remember the location in which it has been stored for reference at a later time. Of course, this information storage activity will prove useless if the receiver forgets that the brochure was received or what was in it. These impediments are likely if the information has been processed superficially, that is, was given only a very limited amount of attention or was poorly comprehended. Information storage also will prove to be useless if the receiver forgets where the document has been stored.

Decision Stages

In hazard awareness programs, as in disaster warnings, the predecisional stages of information processing are followed by the five decision stages—risk identification, risk assessment, protective action search, protective action assessment, and protective action implementation. The PADM emphasizes that authorities should construct risk communication programs so that households can proceed quickly through these five stages of the hazard adjustment process. In addition, they should recognize that people might also engage in the information-seeking activities of information needs assessment, communication action assessment and selection, and communication action implementation.

Risk Identification

The first decision stage, risk identification, is triggered by the receipt of information indicating that an environmental threat exists. As is the case with warnings, recipients must believe that the message refers to a credible threat that demands their attention. However, unlike a warning, risk information about long-term threats generally conveys less of a sense of urgency, especially in connection with climatic and geophysical hazards for which there is a low probability of a high consequence event (e.g., a major hurricane or earthquake). The risk identification stage is less significant in this context because the question that arises in long-term threats is whether an extreme event *could happen* rather than whether an extreme event *is happening* (the question that arises in an actual disaster). Even a modest degree of source credibility is likely to pass this test, so the protective action decision-making process is likely to pass easily to the next stage of the decision process.

Risk Assessment

The second stage, risk assessment, which is also referred to as *risk perception*, has long been considered to be a major factor in motivating individual warning response (Mileti et al., 1975). On the basis of the research cited in their review and other work done subsequently, it has been assumed and sometimes empirically documented that perceived risk is positively correlated with the adoption of hazard adjustments. For example, Perry and Lindell (1990a) report in a study of long-term adjustment to eruptions of the Mt. St. Helens volcano that higher levels of perceived risk to both personal safety and property are associated with the adoption of a greater number of hazard adjustments, and that the magnitude of the correlation is higher for risk to personal safety than for risk to property. These data, however, deal with individuals operating in a setting where threat salience was high because of a recent eruption, much information was available on a variety of hazard adjustments, and the probability of future eruptions was widely understood to be substantial. Other research on the role of risk perception has yielded more mixed results. Some researchers report significant positive correlations of risk perception with hazard adjustment adoption (Mileti & Fitzpatrick, 1993; Mileti & O'Brien, 1992; Showalter, 1993; Turner et al., 1986), whereas others report either weak relationships or no relationship (Farley, 1998; Lindell & Prater, 2000; Lindell & Whitney, 2000; Mileti & Darlington, 1997; Mulilis & Duval, 1995; Mulilis & Lippa, 1990). The apparent empirical inconsistencies might be due to methodological reasons, because there are significant differences among researchers in the ways they define and measure risk perception (Lindell & Perry, 2000). As pointed out in Chapter 3, the PADM defines *perceived risk* in terms of the certainty, severity, and immediacy of disaster impacts to the individual, such as death, injury, property destruction, and disruption of work and normal routines (see Lindell & Perry, 2000; Lindell & Prater, 2000). This definition of perceived risk is very likely to yield results that differ from one that addresses the probability and severity of an event or the probability and severity of exposure.

Of particular importance is the longer, but uncertain, time frame associated with risk assessment in the context of adopting long-term hazard adjustments. In connection with disaster warnings, risk assessment tends to be focused because the time frame for undertaking protection is limited. Decisions about long-term hazard adjustments have a long time frame, allowing other variables to influence a person's perception of danger and, in turn, adoption of hazard adjustments. Thus, a person's risk perception can change over time and, thus, be less influential than other factors in determining the level of hazard adjustment adoption. Weinstein and Nicolich (1993) have argued on the basis of methodological analyses that correlations of risk perception and adjustment adoption will inevitably decline over time. That is because a high level of risk perception would lead to the adoption of hazard adjustments that would, in turn, decrease the respondent's risk. This reduction in risk would lead to a reduction in risk perception, which would reduce the motivation to adopt additional hazard adjustments.

Questions about the influence of risk perception remain even among studies that measure risk in similar ways. For example, Perry and Lindell (1990b) found that the correlation between risk perception and adoption of hazard adjustments by those threatened by volcano hazard was positive but not statistically significant when other variables were controlled. However, the magnitude of this correlation might have been high because the respondents had experienced several volcanic eruptions during the 4 years preceding data collection, and the threat was clearly very salient to them. On the other hand, Lindell and Whitney (2000) and Lindell and Prater (2000) collected data from respondents who had not experienced any recent earthquakes, so procrastination in the adoption and implementation of hazard adjustments would be less threatening. This explanation is supported by Lindell and Prater's (2000) finding that hazard intrusiveness, measured by frequency of thought, discussion, and information receipt about earthquakes, had a significant correlation with hazard adjustment, even though their measure of risk perception did not. It is important to note that many respondents in this study believed that there was a significant probability of a major earthquake occurring within the next 10 years, but this time interval is extremely long in comparison to the time required to implement the seismic hazard adjustments usually recommended by authorities. The longer time frame available for adopting hazard adjustment allows variables other than risk to come into play in the decision process, a consideration that reinforces the need for additional multivariate studies to more carefully specify the relationship of risk perception with other variables that arouse protection motivation. Thus, despite the conflicting evidence, the PADM continues to include risk perception as a decision factor in the adoption of hazard adjustments, based on the proposition that increased levels of perceived risk increase protection motivation and, thus, tend to increase the level of hazard adjustment adoption.

Protective Action Search

The third stage of the decision process consists of protective action search. Of course, the most effective way to ensure that protective action search is successful is for authorities to mention one or more feasible hazard adjustments in their risk communication messages. If they fail to do so, message recipients must recall such adjustments from memory, obtain information about these adjustments from others (such as the media, peers, and authorities), or devise suitable adjustments for themselves. Recalling items from memory can be an error-prone process, but it seems unlikely that highly meaningful material—like the appropriate adjustments for environmental hazards such as earthquakes—would be difficult to recall if those at risk ever knew about these adjustments in the first place. The problem is often that many people were never told in the first place what actions they could take to protect themselves and their property against disaster impacts (Endo & Nielsen, 1979; Jackson, 1977, 1981; Jackson & Mukerjee, 1974; Sullivan, Mustart, & Galehouse, 1977). The process of obtaining information about hazard adjustments from the media, peers, and authorities is, of course, what has been called *information seeking*—which will be discussed later. Finally, protective action search can involve the development of personally innovative hazard adjustments. In this context, the term *personal innovation* refers to a process by which those at risk recognize that a specific activity would be effective in protecting people or property, even though no one else had ever suggested taking such an action for this purpose. For example, some residents of areas affected by the eruption of Mt. St. Helens realized that the weight of ash threatened to collapse their roofs, so they used push brooms to sweep off the ash before it accumulated to dangerous depths. Of course, there have undoubtedly been thousands of people threatened by volcanic ash over the centuries who have had similar insights, but this means that sweeping ash off the roof was only personally innovative, not socially innovative. The disadvantage of relying on personal innovation is that society cannot count on all of the members of the population at risk identifying these hazard adjustments.

Protective Action Assessment

The fourth stage of the decision process consists of protective action assessment. Lindell and Perry (2000) contend that protective action assessment is defined by two categories of variables, efficacy attributes and resource requirements. The *efficacy attributes* refer to the individual's perception of the effectiveness of hazard adjustments as a means of reducing or avoiding negative consequences, whereas the *resource requirements* refer to perceptions of the financial cost, time and effort, specialized knowledge and skill, specialized tools and equipment, and cooperation from others that are needed to implement a hazard adjustment.

The emphasis on the perceived characteristics of hazard adjustments follows a basic tenet of Fishbein and Ajzen's (1975) Theory of Reasoned Action, which posits that a person's attitudes toward an object (a hazard such as an earthquake) is less predictive of that person's behavior than his or her attitudes toward an act (a specific hazard adjustment) relevant to that object. The PADM suggests that at the stage of protective action assessment, alternative hazard adjustments must be judged to be effective in reducing hazard consequences or they will not be undertaken. Specific theoretical support for this contention can be found in Person-relative-to-Event (PrE) theory (Duval & Mulilis, 1999a), as well as in other theories of health protective behavior, such as Protection Motivation Theory (Rogers & Mewborn, 1976). Specifically, PrE theory argues that response efficacy—an estimate of the effectiveness of an action in achieving protection—is expected to be positively correlated with individuals' willingness to adopt that protective action. Similarly, several major models of the variables involved in individual adoption of positive health practices posit that beliefs about an adjustment's efficacy in protecting from disease or illness are key determinants of intended adoption (e.g., Neuwirth et al., 2000).

Though the logic for including efficacy variables as a factor in hazard adjustment adoption has much theoretical support, the number of empirical studies that have included such variables is small. Sorenson and Mileti (1987), in evaluating a range of programs aimed at promoting adoption of protective actions against natural disasters, reported that programs emphasizing actions most directly linked to specific threat outcomes were perceived to be more useful. More directly addressing the notion of efficacy, Hutton (1982) studied the adoption of specific measures to reduce residential water consumption. In this study, a sample of citizens was randomly divided into two groups, one of which was given information on general water use reduction measures, while the other received specific literature on benefits of water-flow restrictors that included a restrictor in the package. Those receiving specific information linking the use of restrictors with the outcome of conservation were much more likely to adopt the measure. Research on household adoption of protective measures against health and disease threats has also reported that adoption is more likely when individuals believe that the measure itself will be effective in reducing or preventing the negative consequences of the disease (Lundgren & McMakin, 1998; Weinstein, 1993). In particular, Peters, Covello, and McCallum (1997) found that people tended not to undergo inoculation if they did not believe that vaccines significantly reduced the probability of contracting a given disease.

Moving to studies of natural hazards, research by Baker and Patton (1974) found that attitudes toward hurricane adjustments were better predictors of adoption of preparedness measures than attitudes toward the hurricane threat. Furthermore, hazard adjustments that were perceived as more likely to be effective were more frequently undertaken. In the area of seismic hazards, Garcia (1989) reported a statistically significant correlation between perception of adjustment effectiveness and adoption. Similarly, Davis (1989) found that perceived adjustment effectiveness showed a higher positive correlation with adoption than either the cost of an adjustment or its difficulty to implement. Perry and Lindell's (1990a) study of the Mt. St. Helens volcano also found that adjustment efficacy was positively correlated with adjustment adoption but negatively correlated with perceived risk (supporting Weinstein and Nicolich's, 1993, contention that adoption of protective actions believed to be effective reduce an individual's sense of danger). More recently, Mulilis and Duval (1995) found that higher levels of response efficacy were positively correlated with adoption of earthquake adjustments. Lindell and Whitney (2000) found that three measures of the efficacy of earthquake adjustments—perceived efficacy in protecting personal safety, perceived efficacy in protecting property, and perceived utility of a measure to protect threats in addition to earthquakes (see Russell, Goltz, & Bourque, 1995)—were positively correlated with the adoption of adjustments. Finally, Lindell and Prater (2002) confirmed Lindell and Whitney's results using a sample of residents from three communities in the Los Angeles area (a high seismic hazard area) and the Seattle area (a moderate seismic hazard area). Once again, the efficacy attributes were significantly correlated with household adoption of hazard adjustments.

In closing this discussion, we conclude that there is substantial empirical evidence to indicate that perceived adjustment efficacy is positively correlated with hazard adjustment adoption. There also is evidence that response efficacy is a multi-dimensional construct that includes efficacy in protecting people and property from the hazard being considered, as well as usefulness for other purposes, especially protection from other hazards. This is important because it implies that future researchers will need to assess different aspects of efficacy, asking "efficacy for what?" to fully understand the conceptual importance of the variable. It also raises the possibility that these efficacy dimensions might have additive effects on the adoption of hazard adjustments. That is, a hazard adjustment (such as maintaining a battery-powered radio) that is moderately effective for coping with a variety of different hazards might be a more attractive investment than another hazard adjustment (such as knowing how to shut off the electric power panel) that is highly effective, but only for a single hazard. The existence of multiple efficacy dimensions also suggests the possibility that they are differentially correlated with adjustment adoption for different types of hazards. It certainly reinforces the notion that much further research on the perceived efficacy of hazard adjustments is required to adequately understand its conceptual significance.

The second set of decision factors that are considered in protective action assessment and selection is resource requirements. Among alternatives with equivalent levels of efficacy, those having the lowest level of resource requirements have a greater probability of being selected. These resource requirements can be generically conceived in terms of financial cost, time and effort requirements, specialized knowledge and skill requirements, requirements for specialized tools and equipment, and the need for cooperation from others (Lindell & Perry, 2000; Lindell & Prater, 2002). The multidimensionality of the resources required to implement hazard adjustments has been the subject of some research, but the relative importance of these attributes for the adoption of different hazard adjustments has largely been neglected. Particularly in the public health literature, there has been a tendency to include multiple dimensions as components of a single measurement scale (Committee on Risk Perception and Communication, 1989). Thus, the discussion that follows identifies specifically which resource requirements were studied.

As was the case with efficacy attributes, a review of research addressing the effect of personal resource requirements on the adoption of hazard adjustments is limited by very sparse empirical literature on the role of these variables. Research evidence is sufficient to support the proposition that an individual's capacity to implement a hazard adjustment is positively correlated with adoption of that adjustment (Dynes & Wenger, 1971; Hutton & Mileti, 1979; Mileti, 1975; Moore et al., 1963; Perry & Lindell, 1997b; Quarantelli, 1965) and that possession of adequate knowledge and resources is positively correlated with adoption (Burton et al., 1978; Fritz, 1961a; Kates, 1977; Kennedy, 1970; Mileti & Sorensen, 1988; Sjoberg, 1962; Sorenson & White, 1980). However, only two of the specific resource requirements mentioned above have received any consistent attention in the literature: the financial cost of an adjustment and its difficulty (or complexity) of implementation.

Research on the effects of financial cost on the adoption of hazard adjustments has mostly been indirect because the available studies have examined the correlation of reported adoption with household income, not the actual cost of each hazard adjustment. For example, Turner and colleagues (1986) reported household income was positively correlated with adopting earthquake preparedness measures through the intervening variable of community bondedness. Edwards (1993) also found that among homeowners in Memphis, Tennessee, household income showed a statistically significant positive relationship with household earthquake preparedness. Bourque, Reeder, Cherlin, Raven, and Walton (1973) studying earthquake preparedness and Neal, Perry, and Hawkins (1982) studying severe winter storms each report that higher socioeconomic status (measured as income) is positively correlated with household preparedness. Farley (1998) has also reported that families with higher socioeconomic status are more likely to undertake earthquake hazard adjustments. A classic study that used the purchase of flood or earthquake insurance as a specific adjustment (Kunreuther et al., 1978) found a positive relationship between income and being a policyholder. Along the same lines, Russell and colleagues (1995) found that family income was positively related to the adoption of earthquake adjustments. Virtually all of these studies involve the inference, rather than the explicit empirical demonstration, that if families with higher incomes are more likely to adopt hazard adjustments, then the cost of the adjustment must be a factor in the adoption decision. Unfortunately, many of these studies—and others—involved at best bivariate analysis of the relationship of family income with the adoption of one or more adjustments. None of the researchers assessed respondents' beliefs about the cost of the adjustment itself and related that to the probability of adopting that adjustment.

There also is limited research on the effects of hazard adjustment difficulty on adoption. After reviewing eight studies of earthquake adjustment adoption in the Central United States, the Committee on Preparedness, Awareness and Public Education (1993) operating under the Central United States Earthquake Consortium, concluded that "more difficult actions, such as structural alterations of homes and securing of water heaters and other hazardous objects, were taken by few people" (p. 96). One problem in interpreting statements such as this is that the "difficulty" of a hazard adjustment is an (unspecified) combination of time and effort requirements, specialized knowledge and skill requirements, requirements for specialized tools and equipment, and the need for cooperation from others. If one examines the component dimensions specifically, there is support for the proposition that adjustments are more readily adopted if they are easy to initiate and require little special knowledge and skill. For example, Edwards (1991) concluded that people were more likely to adopt adjustments that were simple and involved low effort (devising a family protection plan, keeping flashlights and battery-powered radios, talking with children, and protecting dishware) than more complex adjustments (securing water heaters, making building structural changes, obtaining advice from engineers). Similarly, Farley, Barlow, Finkelstein, and Riley (1991) reported that individuals more readily engaged in simple measures (learning utility shut-off procedures and storing water and supplies) than more complex measures (installing fasteners on cupboard doors and securing furniture).

Unfortunately, there appear to have been only two studies that have examined specific resource requirements (cost, knowledge and skill requirements, time and effort requirements, and required cooperation) in multivariate models of hazard adjustment adoption and these reported negative results. Studies of seismic hazard adjustment adoption by Lindell and Whitney (2000) and Lindell and Prater (2002) found that none of the four resource requirements had a statistically significant relationship with adjustment adoption.

In summary, the justification for considering resource requirements as determinants of hazard adjustment adoption is mixed. There obviously is a compelling theoretical rationale for including resource requirements in a model of hazard adjustment adoption. If an individual lacks sufficient resources—whether money, time, or intellectual ability—for a particular hazard adjustment, it simply cannot be implemented. Thus, the negative findings of Lindell and Whitney (2000) and Lindell and Prater (2002) raise significant challenges to the interpretation of the study results as much as they do to the inherent plausibility of the theory. One way to interpret these findings is to acknowledge that most of the 16 hazard adjustments examined in these studies (e.g., storing a 3-day supply of food and water, purchasing and maintaining a battery-powered radio, and learning the location of nearby medical centers) had relatively small resource requirements compared to making major structural modifications to the home.

It also is possible that the importance of resource requirements could be reduced by other variables. For example, very high levels of perceived risk could cause attributes such as time investment or difficulty to be seen as less of an impediment to adoption. However, this seems much more likely to happen during disaster response than during long-term hazard adjustment adoption. Alternatively, external incentives such as government-supported programs could avoid the constraints of limited household resources by making collective resources available to risk area residents. The city of Seattle, Washington, followed this approach in its implementation of Project Impact by establishing neighborhood tool banks that households could use while retrofitting their homes to reduce seismic vulnerability.

At this point, we have again encountered a significant problem with the empirical record. With the exception of financial cost, there has been little research on the role of resource requirements in the adoption of hazard adjustments. Among the studies that have been conducted, there has been a paucity of multivariate analyses that would provide an assessment of the importance of these attributes in relation to other theoretically relevant variables. In addition, the literature is characterized by findings that appear to be inconsistent and sometimes contradictory. Certainly this latter condition is related to the use of varying conceptualizations and measurements of resource requirements, as well as to the general absence of replications. Given these conditions, the appropriate theoretical tactic is to continue to include resource requirements in the hazard adjustment model, but to do so cautiously, emphasizing that further empirical attention is required.

Protective Action Implementation

As was the case during disaster response, protective action implementation occurs when all of the previous questions about risk reduction have been answered satisfactorily. Specifically, those at risk have determined that action should be taken, at least one available option is likely to be effective in achieving protection, and that option is logistically feasible with the available resources. As we have indicated earlier, there is no deadline for implementation that requires immediate action. Thus, the question "Does protective action need to be taken now?" typically produces a negative answer and, in turn, fails to elicit a threat response. Just as evacuation is delayed by those who receive hurricane warnings long in advance of the estimated time required to leave, those who receive advisories of long-term threats tend to await the receipt of information indicating a need for further action. This conclusion is supported by some of the early studies of seismic hazard adjustment, which showed extremely low levels of hazard adjustment adoption (Endo & Nielsen, 1979; Jackson, 1977, 1981; Jackson & Mukerjee, 1974; Sullivan et al., 1977). Lindell and Perry (2000) concluded that more recent studies seemed to indicate higher levels of hazard adjustment, but the evidence is equivocal. Specifically, Lindell and Prater (2000) found that residents of Southern California reported having adopted about half of the hazard adjustments in a 16-item inventory, but the residents of Southern California were not significantly different from residents of Western Washington State in their levels of household seismic hazard adjustment—despite the fact that the former area had experienced a number of damaging earthquakes within the previous 40 years (Sylmar, Coalinga, Whittier Narrows, Loma Prieta, and Northridge) and the latter area had experienced none.

Information Needs Assessment

As is the case with response to an imminent threat, the process of information search begins with an information needs assessment that arises from an individual's recognition that the available information is insufficient to justify proceeding further in the protective action decision process. Lion, Meertens, and Bot (2002) recently addressed this issue by collecting free response data on people's desire for information about five hazards about which their respondents had little or no information. These hazards were genetically modified food, radon in homes, an anti-blood-clotting medication, dioxin emissions from incinerators, and electromagnetic fields from high voltage power lines. The authors found that the major categories of information about which people wanted concerned the hazard agent ("What is it?"), its controllability ("What can be done about it?"), exposure ("Who is at risk, and what level of exposure is dangerous?"), the consequences of exposure ("What are its effects?"), blame ("Who is responsible?"), knowledge ("What research has been done?"), and others' response ("What do others do about this hazard?"). Two of these information categories are quite similar to the known risk (knowledge) and dread (exposure consequences) dimensions identified in research summarized by Slovic (1987), but all of them overlap with features of the PADM, especially the perceived hazard characteristics Lindell (1994a) derived from previous disaster research. Specifically, the hazard agent and its controllability identified by Lion and colleagues (2002) are equivalent to the PADM's agent characteristics, exposure is equivalent to the PADM's impact characteristics, consequences of exposure are equivalent to personal consequences, blame is related to perceived personal consequences, knowledge is equivalent to risk assessment by authorities, and others' response is equivalent to protective action (either recommended by authorities or observed being implemented by others).

Significantly, the authors found that a small but significant portion of the respondents preferred to remain ignorant about these hazards because of lack of personal relevance (i.e., a failure to personalize the risk), avoidance (i.e., emotion-focused coping), or perceived incapability of making use of additional information. Lion and colleagues (2002) also acknowledged that their study addressed "what information people *desire,* not what information they *use*" (p. 774), suggesting that many people are likely to passively monitor the news media rather than actively contact authorities to obtain this information. In this case, the *identified information need* is to be told that the probability of an extreme event is high enough to warrant people's searching for, assessing, and implementing protective actions.

Communication Action Assessment

The next question in the information-seeking process—"Where and how can I obtain this information?"—can be thought of as being guided by a thought process that is very similar to protective action assessment. Specifically, sources and channels are evaluated in terms of the value of the information in relation to the resources required to obtain that information. Information will be most valuable if it is new, valid, and relevant (Turner, 1991), as well as timely. As is the case with protective actions, the resources required are financial cost, knowledge and skill requirements, time and effort requirements, and the necessary cooperation.

In the case of long-term hazard adjustment, identification of a need for information does not necessarily motivate people to put any great amount of effort into the assessment of alternative sources and channels, so it is relatively unlikely that risk area residents will develop a systematic *information search plan.* Instead, the low sense of urgency is likely to lead people to passively monitor their routine information sources and channels. This conclusion is supported by data from Turner and colleagues (1986), which showed that a substantial proportion of their respondents relied on media coverage of the Palmdale Bulge for information about seismic hazards. Unfortunately, many local residents also considered celebrities and mystics to be credible information sources. These misplaced attributions of credibility are a logical consequence of restricted opportunities for physical reality testing. The scarcity of actual earthquakes made it impossible for scientists to prove that their scientific assessments were superior to celebrity pronouncements or mystical predictions—a problem that was especially severe for risk area residents who misunderstood or mistrusted scientific methods. Thus, for those who cannot evaluate complex scientific explanations and who have no particular beliefs about which source (scientists or mystics) is more credible, a logical response to this situation is to monitor the situation passively while waiting for some piece of information that will motivate protective action.

Communication Action Implementation

As was the case for disaster response, the final step in the information search process for long-term adjustment adoption is communication action implementation, which provides *decision information* by answering the question "Do I need the information now?" All too frequently, the answer to this question seems to be negative, so people tend to return to normal activities and, at most, passive monitoring. Here again, the absence of a deadline for action means that this passive monitoring is likely to continue until a credible source sounds a warning, environmental cues of an imminent threat arise (as in the case of hurricanes and floods), or a disaster strikes (as in the case of earthquakes or tornadoes).

❖ SITUATIONAL INFLUENCES ON HAZARD ADJUSTMENT

As described in Chapter 3, there are four categories of variables that influence risk area residents' response to disaster warnings. Although there are a few differences in the variables comprising these four types of variables—environmental cues, social context, message components (source, channel, and content), and receiver characteristics—they also influence hazard awareness programs.

Environmental Cues

Observation of physical cues during normal times is likely to produce a conclusion that conditions are benign rather than threatening, so people tend to procrastinate rather than to take protection action. Indeed, some people are reassured by the absence of threatening environmental cues for earthquakes because they believe this hazard actually will provide such cues before it strikes (Turner et al., 1986; Whitney, Lindell, & Nguyen, in press).

However, observation of others' behavior could motivate protective action if the others are observed implementing long-term hazard adjustments. Such action is likely only if the hazard adjustments are adopted by members of an individual's reference group. A *reference group* "designates the groups to which an individual orients himself, regardless of actual membership" (Singer, 1981, p. 68). In the context of hazard adjustment, reference groups can be broadly seen as representing people that the decision maker considers significant and worthy of emulation. These might be peers (friends, relatives, neighbors, or coworkers), authority figures, or respected individuals that the individual knows personally or whose views are known to the individual via the mass media or informal communication with peers. Of course, the individual selects the reference group, but it nonetheless influences his or her behavior. In terms of the PADM, the adoption of hazard adjustments by reference group members enhances the likelihood that decision makers will pass through the stages of the protective action decision process. Specifically, individuals who observe the adoption of hazard adjustments by reference group members or who hear about reference group members adopting these hazard adjustments are more likely to define risk as high, begin to gather hazard relevant information, and adopt hazard adjustments.

There appear to have been few empirical studies of hazard adjustment that have explicitly addressed relationship between the observation of reference group members' behaviors and the stages of the protective action decision process. Dexter, Willeke, and James (1979) found that respondents formed definitions of flood risk and selected floodproofing techniques "by talking to neighbors and observing their adjustments" (p. 75). In studying residents of volcano hazard risk areas, Greene and colleagues (1981) reported that people who saw relatives undertaking volcano adjustments and gathering information were more likely to view the volcano threat seriously and gather information themselves. Furthermore, Wenger, Faupel, and James (1980) found that people who reported social relationships with others who had undertaken protective measures were more likely to possess higher levels of threat relevant knowledge. Farley and colleagues (1991) similarly found that people who reported knowing others who had undertaken preparations for a damaging earthquake were more likely to believe they were in danger and to undertake protections themselves. In a subsequent study of the Browning earthquake prediction in Midwestern communities, Farley and colleagues (1993) reported that while messages in the news media regarding potential seismic activity influence risk perceptions, people's "plans on what to do about it were based much more on the perceived actions of others" (p. 319). Finally, Mileti and colleagues (1992) and Mileti and Darlington (1997) reported that perceptions of risk and household preparedness were positively correlated with the observation of seismic adjustments by others (primarily friends, relatives, and neighbors).

In many of these studies, it is difficult to clearly identify the relative importance of different mechanisms of the referent group influence. If referent group members are simply observed implementing protective action and the observers view the action as an innovative idea for providing protection from a hazard, then the process would be classified most accurately as behavioral modeling (Bandura, 1977; Wood & Bandura, 1989). This is because the reference group members made no attempt to change the observer's perceptions of the hazard adjustment (thus ruling out informational influence) or the observer's perceptions of the social consequences of the hazard adjustment (thus minimizing normative influence).

It is, of course, possible that the observer might adopt the hazard adjustment because he or she *thinks* that there would be social sanctions for adoption, even if the reference group members actually were indifferent to the adoption of this hazard adjustment by others. In this case, conformity with the wishes of these others involves changes in what Fishbein and Ajzen call the "social norm." This would still constitute modeling because the reference group members made no explicit attempt to change the observer's beliefs or behavior.

These two cases involving behavioral observation should be distinguished from two other cases involving persuasive appeals. In the first case, if reference group members are perceived to be credible sources who have relevant information that changes people's beliefs about the hazard and about alternative hazard adjustments, then this would be called informational influence that proceeds along what Petty and Cacioppo call the "central route" to persuasion in an attempt to change what Fishbein and Ajzen call the "attitude toward the act." In the second case, if the observer ignored the message content altogether, but he or she adopted the hazard adjustment on the basis of its potential social consequences (i.e., the subjective norm), the nature of the influence would be what Petty and Cacioppo call the "peripheral route" to persuasion and the effect would be on what Fishbein and Ajzen call the social norm. In the latter two cases, making the distinction between the central and peripheral routes to persuasion is important because the difference affects behavior—behavioral change that is caused by the central route is more persistent than behavior change achieved via the peripheral route. This is because people's beliefs about the hazard adjustments are likely to be more stable than their motivation to comply with others, the others concern about the intended behavior, or their ability to sanction deviations from their preferences.

Whatever the specific mechanism of influence, the studies cited above do confirm that observation of reference group members' behavior does enhance on the adoption of hazard adjustments. Some of these studies suggest that social influence affects the processes of defining risk and gathering hazard-relevant knowledge and that reference groups (if drawn from friends, relatives, neighbors, and coworkers) could form one part of this process. Moreover, there are strong theoretical reasons—from both reference group theory and social modeling (Bandura, 1977; Wood & Bandura, 1989)—for believing that reference group actions play a role at all steps in the hazard adjustment adoption process. That is, reference groups influence initial exposure to hazard relevant information (the adoption of a hazard adjustment) that is likely to produce an inference that there is a real threat that could produce severe personal consequences (although not soon). In addition, behavioral modeling inherently defines a recommended protective action and, depending on circumstances, might provide any specific information needed to implement that action. Even if observation does not reveal sufficient information about the efficacy of a protective action and its resource demands, it is likely to facilitate information seeking by indicating what source and channel (personal contact with the individual observed) to use in obtaining the needed information.

Social Context

Social context variables have an important effect on the adoption of hazard adjustments because of their relationships to the predecisional processes, decision stages, message characteristics, some psychological reactions, and some situational factors. There are two social context variables that are important in long-term hazard adjustment adoption, *friend and kinship networks* and *community networks.* Unlike the case of disaster response, *family obligations* play a relatively insignificant role in long-term hazard adjustment adoption because the availability of time for response eliminates family member separation as an impediment to protective action.

The importance of friend and kinship networks as an influence on disaster behavior has a long history in disaster research, dating to the early work of Killian (1952), Quarantelli (1960), and Hill and Hansen (1962). In the realm of hazard adjustment, immersion in such networks serves the social psychological function of providing decision makers with sources of information and serving as support in evaluating that information. Drabek and Boggs (1968) reported that interactions with kin both supply additional information (content) about the threat and serve as sources for information confirmation, whereas Perry and Lindell (1990a) stated that the volcano risk area residents they interviewed reported many discussions with friends and relatives: "They report talking about the [information] sources, the [protective] measures themselves, and about how much work and cost is involved in a given measure" (p. 139). The prevalence of such discussions was widespread; Perry and Greene (1982) reported that before the catastrophic May 18, 1980 eruption, 70% of those interviewed claimed to have had multiple discussions with friends, relatives, and neighbors about the hazard. Subsequently, Lindell and Perry (1993) found that residents near Mt. St. Helens who reported high levels of contact with friends and kin were more likely to perceive risk to be high and also were more likely to be able to correctly identify larger numbers of eruption consequences.

Similar findings have emerged in studies of other hazard agents. Mileti and Fitzpatrick's (1993) research on the Parkfield earthquake prediction revealed that approximately half of the residents in three study communities reported discussions with friends and acquaintances formed an important source of information regarding the likelihood of an earthquake and what could be done about it. Turner and colleagues (1986) studied residents of earthquake prone Southern California and found that "discussion of earthquake topics" with peers was positively correlated with earthquake fear, perceived danger, personal understanding of the earthquake threat, and household preparedness. A later study of California earthquake preparedness by Mileti and O'Brien (1992) similarly found that adoption of hazard adjustments after the Loma Prieta (San Francisco) earthquake was related to social contacts that produced higher levels of information quality (number of messages, message specificity, and message consistency).

The second social context variable of interest is the individual's integration into *community networks.* As indicated in Chapter 3, this variable captures the extent to which individuals communicate with members of community organizations, including voluntary associations, formal organizations, and government agencies. The first two of these, voluntary associations and formal organizations, comprise a wide array of types, including religious organizations, ethnic associations, service organizations, and fraternal organizations. Relevant government agencies include those with missions related to emergency preparedness and response (fire, police, emergency medical services, and emergency management), as well as to hazard mitigation and disaster recovery (land use planning, community development, and building construction).

Community network immersion has a long history of being studied in connection with disasters (Drabek, 1986), and findings regarding the effect of community involvement on long-term hazard adjustment are similar to those associated with disaster response. For example, research by Quarantelli (1985); Greene, Neal, and Quarantelli (1989); and Gillespie, Colignon, Banerjee, Murty, and Rogge (1993) suggests that interorganizational networks connecting both established and emergent disaster organizations can greatly enhance the level and quality of hazard relevant information available to those at risk by linking agencies that have disparate sources of expertise. Moreover, individuals' social connectedness achieved through membership in community organizations appears to promote their access to hazard information and to shape individual perceptions of long-term hazard adjustment processes (Tierney et al., 2001). Specifically, Turner and colleagues (1986) reported that community bondedness was significantly correlated with knowledge about earthquakes, threat perception, and salience of earthquake threats. In a direct extension of their previous research on warning response, Perry and Lindell's (1989) report on the communication of volcano hazard information found that a higher level of involvement in community organizations was associated with a greater likelihood that risk area residents will receive multiple messages about the hazard and that one or more of those messages will have come from what is perceived to be a credible source. Perry and Lindell (1997b) replicated these findings in a study of earthquake information that also found the level of contact with community organizations to be positively correlated with perceived risk. Similarly, Perry's (1990) study of volcanic hazard information at Mt. Shasta found that higher levels of community involvement were positively correlated with hazard relevant knowledge, number of messages received, and having heard at least one warning from a credible source. The large-scale study of adjustment to the Mt. St. Helens volcano by Perry and Lindell (1990a) showed that higher levels of participation in community organizations was correlated with higher levels of perceived risk, higher levels of hazard-relevant information, greater numbers of messages received, and higher levels of threat salience.

In summary, immersion in friend, kinship, and community networks can have a significant effect on all stages of the protective action decision-making process. Specifically, these networks provide a large number of individuals who can serve as credible sources of information about hazards and hazard adjustments. Consequently, information from members of these networks is more likely to be heeded and comprehended, thereby influencing people's threat beliefs, protection motivation, protective action decision sets, adaptive plans, and threat response. In addition, such information can affect information search plans and decision information. In most cases, immersion in friend, kinship, and community networks has indirect effects on the protective action decision process via its effects on other variables. These include effects on source credibility; the number of messages received; message clarity, specificity, repetition, and consistency; and receiver characteristics such as threat salience, hazard intrusiveness, hazard relevant knowledge, and perception of protection responsibility.

Message Components

Much of the literature on risk communication has been oriented toward the construction of messages, particularly their content, structure, and repetition

(Committee on Risk Perception and Communication, 1989; Covello & Allen, 1988; Covello, McCallum, & Pavlova, 1989; Gutteling & Weigman, 1996; Handmer & Penning-Roswell, 1990; Krimsky & Plough, 1988; Lundgren & McMakin, 1998). One significant shortcoming of these treatises is that they have neglected the ways in which messages about environmental risks affect the protective action decision-making process. By contrast, interpreting risk communication within the context of the PADM shows how message characteristics influence each of the steps in the hazard adjustment process. Thus, the following sections will examine the three message components—sources, channels, and content—to examine their specific effects.

Message Sources

It is well documented that people receive hazard relevant messages from a variety of sources, and that these sources are evaluated and differentially attended to in terms of perceived credibility (Lindell et al., 1983; Perry & Lindell, 1987; Peters et al., 1997). As indicated in Chapter 3, message receivers make subjective judgments of source credibility that can be divided into two dimensions, expertise and trustworthiness (Hass, 1981). Although this characterization is helpful, it does not explain what specific cues people use in making judgments of expertise and trustworthiness. Perry and Lindell (1989) addressed this problem by collecting free-response data on the attributes that residents of the area around the Mt. St. Helens volcano associated with some of the different sources of volcano hazard information. The responses could be categorized into four themes: past reliability (56% of all responses in one community and 44% in another), special hazard-related skills and information (31% and 33%), integrity (10% and 17%), and concern for citizens (3% and 5%). These data suggest that expertise is judged by special hazard-relevant skills and information, whereas trustworthiness subsumes the categories of past reliability, concern for citizens, and integrity. In a further examination of these data, Lindell and Perry (1992) concluded that there appear to be three different bases on which a source can be judged credible. The first basis is credentials—such as job titles, advanced degrees, or special certification. For example, credibility is often attributed to government environmental hazard managers, university professors, geologists, hydrologists, or meteorologists on the basis of their credentials. A second basis of source credibility can be found in the way a given source is treated by other sources who are known (or believed) to be credible. A source of unknown credibility is more likely to achieve a degree of public acceptance if that source is treated with respect by sources of known credibility as, for example, when a source is cited in the news media. Finally, a source can be considered to be credible because of a past history of reliable performance. This is most often the case for local officials such as a sheriff, a fire chief, an emergency manager, or a public health director.

There are two important issues related to source credibility, the first of which concerns the identification of sources that are perceived to be the most credible. As early as 1969, Drabek reported that messages from authorities (fire and police personnel) were more likely to be seen as credible than were messages from other sources. Similarly, Mileti (1975) found that messages from official sources (listed as "police, state police and fire fighters") were more likely to be believed (p. 21). Perry and Lindell (1989) studied source credibility among citizens living near Mt. St. Helens and found that local authorities (county sheriff and county emergency services) were seen as the most credible sources of volcano threat information, followed by nonlocal authorities (U.S. Geological Survey and Army Corps of Engineers), then mass media and, finally, peers.

The available data suggest that source credibility influences the stages of the protective action decision-making process. Specifically, source credibility is positively correlated with both hazard knowledge and perceived risk. Sorenson (1983), based on a study of Hawaiian students, found that perceived source utility (which appears to be equivalent to the expertise dimension of credibility) was positively correlated with level of hazard knowledge. Perry and Lindell's (1990b) study of long-term adjustment to volcano hazards found that citizens who received messages from what they perceived to be credible sources were more likely to develop a sense of personal vulnerability (perceived risk) and to develop higher levels of hazard knowledge (defined specifically as information about the likely consequences of volcanic threats). Similar findings have been reported in the context of tsunamis (Anderson, 1969), tornadoes (Moore et al., 1963; Stallings, 1971), hurricanes (Windham et al., 1977), volcanoes (Carter et al., 1977), and a broad category of technological accidents (Rosenthal, 1990).

There are a number of predecisional processes and stages of the protective action decision-making process where the effects of source credibility are unclear. On the one hand, it seems likely that high credibility would increase attention to a source's message, but the Elaboration Likelihood Model suggests that high credibility would decrease attention because the source's credibility would make it unnecessary to attend to and comprehend the message (Petty & Cacioppo, 1986a). In addition, source credibility appears to contribute to the individual's propensity to accept the source's threat belief, but the level of perceived risk and protection motivation will depend on the source's message; risk perception will increase if the source advocates a greater perception of risk, but it will increase if the source minimizes the risk. The distinction between sources advocating an increased or decreased risk perception is rarely an issue with natural hazards because it is almost invariably the case that authorities are attempting to increase the risk perceptions of risk area residents. However, this is frequently an issue with technological hazards, where facility operators are attempting to decrease the risk perceptions of risk area residents.

Similarly, perceptions of the attributes of alternative hazard adjustments will depend on the content source's message; favorability of the protective action assessments and likelihood of adoption will increase or decrease depending on the source's position. By contrast, information seeking is generally expected to be inversely related to source credibility. High source credibility is expected to reduce people's need for additional information about what was presented in the message, but it could stimulate information seeking regarding information that was not addressed. For example, highly credible sources might have no difficulty in elevating people's risk perception and protection motivation, but they may stimulate information seeking about appropriate protective actions if they did not have any to recommend.

Message Channels

Research on the adoption of hazard adjustments has devoted relatively little attention to the choice of message channels for conveying information about long-term hazards and hazard adjustments. In one study, Wenger (1980) reported that the principal channel for information about hazards is the mass media, and this was confirmed by the data Turner and colleagues (1986) collected in the course of their monitoring of the Palmdale Bulge. Mileti and Darlington (1997) reported that adoption of seismic hazard adjustments was positively correlated with the number of information channels available to individuals.

One of the challenges in interpreting these results is that most studies (or perhaps the situations they are studying) make it difficult to distinguish between a communication channel and an information source. Theoretically, the distinction is clear. An *information source* is a person or organization that uses expertise to identify a threat and to collect and disseminate information about it. By contrast, a *communication channel* represents the technological means by which a message is disseminated. Thus, for example, emergency management authorities, police, firefighters, friends, relatives, neighbors, and political authorities are all sources. Channels include print media (newspapers, brochures), electronic media (television, radio, Internet), loudspeakers, telephones, public meetings, and face-to-face conversations. One reason the distinction between source and channel becomes muddled in practice is that some sources are "channel bound." That is, some sources commonly—even exclusively—use the same channels. Political and emergency authorities tend to use public meetings and brochures, whereas peers tend to use face-to-face and telephone conversations. Moreover, when one source (e.g., a radio announcer) is relaying a message from another source (e.g., a local emergency management coordinator), warning recipients sometimes cannot distinguish among the original source (the local emergency management coordinator), the intermediate source (the radio announcer), and the channel (the radio). To further complicate this issue, the media sometimes report that they are relaying a message from authorities and then proceed to comment on the information in the message from their own perspective (Lindell & Perry, 1992).

The tendency to confound message sources and channels makes it even more difficult to assess the effects of information channels on the stages of the protective action decision-making process. Given the prominence of the mass media as hazard information sources, one can safely conclude that television and radio (and to a lesser extent, newspapers) are excellent channels for achieving the reception of hazard information. However, attention is likely to be limited—especially in newspapers, where editors can vary the size and placement of articles and where readers can use the headlines to guide them in avoiding stories that they consider uninteresting. The mass media rarely have a problem with comprehension, at least in terms of using language and concepts that cannot be understood by the typical reader, listener, or viewer. If anything, the complaint from environmental hazard managers tends to be that reporters oversimplify complex issues. A problem with the mass media is that it can be difficult to get coverage of hazards and hazard adjustments because the news media tend to have limited interest in these issues before a disaster strikes.

All of the available channels appear to be able to influence threat beliefs, protection motivation, protective action decision sets, adaptive plans, and hazard adjustment adoption. Similarly, they all appear to be able to assist in developing identified information needs, information search plans, and decision information, although some of them (e.g., face-to-face contacts, public meetings, telephone conversations, and the Internet) provide greater opportunities for feedback than do others (e.g., television, radio, and newspapers). Any observable effects of channels on the protective action decision-making process are most likely to arise from two factors. The first of these is a channel's inherent limitation in the types of verbal, numeric, and graphic information that it can transmit, whereas the second factor is the confounding of sources and channels noted earlier. To the extent that certain channels are used by specific sources that transmit specific types of messages, systematic differences in channel effects on the protective action decision-making process will be observed.

Message Content

Risk communication in connection with long-term hazard adjustment is directed toward a very lengthy protective action decision-making process that is measured in months to years, rather than the minutes to hours characteristic of disaster response. This extended time horizon provides excellent opportunities for dialogue among sources and receivers but, because the level of scientific understanding of some hazards is often inadequate, such exchanges are "often riddled with disagreements, apathy, misunderstanding and suspicion" (Ng & Hamby, 1997, p. 473).

An important practical issue for environmental hazard managers and a significant conceptual issue for researchers lies in sorting out what information people need and how they process the information that is presented. As noted earlier, people need information about the characteristics of the hazard and appropriate hazard adjustments, so it is important to focus hazard awareness programs on information that is relevant to protection motivation and the choice of hazard adjustments (Mileti & Peek, 2000). Some earthquake risk communication documents, such as *Putting Down Roots in Earthquake Country* (Southern California Earthquake Data Center, n.d.), have adopted this approach of attempting to heighten risk perceptions by providing factual information about the probability that a major disaster will occur within a specified period of time. This information about the hazard is followed by descriptions of methods for emergency preparedness and hazard mitigation.

There are some important limitations to this approach, as evidenced by Mileti and Fitzpatrick's (1993) assessment of a seismic hazard mitigation program for residents in three Central California towns. Mileti and Fitzpatrick found that few of those who received an earthquake brochure advising them of the Parkfield earthquake threat remembered specific details about the earthquake hazard, although most of them did recall the recommended protective actions. Significantly, this result is consistent with research on social cognition that has found that memory for overall impressions is better than memory for specific details relevant to those impressions (Fiske & Taylor, 1991). Of course, this does not necessarily mean that it is unnecessary to present the details in the first place because these might be necessary to support the conclusion that the high level of personal risk requires protective action. Then, once the argument has been made convincingly, the details about the threat can be forgotten because they are no longer necessary.

In an evaluation of another seismic hazard awareness program, Mileti and Darlington (1997) found that only a few residents of the San Francisco Bay area adopted new seismic adjustments that were described in the brochure. One interpretation of these results is that the process of hazard adjustment adoption is very slow, so few people will adopt a new hazard adjustment in a given period of time. Alternatively, it might be that conventional methods of risk communication will have little influence if they are perceived to lack novelty, validity, or relevance (Turner, 1991). In particular, residents of areas with a well known seismic risk might believe that they already know everything they need about earthquakes, so additional information on this topic is overlooked even if it actually would be useful.

Most of the studies of hazard adjustment have tacitly assumed that the role of hazard awareness programs is to provide information that will create beliefs where none existed previously, but researchers have documented the existence of erroneous beliefs about people's behavior in disasters (Wenger et al., 1980) and various aspects of seismic activity (Turner et al., 1986; Whitney et al., 2003). That is, risk communicators must sometimes overcome old beliefs, which could be much more difficult than just establishing new ones.

Once again, the cognitive processing model is useful in identifying multiple obstacles to belief change. In addition to the possibility that people do not receive accurate information, there are these possibilities: (1) that they do not heed the accurate information they do receive because they do not recognize it as novel (i.e., different from what they currently believe); (2) that they do not comprehend it; (3) that they do not believe it because they do not consider it to be valid; or (4) that it has no perceived relevance to their personal safety or property. To address the possibility that erroneous beliefs can persist because message recipients do not recognize information about a well-known risk as new and different, Whitney and colleagues (in press) conducted an experiment in which one group of participants was given only factual information (the "facts only" condition), and the other group of participants received information that presented a common myth about earthquakes (labeled as such), followed by accurate information on the same topic (labeled as fact) (the "myths vs. facts" condition). Whitney and his colleagues found evidence that the "myths vs. facts" condition was more successful in changing people's beliefs than the "facts only" condition, but both formats were effective in increasing the level of seismic hazard adjustment.

Another way of understanding this problem is to examine *message style* characteristics (Mileti & Peek, 2001; Mileti & Sorensen, 1987). These factors include four primary components: the *clarity* and *specificity* of message content, the *repetition* of messages, and the *consistency* of content across messages. *Clarity* is characterized by the use of a basic vocabulary, avoidance of technical terminology, and simple declarative sentences. *Specificity* reflects the inclusion of enough detail that those receiving the message can accurately determine if they are at risk. *Repetition* refers to multiple reception of identical information within or across sources as well as within or across channels. *Consistency* means that all the information within a single message or in all of the messages (whether these are from the same or different sources over the same or different channels) leads to the same conclusion.

The discussion that follows is based on two major premises. First, although many different sources might be sending and relaying messages, the most important of these are messages sent by governmental authorities in emergency management, public safety, and public health. These agencies provide a presumptively credible standard against which to judge the messages of other sources (e.g., peer groups, mass media, nongovernmental organizations, and private corporations). Second, messages are sent via multiple channels, with some sources consistently using channels that systematically differ from those used by other sources. While in some cases the channel chosen can affect the use of the information—for example, Perry (1990) and Perry and Nelson (1991) have argued that written information is more likely to be retained—it is likely, perhaps even desirable, that authorities will use electronic media and public meetings as well. Hence, we are more concerned here about message content and repetition than about the specific channels used. This latter issue will be addressed more directly in Chapter 5 when we examine the differential utility of hazard awareness programs.

There is a substantial body of literature on the structure of disaster warnings that shows that message clarity, specificity, repetition, and consistency are positively correlated with recipients' threat beliefs, hazard knowledge, risk perceptions, and warning compliance (Drabek, 1969; Fritz, 1968; Fritz & Williams, 1957; Lindell & Perry, 1992; Mileti, 1974; Perry, 1979a; Perry et al., 1981). Thus, one would expect that these findings also apply to information about long-term hazard adjustments and, indeed, this is the case. Haas and Trainer (1974) found that the provision of specific information regarding tsunami threats in Alaska enhanced recipients' perceptions of danger, Bauman (1983) found a positive correlation between the amount and specificity of risk information with perceptions of flood risk, and Ruch and Christensen (1980) reported that specific written information about hurricane threats increased recipients' knowledge of local hurricane consequences. Perry and Greene (1982) reported that receipt of community-specific information about the volcano hazard at Mt. St. Helens was positively correlated with both perception of volcano risk and contacts with authorities to seek additional information. In turn, information seeking was positively correlated with hazard knowledge. Furthermore, Perry (1990) found that receipt of specific information by risk area residents near the Mt. Shasta volcano in California was positively correlated with hazard knowledge and contacts with authorities to seek additional information. Similarly, Perry and Lindell's (1990a) study of Mt. St. Helens found that risk area residents who reported receiving clear and specific information from authorities also reported higher levels of hazard knowledge. Finally, Mileti and colleagues (1992) reported that the results of their study of the Parkfield earthquake prediction indicated that message style characteristics influenced people's hazard knowledge, risk perceptions, and, in some cases, hazard adjustment adoption. In particular, these researchers found that receipt of messages that were clear and specific regarding earthquake consequences and that recommended protective actions increased perceptions of near-term risk from earthquakes.

With respect to repetition, studies of warning behavior have found that people who report hearing multiple warnings are more likely to perceive themselves at risk (Drabek, 1969; Mileti & Beck, 1975; Mileti & Sorenson, 1988; Perry et al., 1981; Quarantelli, 1980). With the extended forewarning of hazard impact that characterizes risk communication directed toward long-term hazard adjustment, message repetition becomes critically important. For decades, researchers have documented that people's initial reactions to a message indicating environmental danger is to reinterpret the message to indicate either that there is no real danger or that it does not apply to them personally. This phenomenon is described in the literature as a "normalcy bias" (see, e.g., Committee on Socioeconomic Effects of Earthquake Predictions, 1978). Often, it is only after receiving multiple messages or confirming warnings through contacts with other sources that warning recipients begin to achieve what the PADM defines as a "threat belief and protection motivation" (Lindell & Perry, 1992). Warrick's (1981) study of ash fall threat in four communities reinforces the notion that single messages are problematic:

> The initial warning about the ash fall issued by the Washington State Department of Emergency Services had absolutely no utility at any of the community study sites. Recipients . . . felt that it did not apply to their community, or they waited for more extensive confirmatory information. (p. 103)

Similarly, Saarinen and Sell (1985), describing the attempts to inform local officials of the potential for eruptions at the Mt. St. Helens volcano, reported that "on receipt of the first warning information, most respondents did not seriously consider it a threat to public safety" (p. 94). The authors went on to emphasize that it was only after several weeks—during which planning meetings were held and more messages were issued from the U.S. Geological Survey—that most individuals began to systematically assess their vulnerability.

Other studies of volcanic hazards have also produced findings indicating that receipt of multiple messages regarding a hazard is positively correlated with hazard knowledge and risk perception (Blong, 1984). Hodge and colleagues (1978) studied citizens living near the Mt. Baker volcano in Washington and reported that, although most people did not believe themselves to be at risk, those who did perceive risk to be higher had received multiple messages from multiple sources regarding eruptive dangers. Murton and Shimabukuro (1974) studied Hawaiians living near the frequently eruptive east rift zone on the island of Hilo. Although long-time residents were accustomed to periodic lava flows from the rift, it was reported that newcomers reported low levels of risk perception until after they had received several messages regarding the eruptive threat. Greene and colleagues (1981) studied perceptions of threat from the Mt. St. Helens volcano prior to the cataclysmic eruption of May 18, 1980 and also reported that risk area residents who had received multiple messages about the eruptive threat were more likely to have elevated perceptions of risk.

The data on volcanoes are reinforced by studies of earthquake threats. Studies of earthquake perception in California by Turner and colleagues (1979) found that the receipt of multiple hazard-relevant messages was correlated with higher levels of perceived risk. Similarly, Mileti, Hutton, and Sorenson's (1981) study of response to earthquake predictions revealed a positive correlation between the number of messages received and both risk perception and information-seeking behavior. Mileti and Fitzpatrick's (1993) studies of the Parkfield earthquake prediction also found a positive correlation between the number of messages and risk perception, and they concluded that "the public needs to get the message from as many different sources and through as many different channels as possible" (p. 87). Mileti (1999) argued that the empirical data so strongly support the connection of multiple message receipt with outcomes such as hazard knowledge, risk perception, and eventual hazard adjustment that all efforts at promoting hazard adjustment should plan on incorporating multiple messages sent by multiple sources via multiple channels.

The last message style characteristic to be considered here is consistency. Disaster response studies have demonstrated that receipt of waning messages that are consistent with each other with respect to the location, timing, and severity of impact, and especially with respect to recommended protective actions, are more likely to increase people's risk perceptions and protective actions than are less consistent and specific messages (Drabek, 1986; Flynn, 1979; Mileti et al., 1975; Perry et al., 1981; Quarantelli, 1980). Thus, as one would expect, a positive correlation between message consistency and risk perception has also been found in studies of hazard adjustment behavior. Turner and colleagues (1981) found that citizens who reported receipt of earthquake-related messages that were mutually consistent also tended to rate the probability of a damaging earthquake higher than did citizens who did not receive consistent messages. In a study of the adoption of flood hazard adjustments, Waterstone (1978) found that those who received and remembered two consistent messages (brochures from authorities) had higher levels of hazard knowledge and were more concerned about the likelihood of flooding than those who did not.

In summary, existing research indicates that message content per se does not affect message reception, but message repetition does. Message content can significantly affect attention and comprehension, so poorly constructed messages might not even pass from the predecisional processes to the decision stages. Moreover, message content influences threat beliefs, protection motivation, protective action decision sets, adaptive plans, and hazard adjustment adoption. Finally, information content affects the identification of information needs, the identification of sources and channels for information search plans, and the decision information that is obtained.

Receiver Characteristics

Disaster Experience

There is a long history of speculation and research about the role of people's previous disaster experience on hazard adjustment. The explanation for the effect of personal experience is that it produces more vivid memories than does a pallid description of events (Fiske & Taylor, 1991; Nisbett & Ross, 1980). The challenge in assessing the effect of experience on the protective action decision process is to measure experience in research studies in a way that reflects its impact on disaster victims. Thus, measuring experience as people's "having been in" an event (such as Hurricane Andrew) provides less information than measuring experience in terms of personal exposure to specific environmental conditions (such as 120 mph wind) or, more suitably, in terms of personal consequences such as casualties (death and injuries), property damage (to structures, contents, and vehicles), and/or disruption of normal activities (e.g., work, shopping, and travel). The experience of such personal consequences constitutes a significant event for the individual, and thus one that is likely to be remembered as incontrovertible personal evidence of the hazard's potential impacts. At least three dimensions of experience appear to be important, the first of which is defined by the types of impacts—casualties, property damage, and disruption to normal activities. The second dimension concerns the intensity of an individual's involvement with the event. In the case of casualties, this range can be exemplified by a continuum that generally decreases in psychological significance as one proceeds from impacts suffered by oneself to those suffered by more distant family members and, finally, to those suffered by peers. More remote in their psychological significance would be injuries experienced vicariously by viewing victims on television, hearing them on radio, or reading about them in newspapers. The most remote in their impacts would be injuries "experienced" as pallid statistical summaries of the number of injuries reported in the news media. The third dimension is defined by the temporal distribution, that is, the recency and frequency of impacts over time. Thus, the more recent and frequent the effects, the greater the psychological impact.

The majority of household hazard adjustment studies conducted over the past 30 years that have dealt with disaster experience have found that it is positively correlated with hazard knowledge, risk perceptions, development of adaptive plans, and adoption of hazard adjustments (Tierney et al., 2001). For example, research on floods has found disaster experience to be positively correlated with risk perception (Drabek & Boggs, 1968; Perry et al., 1981) and intention to undertake preparedness measures (Perry et al., 1981). Research also indicates that the previous experience of hurricane damage is positively related to threat belief and risk perception (Norris, Smith, & Kaniasty, 1999; Riad et al., 1999; Windham et al., 1977).

Similarly, Perry and Lindell (1990a) found that residents near the Mt. St. Helens volcano who reported damage from previous eruptions judged their personal risk as higher, were able to identify larger numbers of volcano adjustments, and were more likely to have adopted multiple hazard adjustments. In studies of earthquakes, several studies have documented that individuals who have experienced damage are more likely to define future risk as high, seek information about hazard adjustments, and adopt those hazard adjustments (Dooley, Catalano, Mishra, & Serxner, 1992; Jackson, 1981; Russell et al., 1995; Showalter, 1993; Turner et al., 1986). In connection with the 1989 Loma Prieta earthquake, Burger and Palmer (1992) found that university students whose families had experienced damage were more likely than those whose families did not experience such damage to believe there was a high risk of future damaging events. These findings were replicated by Helweg-Larsen (1999) on a sample of students who had experienced the Northridge earthquake.

One important finding is that disaster experience sometimes has been found to have a stronger correlation with hazard adjustment than with either perceived risk or hazard intrusiveness. Moreover, the correlation of disaster experience and hazard adjustment remains statistically significant even when controlling for perceived risk and hazard intrusiveness (Lindell & Prater, 2000). Thus, disaster experience seems to have a direct effect on hazard adjustment that is independent of its indirect effects through these other variables, which suggests that there are additional unidentified variables that mediate the effect of disaster experience on hazard adjustment.

It is important to recognize that the evidence for an effect of disaster experience on the protective action decision-making process has focused on the early stages of the process, particularly on risk identification and risk assessment. It is therefore not surprising to find that some studies have found disaster experience to be weakly related or unrelated to the adoption of hazard adjustments (Mileti & Darlington, 1997; Mileti & O'Brien, 1992; Palm & Hodgson, 1992; Palm, Hodgson, Blanchard, & Lyons, 1990; Russell et al., 1995). The latter results can be explained by the large number of steps (i.e., the large number of intervening variables) that lie between disaster experience and hazard adjustment in the protective action decision-making process. Moreover, these weak or nonsignificant correlations can also be explained by methodological differences among studies in the method used to measure disaster experience (i.e., as events, exposures, or personal consequences).

Finally, Quarantelli (1984) has questioned whether experience with the impacts of one type of hazard agent generalizes to other types of hazard agent. Specifically, he argues that disaster experiences that contradict long and strongly held individual beliefs might be perceived to be anomalies and not relevant for future experiences—an argument that is consistent with research on social cognition (Fiske & Taylor, 1991). Nonetheless, it appears appropriate to conclude that disaster experience is positively correlated with threat belief, hazard knowledge, and risk perception. Moreover, it seems plausible that disaster experience is positively correlated with attention to environmental cues and risk communication, protective action search, protective action assessment, and information-seeking activities (and, thus, reception of risk communication). There is no evidence or theoretical rationale for expecting disaster experience to be correlated with exposure to environmental cues or comprehension of risk information.

Hazard Knowledge

Chapter 2 described four core dimensions of perceived risk (certainty, severity, immediacy, and duration of personal consequences), but these are not the only beliefs that people have about hazards. As indicated earlier, Lindell (1994a) found evidence that people also distinguish among environmental hazards in terms of the characteristics of the hazard agent (likelihood of a major event, ease of reducing risks, and likelihood of release prevention) and disaster impact (existence of environmental cues, speed of onset, scope of impact, and duration of impact). This information, which we call *hazard knowledge,* is generally descriptive of a hazard's genesis, its mechanisms of exposure, and the types of hazard adjustments that can avoid its impacts. It also can include the information about the number and types of specific threats associated with a hazard. For example, many of those at risk from volcanic eruptions know that they could be harmed by ashfall, pyroclastic flows, and mudflows and/or floods (Greene et al., 1981).

Hazard knowledge will be highly correlated with risk perception if it serves as the basis for people's judgments of the certainty, severity, immediacy, and duration of personal consequences. Alternatively, hazard knowledge will be unrelated to risk perception if the hazard knowledge was received from one source (e.g., an authority) and the risk assessments were received directly from another source (e.g., a peer) rather than being derived deductively from the hazard knowledge. People might not notice any inconsistencies between the hazard knowledge and risk perceptions if they give only limited attention to the issue or, more generally, because of inherent limits to the rationality of judgment (Feldman & Lindell, 1990; Yates, 1990). Indeed, it is possible that hazard knowledge could influence people's adoption of hazard adjustments even if it is not incorporated into their risk perceptions.

It is important to note that there is a related literature on hazard awareness, but this concept overlaps only partially with hazard knowledge. *Hazard awareness* tends to be thought of largely in terms of a person's recognition of the existence of an environmental threat (Saarinen, 1982). Thus, hazard awareness is more closely related to the concept of a threat belief, as described in previous chapters. *Hazard knowledge* differs from hazard awareness in that it characterizes the depth of an individual's understanding of the hazard. This approach is consistent with Mileti and Sorenson's (1987) argument that people's protective responses can be predicted more accurately from their perceptions of threat consequences than from their awareness that a hazard exists. Moreover, research summarized by Drabek (1986; see also Faupel, Kelley, & Petee, 1992) suggests that people with higher levels of hazard knowledge are more likely to adopt hazard adjustments, and this conclusion is supported by research studying different types of hazards adjustments. In studying the purchase of hazard insurance, Britton, Kearney, and Britton (1983) found that respondents with higher levels of hazard knowledge were more likely to purchase insurance. Palm (1981) obtained similar findings when studying homeowner purchases of earthquake insurance. Likewise, Turner, Nigg, Paz, and Young (1979) reported that higher levels of hazard knowledge were positively associated with adoption of specific emergency preparedness measures. Furthermore, Perry and his colleagues found a positive relationship between hazard knowledge and the adoption of preparedness measures in studies of communities struck by floods (Perry et al., 1981) and threatened by volcanic eruption at Mt. St. Helens (Perry et al., 1982b).

According to the PADM, people are likely to have acquired higher levels of hazard knowledge through active information seeking and, thus, also are likely to have more information about hazard adjustments. However, individuals with higher levels of hazard knowledge can be overconfident about their hazard invulnerability (see Svenson, 1981; Weinstein, 1989). For example, Kunreuther and his colleagues (1978) reported that some purchasers of hazard insurance became overconfident about the security achieved by the purchase and tended to shun further adjustments. An individual's overly optimistic assessment of his or her own skill and knowledge, especially if it follows from the adoption of a single adjustment, might well hinder that individual from making further adjustments (Harris, 1996). Both lines of reasoning, however, underscore that a connection exists between hazard knowledge and adjustment adoption.

Hazard Salience

Hazard salience is an important concept because it provides an internal stimulus for actions that take place in the absence of an external stimulus. In the case of environmental hazards, hazard salience is invoked to explain why some individuals but not others adopt hazard adjustments (apparently spontaneously) without an immediately preceding stimulus of risk communication or environmental cues indicating a potential for disaster impact. The problem is that the effects of hazard salience have more often been *assumed* on conceptual grounds than actually studied. For example, a stated goal of many hazard awareness programs is to create hazard salience in the risk area population, but this variable has rarely been measured as a program outcome (Sorenson & Mileti, 1987).

Drabek (1986), writing in his encyclopedic review of disaster studies, argued that the empirical record suggests that hazard salience is *probably* related to both hazard knowledge and perceived risk, but he also stated that variations in theoretical definitions and methods of measurement preclude an unequivocal conclusion. In particular, there seems to be agreement that *salience* refers to the prominence of an object in relation to its background, but this has been interpreted in four distinctly different ways. First, salience is sometimes used to refer to a physical object or phenomenon that stands out against an environmental background, as when one tall person is seen in a group of shorter ones or when information about the price of an item is easier to see than its quality. Salience is important because it appears to distort people's judgments. For example, Tversky and Kahneman (1974, 1981) and Kahneman and Tversky (1979) reported that, in judging risk, people have a tendency to overvalue low probability salient information, yet undervalue high probability nonsalient information.

The second interpretation of salience arises in connection with social issues or personal concerns that are judged to be more important to an individual. In the context of environmental hazards, high salience enhances the likelihood that people will attend to an environmental hazard as a personal concern. Thus, people who rate an environmental hazard as high in importance or as causing great personal concern find the issue to be more salient and, consequently, will be more likely to identify the hazard as a real threat and have a high level of protection motivation. The meaningfulness of this definition of salience is supported by Farley's (1998) study of the Browning earthquake prediction, which found that people who expressed "concern" about the risk of a damaging earthquake were more likely to possess higher levels of hazard knowledge. However, Russell and colleagues (1995) also used "personal concern about earthquakes" as their measure of salience, but they found that this variable did not significantly predict adoption of seismic hazard adjustments in most cases.

The third usage of salience refers to the frequency with which people report thinking about an issue. Perry and Lindell (1990a) adopted this method of measuring the salience of the volcano threat to residents of the risk area around Mt. St. Helens, finding salience to be positively, but not significantly, correlated with adoption of volcanic hazard adjustments. However, they did find that hazard salience was positively (and significantly) correlated with both hazard knowledge and perceived risk. Using the same measurement methods, Perry's (1990) study of the Mt. Shasta volcano found that the salience of the volcano hazard was positively related to risk perceptions and information seeking (defined as number of citizen-initiated contacts with information sources). This method for measuring hazard salience was extended by measuring the extent to which people think about and discuss (Lindell, 1994a; Lindell & Prater, 2000) and receive information (Lindell & Prater, 2000) about a hazard—which the latter authors referred to as "hazard intrusiveness" to distinguish it from other measures of hazard salience. This definition could prove to be problematic because the last component of hazard intrusiveness (passive information receipt) is rather similar to (active) information seeking. Nonetheless, Lindell and Prater (2000) found that hazard intrusiveness had a stronger correlation with seismic hazard adjustment than did perceived risk, disaster experience, and many demographic variables. If future studies replicate these results, the concept of hazard intrusiveness might sharpen the more general notion of hazard salience. In the interim, hazard salience is retained in the PADM as a determinant of hazard knowledge and risk perception.

Personality Characteristics

As noted in Chapter 2, the generally preferred solution to the question "What can be done to achieve protection?" is an action that will be taken by someone else. This seems to have been particularly true for seismic hazard adjustments in the 1970s (Jackson & Mukerjee, 1974; Kunreuther et al., 1978; Sullivan et al.,1977), but recent evidence suggests that people are accepting increased responsibility for protecting themselves from disaster impacts (Lindell & Perry, 2000). This raises the issue of individual differences in the personality characteristic of *personal protection responsibility,* which refers to people's beliefs about their own levels of responsibility for self-protection from a hazard. It is generally expected that those who consider self-protection to be a personal responsibility are more likely to undertake long-term hazard adjustments. Empirically, the role of personal protection responsibility can be traced to the early work of Jackson (1977, 1981) who found that residents of California earthquake risk areas judged that the responsibility for coping with earthquakes lay with government; only 10% of his respondents felt that households were responsible for their own protection. Mulilis and Duval (1995) and Duval and Mulilis (1999) later found strong positive correlations between perception of personal protection responsibility and the adoption of earthquake hazard adjustments, whereas Mulilis and Duval (1997) extended these findings to the implementation of tornado preparedness measures. Furthermore, Lindell and Whitney (2000) found that ratings of personal responsibility for seismic safety were positively and statistically significantly related to seismic hazard adjustment intentions.

Although these studies provide empirical support for the claim that perception of personal protection responsibility is positively correlated with the adjustment adoption, the small number of studies involved suggests that much remains to be learned about this variable. It is possible, for example, that people's absolute levels of personal protection responsibility vary with the hazard agent involved—possibly as a function of hazard familiarity (Slovic, 1987) and the perceived resource requirements of the available hazard adjustments. Thus, individuals might perceive higher levels of personal protection responsibility in connection with hazards that are familiar and amenable to simple and technologically less sophisticated adjustments. This would account for why hazards such as floods, tornadoes, hurricanes, and earthquakes seem to elicit personal protection responsibility, whereas unfamiliar hazards requiring complex protective actions such as toxic chemicals or radiation do not.

The perceived locus of personal protection responsibility is generally not a consideration in disaster response simply because the time available for responding is so limited that it is not possible for anyone other than the warning recipients to take responsibility for their protection. Moreover, protective action in emergencies is limited to responses such as evacuation and sheltering in-place. By contrast, most community protection works, land use practices, and building construction practices simply cannot be implemented in the limited time available after a disaster warning. When these long-term hazard adjustments are feasible, the question arises as to whether government and industry share responsibility (or have exclusive responsibility) for protection from these hazards. There appears to be a trend, at least with respect to earthquake hazard in California, for risk area residents to assume increasing responsibility for self-protection—at least for the first 72 hours after impact (Lindell & Perry, 2000). However, there appears to be widespread sentiment that the operators of facilities such as chemical plants and nuclear power stations should be responsible for protecting nearby residents from the hazards that they impose on others. Facility operators can engage in a number of hazard mitigation actions such as locating a plant in less densely populated areas, designing it to use less hazardous materials or to reduce the probability of accidental releases, or changing operating procedures so smaller quantities of hazardous materials are available for release (Ashford et al., 1993).

In summary, the PADM makes no predictions about the effect of personal protection responsibility on the receipt of hazard information or on the comprehension of such information once it is received, but one would expect that people who are high on personal protection responsibility would be more likely to attend to any hazard information that they receive. With respect to the decision stages, this personality characteristic is likely to have no effect on risk identification or risk assessment. It would have an effect on protective action search, but it would have no effect on protective action assessment. In addition, it would have an effect on protective action implementation, but not on information needs assessment or communication action assessment. Finally, one would expect people's personal protection responsibility to have an effect on their communication action implementation.

The second personality characteristic that has received attention as a predictor of hazard adjustment adoption is *locus of control*, whose negative end point (external control) also has been labeled *fatalism*. As is the case with disaster response, fatalism is predicted to be correlated with the development of an adaptive plan and the adoption of hazard adjustments. There are differences in the literature regarding the assumed causal status of this variable, with research on disaster response finding that fatalism is linked directly to the development of adaptive plans and indirectly, via its relations with adaptive planning, to protective action. Accordingly, Perry and Mushcatel (1986) reported that an internal locus of control was positively correlated with adaptive planning behaviors for floods. Similarly, Sims and Bauman (1972) reported that an internal locus of control was positively related to willingness to develop an adaptive plan for protection from tornadoes. On the other hand, some warning studies found that locus of control was correlated with both possession of an adaptive plan and protective action. Perry and Greene (1982) found that residents near the Mt. St. Helens volcano with an internal rather than external locus of control were more likely to have an adaptive plan and to comply with an evacuation warning. Similarly, Hodge, Sharp, and Marts (1979) found that Hawaiians with an internal rather than external locus of control were more likely to comply with evacuation warnings of lava flows. Unfortunately, the empirical record does not support an unequivocal determination of causal antecedence among locus of control, possession of an adaptive plan, and protective action, but the temporal ordering of the variables suggests that they form a causal chain in which locus of control causes adaptive planning, which, in turn, causes the implementation of protective action.

When we focus on long-term hazard adjustment, the issue of causal ordering is less critical than it is in the warning context, but it is still of interest. The PADM suggests that locus of control would affect the evaluation of personal resources during the protective action assessment stage. Furthermore, the principal dependent variable in warning studies is disaster response, but adaptive planning is a long-term hazard adjustment (specifically, an emergency preparedness action rather than a hazard mitigation or disaster recovery action) that has been undertaken prior to disaster impact. Consequently, warning response research can be interpreted as documenting a positive relationship between an internal locus of control (low fatalism) and undertaking specific protective measures.

Research on the adoption of seismic hazard adjustment confirms the prediction that locus of control is correlated with hazard knowledge and perceived risk. Specifically, Simpson-Housley and Bradshaw's (1978) studies of earthquake preparedness revealed that a sense of fatalism (external locus of control) was inversely related to hazard knowledge (those who were higher in fatalism knew less about earthquake threats) and to risk perception (those who were higher in fatalism believed that seismic risk was lower), as well as to hazard adjustment (those who were higher in fatalism tended to adopt fewer hazard adjustments). Similarly, Turner and colleagues (1979) found that California residents who were high in fatalism were less likely to possess information on earthquake threats and also less likely to report adopting hazard adjustments. Subsequently, Turner and colleagues (1986) reported that fatalism was negatively correlated with the number of household adjustments to earthquakes. Farley and colleagues (1993), studying preparedness responses to the Browning earthquake prediction, also reported that higher levels of fatalism were correlated with lower levels of hazard adjustment adoption. In his later review of several studies of earthquake preparedness in the Midwest, Farley (1998) confirmed that an internal locus of control was positively related to undertaking seismic hazard adjustments.

This discussion of the research on locus of control should be qualified by two comments. First, as noted in the previous chapter, it is likely that the results of studies examining locus of control or fatalism should probably be interpreted in terms of the respondents' self-efficacy. That is, those who believe that they have the resources to successfully implement hazard adjustments and communication actions are more likely to attempt to implement them. Second, there is reason to question whether fatalism is a causal variable or a dependent variable. Specifically, it is possible that a fatalistic attitude arose only after the individuals considered an environmental threat such as earthquake hazard and found that they knew of no seismic adjustments at all, or no adjustments that they deemed to be effective, or no effective adjustments that were feasible within their personal resource constraints (Jackson & Mukerjee, 1974; Kunreuther et al., 1978; Sullivan et al., 1977). If this interpretation were correct, fatalism would arise as a result of, not a cause of, the perception that no effective adjustments were available. The distinction among these explanations is very important because personality characteristics such as fatalism are enduring attributes that cannot be changed, whereas lack of knowledge is a state that can potentially be changed through risk communication programs. Again, there is insufficient empirical research available to effectively determine which interpretation is correct; additional studies that include measures of fatalism and changes in information about hazards are necessary to conduct adequate analyses.

In summary, the PADM predicts that fatalism will be negatively related to the receipt of hazard information and to the attention to such information, but that it will be unrelated to the comprehension of such information once it is received. With respect to the decision stages, the relationship of fatalism with risk identification has not been reported, but it does have a significant relationship with hazard knowledge and risk assessment, perhaps because fatalists engage in the defensive function of distorting the available information so that it minimizes threat belief and perceived risk (Janis & Mann, 1977). The PADM predicts that fatalists will engage in lower levels of protective action search than others and will judge the available protective actions as less effective and more demanding of resources. In addition, fatalists are less likely than others to implement protective actions and more likely to consider the available information to be adequate and to search for information from fewer sources and channels. Finally, one would expect fatalists to implement fewer communication actions than those who are not fatalists.

Demographic Characteristics

The role of demographic characteristics is at least as challenging to understand as that of personality variables. In studying hazard adjustment, researchers have tended to include demographic variables for two reasons. First, some demographic variables, such as having children in the home, home ownership, or hazard-related employment, are included because they might increase a household's vulnerability to disaster impact and, thus, increase protection motivation and hazard adjustment. The second reason is that some demographic characteristics, such as ethnicity, age, or gender, might bear on the way the threat is viewed or defined or on the way in which decisions are made about protection. Consequently, ethnic groups might differ in their views of environmental threats, women might use a different decision calculus than men, or older people might be more risk tolerant than younger ones. The PADM identifies receiver characteristics (in this case, demographic variables) as having a direct influence on the early stages of the protective action decision-making process, such as threat belief and protection motivation. Thus, one would expect that variables like home ownership and having children in the home would be positively related to levels of threat belief, risk perception, and personal protection responsibility. Similarly, ethnicity (as a surrogate for ethnic identity), age, and gender would be expected to affect hazard knowledge and risk perception. This does not mean that people's demographic characteristics cannot have statistically significant correlations with adjustment adoption. Rather, it is likely that these correlations will be mediated by other variables.

Indeed, clarifying the role of people's demographic characteristics in the protective action decision-making process requires both theoretical and empirical efforts. The theoretical issues are defined by the causal modeling concept of specification error (Blalock, 1969). Demographic variables are usually considered to be exogeneous because they temporally precede virtually all other variables in models of hazard adjustment. As mentioned in connection with warning studies, the discovery that a variable whose value was set at birth (sex) is correlated with something occurring much later in time (hazard adjustment) fails to explain what has happened since birth that might intervene between these two variables to explain the apparent relationship. The absence of information about intervening variables in a model constitutes a specification error. This reasoning does not categorically deny the importance of demographic variables, but it suggests that they might be providing clues to other conceptually important variables that, once controlled, might erase the (otherwise spurious) relationship between a demographic variable and any of the predecisional processes and decision stages of the protective action decision-making process. Understanding the relationship between the demographic variables and intervening variables provides depth to the theoretical formulation, but as Lieberson (1982) reminds us, the goal of causal modeling ultimately is to predict a given target dependent variable. Here, the target variable is hazard adjustment, and the theoretically derived proximal causes are psychological variables. If any demographic variable is to have a direct effect on hazard adjustment adoption, then one would need to develop a rationale that connects the two variables without intervening variables.

Very few researchers who have reported significant correlations between demographic variables and hazard adjustment have ever taken the additional step of developing theoretical rationales to support their findings, and fewer still have devised explanations for direct linkages. The absence of such linkages raises another issue: Demographic variables tend to be intercorrelated, and so a compelling theoretical logic is needed to disentangle their effects (Blalock, 1982). Finally, the empirical record contains studies that sporadically include demographic variables but that are not part of multivariate analyses that would permit the assessment of their statistical importance compared to other substantive variables. In many cases, this precludes even the most elementary tests of spuriousness.

With these qualifications, we will briefly review empirical studies of the effects people's demographic characteristics have on hazard adjustment. As is the case in warning studies, the demographic variables used in research on long-term hazard adjustments have a very mixed record of empirical importance. A given demographic variable is sometimes found to have a statistically significant correlation—positive or negative—and sometimes not. This empirical pattern is consistent with the arguments regarding specification error developed above, although it also can result from the fact that many studies report only the statistically significant correlations. This practice makes it difficult to determine from any given study if a demographic variable was measured, but was not statistically significant, or was not measured at all.

Perry and Lindell (1990a) reported that two demographic variables were significantly related to hazard knowledge and risk perception among those threatened by the Mt. St. Helens volcano. These were the presence of school-aged children in the home (which was positively correlated with hazard knowledge and risk perception) and volcano-related employment (which was negatively correlated with risk perception and positively correlated with hazard knowledge). Turner and colleagues (1986) also found that the presence of school-aged children in the home was positively correlated with perception of risk from earthquakes. Major (1999) found that female gender was associated with higher levels of risk perception from a possible earthquake on the New Madrid fault. Hodge and colleagues (1979) found that Hawaiian females were more likely to "overestimate hazards" from lava flows than were males (p. 241). Hanson, Vitek, and Hanson (1979) reported that age was positively related to the perceived risk of tornadoes. Moreover, Lindell and Prater (2000) reported that home ownership was positively correlated with seismic risk perception, but they also found statistically nonsignificant relationships for children in the home, marital status, education, age, and income.

Other empirical studies have concentrated on the relationship between demographic variables and the adoption of hazard adjustments. It is in these cases that the pattern of relationships between demographics and adjustments is most variable. Dooley and colleagues (1992) reported that children at home, marital status (i.e., married), and age were positively related to adoption of seismic hazard adjustments. Mileti and O'Brien (1992) identified female gender, and Farley and colleagues (1993) identified educational attainment, as being correlated with multi-item measures of seismic hazard adjustment. Similarly, Edwards (1993) found positive relationships of school-aged children at home, income, and education with earthquake preparedness. Russell and colleagues (1995) also reported that income, education, and home ownership were positively related to seismic hazard adjustment. Lindell and Whitney (2000) reported that hazard adjustment was correlated positively with age, correlated negatively with apartment residence, and uncorrelated with gender. Lindell and Prater's (2000) research on earthquake-prone communities found that age (positively), marital status (married more likely), and income (positively) were significantly related to adjustment.

In contrast to these studies, Palm and colleagues (1990) studied a single seismic adjustment—purchase of earthquake insurance—in several California counties having different risk levels. They reported inconsistent findings regarding the relationship of demographic variables to insurance purchase. Using ten demographic variables, these researchers reported that only education was significant in two of the counties, whereas age and presence of children in the home were statistically significant in only one county. Finally, Jackson's (1977, 1981) studies of earthquake perception and adjustment in California found that none of the demographic characteristics measured were related to seismic adjustment adoption. Brinkmann's (1975) review of research on hurricane response, as well as Kunreuther and colleagues' (1993) research on hazard insurance purchases, specifically reported that education and income were unrelated to hazard adjustment adoption.

In summary, this review of the effects of demographic variables indicates that there is empirical evidence that some demographic characteristics—particularly the presence of children in the home, home ownership, and being employed in a hazard-related occupation—are related to hazard knowledge and risk perception. The effects of children in the home and home ownership suggest that additional vulnerabilities are important in risk perception, whereas the role of hazard-related occupation supports the role of an aspect of personal experience that is different from the effect of disaster experience. The difficulty is that only a few studies have tested these variables in multivariate models, so more replication is needed before inferring firm support for the PADM's predictions. This conclusion appears to be especially appropriate when demographic variables are correlated with hazard adjustment. In reviewing the results of 23 studies of earthquake hazard adjustment, Lindell and Perry (2000) concluded that demographic characteristics have small correlations with hazard adjustment, which are statistically significant only in very large samples. Consistent with our previous discussion of specification errors, the extant research suggests that demographics are exogeneous variables whose patterns of correlation indicate the presence of intervening variables that are themselves correlated with both demographic variables and hazard adjustment. With regard to hazard adjustment itself, the utility of demographic variables might lie primarily in identifying segments of the population that are differentially disposed to adopting hazard adjustments. Such information could be used to target the delivery of risk communication programs.

Ethnicity

People's reported ethnicity, which is an approximate measure of their identification with an ethnic group, has sometimes been found to be important at different stages of the protective action decision process. Caution is required in interpreting the results of research on ethnicity and hazard adjustment, however, because the relationship is complicated by defects in research design and analysis, as well as in the conceptualization of this variable. The principal research design issue is that most studies of disaster behavior have failed to measure ethnicity. Furthermore, among studies that did measure ethnicity, most reported bivariate correlations between ethnicity and hazard-relevant variables; only a few used multivariate analyses to distinguish between the direct and indirect effects of ethnicity. Moreover, when these studies did document differences among ethnic groups, they tended to rely on speculation rather than analysis or theory to account for such differences.

These problems are compounded by difficulties in conceptualizing ethnicity. One difficulty is that ethnicity is a multidimensional concept, so comparisons between minority and majority groups are becoming increasingly ambiguous. Another difficulty is that the distribution of ethnic groups is not geographically uniform, so some places are almost completely homogeneous (e.g., the Midwest, with its White communities), others have two or three primary ethnic groups (e.g., the Southwest, with Whites, Mexican Americans, and African Americans), and only a few are extremely diverse (e.g., Hawaii). Moreover, which group is numerically the majority can vary from one community to another, and the differences among minority groups are in many cases as great as the difference between majority and minority groups (Middleton & Putney, 1970; Perry & Nelson, 1991). Finally, there is increasing intermarriage among racial and ethnic groups, producing children whose ambiguous ethnic identities frustrate easy classification either by themselves or others. These considerations introduce the possibility that even members of what ostensibly is the same ethnic group might vary with respect to ethnic identity and subcultural practices in different geographic locales. In some cases, such as among Whites who immigrated from Europe over a century ago, ethnic identity has waned so much that sociologists have questioned whether it has any impact at all (Lieberson, 1985).

Moreover, the conceptual status of ethnicity or ethnic identity is an important issue in itself. Some researchers have implied that ethnic group membership in the United States so thoroughly structures an individual's experience and development that it might be necessary to develop a different conceptual framework to understand the behavior of each group. The differences in ethnic groups can be viewed from at least two perspectives, however. For practitioners, even subtle differences can be important when the goal is to ensure that credible sources disseminate understandable risk communication messages that will increase recipients' protection motivation and adoption of hazard adjustments. At this molecular level, one would like to know the credibility that each group attaches to different information sources, the communication channels that they prefer, the language variations that exist in a community, the existing levels of hazard knowledge, and so on.

By contrast, theorists are concerned about the effect that ethnic differences might have on attitudes, beliefs, and behaviors that are specifically relevant to adjustment decisions. Consequently, the task is not just to specify what differences exist among ethnic groups but also to identify what stages in the hazard adjustment process are affected by ethnic identity. We want to avoid spurious inferences by identifying the mechanisms through which ethnic differences influence hazard adjustment. In turn, this will allow us to conceptualize the identified mechanisms as variables that can be incorporated into more complete explanations. For example, during disaster recovery, it is not so much ethnicity but discriminatory practices and segregation that are important variables (Peacock & Girard, 1997). When ethnic identity appears to have direct impacts on hazard adjustment, thereby demanding its inclusion in a theoretical model, we want to be able to explain *why* the effects exist. The PADM provides some insights into this latter path; although we do discuss specific ethnic differences, our principal concern is with their place in the theoretical model. Thus, the studies reviewed here illustrate the effects of ethnicity on five variables important in the adoption of hazard adjustments—message comprehension (a predecisional variable), risk perception (an early stage of the protective action decision-making process), hazard adjustment adoption (the last stage of the protective action decision-making process), source credibility (a message component), and disaster experience (a receiver variable).

We note at the outset that theory predicts and empirical evidence confirms the existence of intercorrelations among the social context variables; ethnicity is related to immersion in kin and friendship networks, as well as to community involvement. Unfortunately, existing studies cannot sort out the differential importance of these factors. It has long been known that, in disasters, ethnicity has an impact on people's relationships to their kin—Clifford (1958) reported that Mexican Americans had a much stronger tendency than did Whites to confer with and help their kin following the flooding of the Rio Grande. Other studies have shown that African Americans tend to be more immersed in kin networks than are Whites (Babchuk & Ballweg, 1971; Bennett, 1973; Perry & Perry, 1959; Staples, 1976; Staples & Mirande, 1980). These findings were confirmed by Morrow's (1997) recent study of Hurricane Andrew, which reported that both African Americans and Hispanics were more likely than Whites to be involved (either giving or receiving) in post-disaster assistance with relatives. These findings from disaster research are consistent with studies reporting that minority ethnic and racial groups in the United States tend to have larger, as well as more cohesive, extended families (Angel & Tienda, 1982; Ruggles, 1994). Lindell and Perry (1992) summarized the issue when they noted that researchers "must appreciate the exigencies imposed on minority families as a function to adapting to the majority milieu, and consequently the different functions the family must serve for [minority] citizens" (p. 141). It also has been reported that ethnic group membership has an impact on levels of community involvement, and that one needs to distinguish between the Anglo vision of community and the community structures that grow from identification with a specific ethnic group. In some parts of the Southwest, for example, "Chicanos por la Raza" is an important community organization that might be overlooked by those who are not familiar with the Mexican American movement. Olsen (1970) noted a tendency of African Americans to be more involved than Whites in community organizations, particularly voluntary associations related to the ethnic community. Sotomayer (1971) noted a similar tendency in Mexican Americans, while Wright and Hyman (1966) found the same result in multiple minority groups. Tomeh (1973), who controlled for social class, also reported higher levels of involvement in voluntary associations in African Americans. More recent research on urban ecological networks has tended to reinforce the findings of differential participation rates among Whites, African Americans, and Hispanics (Bolin & Bolton, 1986; Dash, Peacock, & Morrow, 1997; Logan & Molotch, 1987; Oram, 1966). Riad and colleagues (1999) found that differential access to social and community support networks among minorities tended to reduce their ability to successfully cope with disasters. All of the above findings remind us that, at some point, definitive conclusions about the role of ethnicity in hazard adjustment can be drawn only after multivariate studies have been conducted to sort out the differential importance (or at least the interrelationships) of the different social context variables by controlling for the influence of other variables.

First of all, it is important to recognize that ethnicity is correlated with language ability (in the United States, command of English) and that language ability is related to people's ability to comprehend information about environmental hazards. This is a critical issue in the risk communication process, especially when bilinguals are not immediately available to interpret messages. In such cases, an inability to understand a message causes a delay in the initiation of protective actions, failure to take any action, or initiation of actions that do not accomplish threat protection (Perry et al., 1981).

Messages about long-term hazard adjustment are disseminated long before a disaster impact is expected, which reduces the problem slightly but does not eliminate it completely. Added time increases the probability that message recipients can obtain translations, but non-English speakers are most likely to obtain translations from kin and friendship networks. A limited English proficiency in these bilinguals could result in imprecise translations (Perry, 1987). For example, considerable difficulties in explaining threats from a proposed toxic waste incinerator arose in Kettleman City, California, when authorities failed to provide Spanish-language information to the 70% of the community residents whose first language was Spanish (Crowfoot & Wondolleck, 1990). As Aguirre, Anderson, Balandran, Peters, and White (1991) have argued in connection with tornado-related messages in Saragosa, Texas, the only effective way in which environmental hazard managers can address such problems is by identifying the different language groups in their communities and producing multilanguage hazard information. Unfortunately, the issue of language does not disappear when multiple translations are present. Jardine and Hrudey (1997) found that technical risk terms that had been translated into colloquial English created significant misunderstanding between environmental hazard managers and information recipients.

In addition, ethnicity appears to be related to risk perception, but no studies conducted to date have provided a clear explanation for why this is the case. Vaughn and Nordenstam (1991) found that African Americans were more likely to perceive risk from nuclear power plants as high when compared to other ethnic groups. Similarly, Vaughn and Seifert (1992) reported that minority citizens judged risks from pesticides and air and water pollutants to be higher than did majority citizens. The Hodge and colleagues (1979) study of volcano hazard in Hawaii found that Philippine Americans and Portuguese Americans perceived the risk from lava flows to be higher than did other ethnic groups. Turner and colleagues (1986) reported that "non-Anglos (Blacks, Mexican Americans, and other minorities) are more fearful [of the earthquake threat] than are White Anglos" in Southern California (p. 161). In a multivariate study of seismic hazard adjustments, Lindell and Prater (2000) found that a Mexican American (but not African American or White) ethnicity was positively correlated with seismic risk perception. Norris and colleagues' (1999) study of hurricane preparedness in four Southeastern U.S. cities found that "Black residents were more likely than White residents to have a plan of action, but less likely to have basic [preparedness] supplies on hand" (p. 28).

Despite the higher levels of risk perception among ethnic minorities, studies by Turner and colleagues (1986) and Farley (1998) found that Whites were more likely than minority residents to have undertaken seismic hazard adjustments. Similarly, Edwards (1993), Russell and colleagues (1995), and Mileti and Darlington (1997) found that adoption of earthquake adjustments was more common in Whites than in other ethnic groups. Lower levels of hazard adjustment in the presence of higher levels of perceived risk suggests the presence of fatalism, an explanation supported by data from Turner and colleagues (1986). However, there also are other explanations, such as a low level of personal protection responsibility or impediments to hazard adjustment adoption. In addition, it might be that variations in attributions of source credibility, income, and personal understanding of hazard exposure mechanisms also might be mediating variables (Tierney et al., 2001).

Ethnicity also is related to message components, particularly perceptions of source credibility. More than three decades ago, McLuckie (1970) contended that "different classes or ethnic groups have varying conceptions of what constitutes adaptation to a threat, or credibility of organizations" (p. 38). Turner and colleagues (1986) found that African American residents of Southern California earthquake risk areas tended to be more skeptical of government messages than were either Mexican Americans or Whites. At the same time, these researchers found that African Americans and Latinos were more likely than Whites to depend on the mass media for information about earthquake predictions. Perry and Lindell (1991) studied two flood-prone communities and reported that as the "most credible sources," White respondents tended to identify public authorities (police and fire departments) and mass media, African Americans identified authorities and social network sources (friends, relatives, and neighbors) but not media, and Mexican Americans selected social networks to the exclusion of other sources. In a subsequent examination of data on the same three ethnic groups in Denver, Lindell and Perry (1992) described similar findings, but they noted that two intervening variables needed to be taken into account in interpreting the findings. First, they argued that idiosyncratic relationships between given ethnic groups and authorities in a given community affected the credibility attributed to risk communication sources. Second, social network contacts appeared to be afforded higher relative levels of credibility when assessing threats with which the residents were more familiar (for example, seasonal flooding as compared with a nitric acid spill). The interaction among ethnicity, threat familiarity, and source credibility is supported by research on pesticides (Hawkes & Stiles, 1986) and chemical threats (Fowlkes & Miller, 1987). One should note, of course, that these studies deal with only three ethnic groups and a handful of hazard agents. The important theoretical issue here is that ethnicity is related to judgments of source credibility; the practical issue is that environmental hazard managers must account for community-specific issues of ethnicity in designing risk communication programs.

There also is some evidence that ethnicity is related to disaster experience. The relationship of these variables appears to be intertwined with the tendency of minority groups to fall into lower income categories that by necessity live in more hazardous geographical areas (Blaikie et al., 1994). At present, there is little research that enables us to control for ethnicity, that is, to distinguish empirically the disaster experiences of lower income Whites and minorities from those of higher income Whites and minorities (Lindell & Perry, 1992). Research conducted under the rubric of "environmental justice" has pointed out that minorities—perhaps for reasons of low income and/or discrimination—tend to occupy substandard housing or live in hazard-prone areas (Capek, 1993). Bullard (1994) found that African Americans in five communities with hazardous waste disposal sites were more likely to reside near the sites. This research suggests that ethnic minorities might have higher rates of disaster experience than Whites (Vaughn, 1995), but a more recent study suggests that ethnic differentials in hazard vulnerability, and thus disaster experience, might be more likely for technological hazards such as chemical facilities than for natural hazards such as floods and hurricanes (Hwang & Lindell, 2003).

Finally, there are additional complicating factors in the form of intercorrelations among the possible explanatory variables. As we indicated above, there is some evidence that locus of control is related to ethnicity. Sims and Bauman (1972) found that an external locus of control was more prevalent among African Americans, which Turner and colleagues (1979) confirmed by observing that African Americans and Mexican Americans "were more fatalistic about earthquake danger, skeptical about science and the predictability of earthquakes" than were Whites (p. 3). Moreover, Ives and Furseth's (1983) research on flood hazard adjustments reported that "a significant subgroup of African Americans, however, view flooding as an uncontrollable natural event and are less confident in their ability to deal with the hazard" (p. 525). Although Perry and Mushcatel (1986) reported that African Americans and Mexican Americans were more likely to possess an external locus of control than were Whites, they documented considerable variation in locus of control scale score in both minority groups. Furthermore, it appears that locus of control varies not only between minority and majority groups but also among minority groups. Finally, the overwhelming majority of studies have examined only three American ethnic groups, so it is unclear if locus of control varies in the same way among other ethnic groups. To adequately assess the casual links among these variables will require considerably more multivariate research.

In summary, these studies suggest that ethnicity is linked with a number of the predecisional processes and decision stages in the protective action decision-making process. There appear to be effects of ethnicity on reception of hazard information and message comprehension, but there are likely to be only indirect effects on attention (via fatalism). Ethnicity also appears to be related to threat belief, perceived risk, and the implementation of protective actions. The latter suggests that there might be a lower level of protective action search and less favorable protective action assessments, but these implications have not been tested. It is unclear if there are ethnicity-linked differences in the level of information needs assessment and communication action assessment, but there do seem to be differences in the types of sources and channels involved in the communication action assessment. However, it is unknown if there are differences in the level of communication action implementation. Finally, there is evidence of ethnic differences in locus of control and disaster experience. Since variations may exist not only between majority and minority groups, but also among different minority groups, it is clear that further research is needed to better define the relationships that ethnicity has with the stages of the disaster response process.

5

Approaches to Influencing Hazard Adjustment Adoption

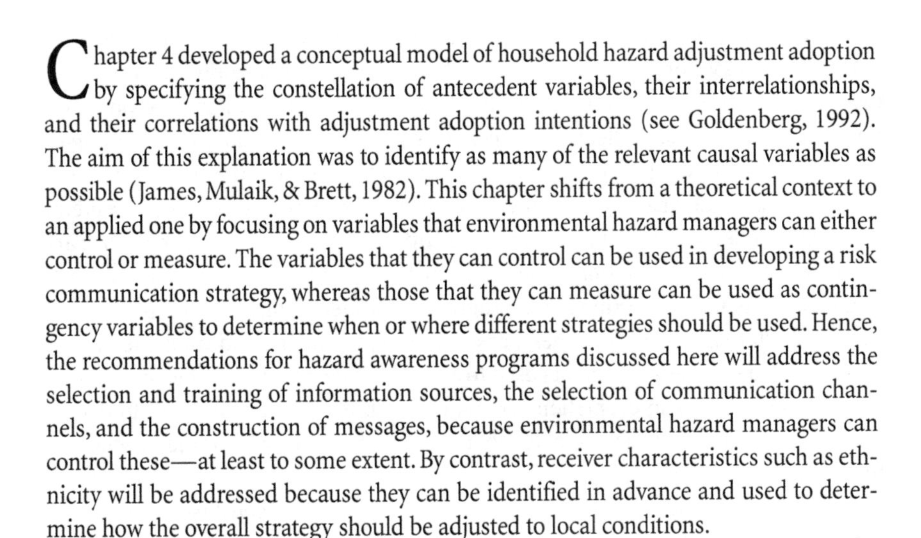

Chapter 4 developed a conceptual model of household hazard adjustment adoption by specifying the constellation of antecedent variables, their interrelationships, and their correlations with adjustment adoption intentions (see Goldenberg, 1992). The aim of this explanation was to identify as many of the relevant causal variables as possible (James, Mulaik, & Brett, 1982). This chapter shifts from a theoretical context to an applied one by focusing on variables that environmental hazard managers can either control or measure. The variables that they can control can be used in developing a risk communication strategy, whereas those that they can measure can be used as contingency variables to determine when or where different strategies should be used. Hence, the recommendations for hazard awareness programs discussed here will address the selection and training of information sources, the selection of communication channels, and the construction of messages, because environmental hazard managers can control these—at least to some extent. By contrast, receiver characteristics such as ethnicity will be addressed because they can be identified in advance and used to determine how the overall strategy should be adjusted to local conditions.

There are numerous hazard awareness programs throughout the United States that are supported by federal, state, and local agencies, as well as by nongovernmental agencies such as the American Red Cross. The efficacy of these programs is often simply assumed, so few studies have been conducted on whether these programs follow the principles of effective risk communication and are successful in promoting effective hazard adjustments. One obstacle to judging the effectiveness of hazard awareness programs is that only a minority of them appear to have been evaluated, and few of those who have evaluated their programs have published their findings in the research literature (Douglas, Westley, & Chaffee, 1970; Michaels, 1990). Thus, published reviews are based on only a very small, and thus possibly biased, set of hazard awareness programs. In any event, these reviews (Center for Natural Phenomena Engineering, 1994; Expert Review Committee, 1987; Faupel et al., 1992; May, 1991; Perry, 1990; Saarinen, 1982; Schulz, 1993; Sims & Baumann, 1983; Sorensen & Mileti, 1987) have reported inconsistent results—successes, failures, and inconclusive findings. Some of these inconsistencies can be attributed to variations in the characteristics of the programs—information sources, communication channels, and message content—as well as variations in audience characteristics such as hazard experience, education, and ethnicity. Other inconsistencies are attributable to the design of the evaluations, with most evaluations being weak quasi-experimental designs rather than stronger pretest-posttest or treatment-control group designs (Cook, Campbell, & Perrachio, 1991).

A final source of inconsistency in results is variation in the criteria used to evaluate the effectiveness of hazard awareness programs. The least stringent criteria are exposure (i.e., the number of persons reached by the program) and audience reactions (i.e., audience members' ratings of their enjoyment of the presentation). For example, many environmental hazard managers define their hazard awareness programs as successes on the basis of the number of talks given to community groups, the number of brochures handed out, and the like. More significant evaluation criteria include such message effects as beliefs about the hazard, attitudes toward mitigation and preparedness actions, and actual adoption of the recommended adjustments. Unfortunately, these measures have been assessed in many different ways whose relevance to the adoption of hazard adjustments is sometimes unclear. Even when the actual adoption of hazard adjustments is used as a criterion, the list of adjustments used to evaluate one program can differ significantly—in terms of such characteristics as effectiveness, cost, time requirements, and implementation barriers—from those adjustments used to evaluate other programs. The net result of these inconsistencies in evaluation criteria is that it is extremely difficult to determine if a program's outcomes are due to its actual effectiveness or to the leniency of the evaluation criteria.

Despite their inadequacies, it is possible to draw some conclusions from the available studies of hazard awareness programs by supplementing them with information from cross-sectional studies of factors associated with the adoption and implementation of hazard adjustments. To present these conclusions, this chapter begins by examining the contextual issues affecting the development and operation of a local program for environmental risk communication. It continues by reviewing the conclusions associated with three distinct phases in the development and implementation of an environmental risk communication program—the continuing hazard, an escalating crisis, and emergency response. The continuing hazard is a phase in which there is a stable probability (usually low) that a catastrophic incident will occur that threatens the public safety, property, and the environment. This phase is characterized by hazard mitigation and emergency preparedness activities.

For most hazards in which there is some forewarning, the continuing hazard phase eventually evolves into an escalating crisis, where there is a significantly increased probability of an incident that will threaten the public's health, safety, or property. The escalating crisis phase frequently requires activities such as activation of a crisis communication team and active monitoring of the situation by those at risk. Finally, an escalating crisis might evolve into an emergency response in which members of the population at risk must take action to protect themselves and their property. Each of these phases has different tasks associated with it that need to be addressed in order to develop an effective environmental risk communication program.

❖ THE CONTEXT OF ENVIRONMENTAL RISK COMMUNICATION

Environmental risk communication exists within the context of environmental hazard management, and both of these are local endeavors. Thus, the focal actor is a local (usually municipal) government, but this does not imply that environmental hazard management activities cannot be undertaken by county, state, and federal government agencies, businesses such as chemical facilities and nuclear power plants, or nongovernmental organizations such as the Red Cross. Certainly, external support (particularly state and federal support) of many forms is made available to local jurisdictions in any environmental emergency, but local government must respond first because there is an inevitable time lag before external assistance will arrive. For example, the current version of the *National Response Plan* (Federal Emergency Management Agency, 2003) explicitly notes that local jurisdictions must be prepared to operate without external assistance for approximately 72 hours after disaster impact. Moreover, the emergency response will proceed most efficiently and effectively if there is a strong local organization into which external resources can be integrated when they arrive (Perry, 1985). Finally, local government involvement in environmental risk communication is important because disaster impacts are likely to persist after any state and federal assistance has been exhausted. The issue was succinctly summarized by Ben Bena, the Cowlitz County Director of Emergency

Figure 5.1 The Local Environmental Hazard Management System and Its Context

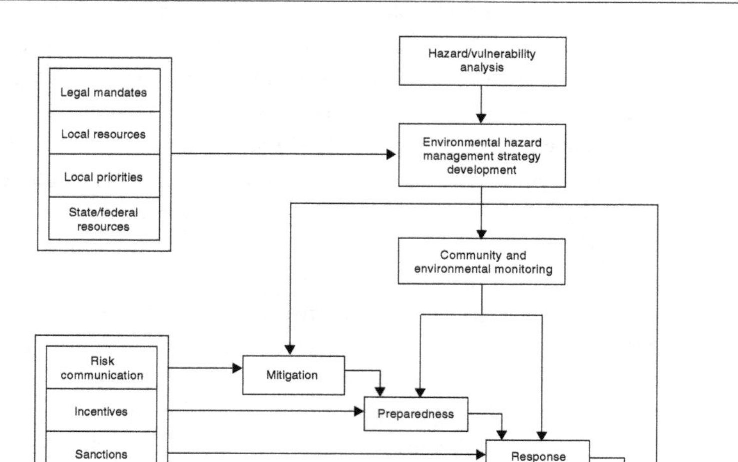

Services, shortly after the 1980 cataclysmic eruption of the Mt. St. Helens volcano: "The feds came and have been helpful, but they left and we're still here with the ash, the ruined rivers, the downed trees, the destroyed buildings, and the dislocated people" (Perry, 1981).

Nor should this emphasis on local government be misunderstood to mean that environmental hazard management is the exclusive responsibility of government. In fact, a strong local program of hazard mitigation, emergency preparedness, emergency response, and disaster recovery must achieve high levels of hazard adjustment by households and businesses. The conceptual foundation for designing a local program to achieve this objective was addressed in Chapter 4, where we summarized the factors that influence household adoption of hazard adjustments. To understand household adjustment in the context of the community, one needs to examine the local environmental hazard management system and its context. Figure 5.1, which presents a flow chart containing the principal elements of this system, enables us to situate risk communication in the context of the tasks demanded and the tools available for local governments to manage their environmental hazards. This flow chart does not identify all stakeholders and processes but, instead, highlights the key parts of the system that are relevant to environmental risk communication.

The process of environmental hazard management begins with a hazard/vulnerability analysis that identifies the environmental hazards to which the jurisdiction is exposed and assesses the level of risk associated with each geographic area within that jurisdiction (Federal Emergency Management Agency, 1997). Further, the hazard/vulnerability analysis identifies the people (i.e., the geographic and demographic segments of the population), property (building types and economic sectors), and infrastructure (electric power, fuel, water and wastewater, telecommunications, and transportation) located in the areas of highest risk and projects the potential consequences of different intensities of hazard impact (Greenway, 1998; Ketchum & Whittaker, 1982). Once this is done, the magnitudes of these consequences are adjusted for their probability of occurrence in setting priorities for risk reduction (Federal Emergency Management Agency, 1997). Based on this foundation, the community can develop an environmental hazard management strategy that indicates which hazards are significant enough to require active management and, further, the relative emphasis that should be given hazard mitigation, emergency preparedness, emergency response, and disaster recovery.

Establishing an environmental hazard management strategy is a complex process that involves myriad considerations and input from a variety of actors (Birkland, 1997; May & Williams, 1985; Stallings, 1995). In particular, development of an environmental hazard management strategy requires the identification of constraints and selection of specific tools that can achieve the selected goals within prevailing constraints. This can be achieved by means of a variety of mechanisms, but the most effective means is for a policy entrepreneur to mobilize a constituency that is powerful enough to place community hazard vulnerability on the public agenda and keep it there long enough for policy adoption to take place (Prater & Lindell, 2000). The ideal constituency for environmental hazard management includes technical expertise, political expertise, and personal commitment. Many times, the requisite expertise and commitment can be found in Local Emergency Planning Committees (Lindell & Brandt, 2000; Lindell & Perry, 2001; Lindell, Whitney, Futch, & Clause, 1996) or in disaster planning committees established by local Emergency Management Coordinators (Drabek, 1987, 1990; Gillespie et al., 1993).

As Figure 5.1 indicates, the nature of the environmental hazard management strategy that is developed depends on legal mandates, local resources (including staff time and budgets), local priorities, and state and federal resources (especially funding and technical assistance). Policy entrepreneurs can use legal mandates requiring them to protect the public health and safety as a legitimate basis for initiating the development of an environmental hazard management strategy. At the same time, they can use what limited discretionary staff time and budget they have to increase the local priority of environmental risk reduction by contacting other hazard-relevant organizations in the public and private sectors to inform them about community vulnerability and to invite them to participate in the strategy development process. This lateral communication process can be supplemented by upward communication to senior appointed and elected officials, as well as by downward communication to neighborhood associations and civic organizations. After policy entrepreneurs achieve preliminary successes, they can use these to justify the receipt of additional technical resources from other sources.

The environmental hazard management strategy that is formulated determines how much the community will rely on hazard mitigation, emergency preparedness, emergency response, and disaster recovery. If there is a substantial reliance on emergency preparedness and response, then the community will need to make a significant investment in community and environmental monitoring, especially if it is exposed to hazards having a rapid onset. Most obviously, this is because such events require prompt activation of local emergency services (fire department, emergency medical services, hazardous materials teams, police and emergency managers) under an agreed on incident management system (Brunacini, 1985; Kramer & Bahme, 1992). In particular, continual environmental monitoring is required to support population protective actions such as evacuation and sheltering in-place, which require rapid detection and dissemination of warnings to the population segments at greatest risk (Sorensen, 2000). Moreover, hazard mitigation and disaster recovery also necessitate continual community and environmental monitoring. In the case of hazard mitigation, such monitoring is needed to determine if environmental risk areas are increasing in size (e.g., increases in the extent of floodplains because of upstream development) or if urban development is encroaching into existing risk areas. Similarly, preparedness for disaster recovery requires community monitoring to collect the data that will be needed immediately after disaster strikes to implement a timely and effective recovery (see Schwab et al., 1998).

A significant portion of the community strategy for environmental hazard management can be implemented by government agencies, but a high level of vulnerability reduction can be achieved only if households also are involved in hazard mitigation, preparedness for emergency response, and preparedness for disaster recovery. Household adoption of all three types of vulnerability reduction strategies can be promoted by means of risk communication, incentives, sanctions, and/or technological innovations. Risk communication leads to the adoption of household hazard adjustments when people are made aware of the *intrinsic consequences* of implementing (or failing to implement) hazard adjustments. That is, environmental risk communication attempts to change people's beliefs about environmental hazards and, especially, about the potential consequences that those hazards could have for them if they fail to take actions that reduce their vulnerability. In addition, environmental risk communication attempts to change people's beliefs about the intrinsic consequences (i.e., the efficacy and resource requirements) of alternative hazard adjustments. In general, risk communication programs, especially those designed to promote awareness of natural hazards, have been based on the assumption that people make incorrect decisions because they are uninformed about the hazards to which they are exposed. Thus, it has been assumed that disseminating scientific information about hazard agents (e.g., earthquakes and hurricanes) and examples of their impacts (damaged buildings and fallen power lines) will change people's beliefs about that hazard. In turn, it is assumed that these altered beliefs will motivate them to adopt appropriate hazard adjustments. As indicated in Chapter 4, these assumptions substantially oversimplify the adoption process because an exclusive focus on the message ignores the roles of source, channel, and receiver characteristics. Moreover, as Chapter 4 has also indicated, even if the information dissemination process is effective in changing beliefs about the hazard, this does not ensure that people will be aware of appropriate hazard adjustments, have accurate beliefs about them, or be motivated to adopt them.

Incentives provide *extrinsic rewards* for implementing a specific hazard adjustment. The most common incentives—financial rewards such as grants, loans at subsidized interest rates, and tax credits—have both advantages and disadvantages. On the one hand, they could induce the adoption of additional hazard adjustments by lowering the cost of implementation. On the other hand, financial incentives increasingly raise objections that the government is subsidizing exposed populations who should be providing for their own protection. However, the net effect of well-designed incentives is that households and businesses in hazard-prone areas benefit by reducing their vulnerability, but society as a whole also benefits because less tax money is spent on disaster assistance. Unfortunately, financial incentives might not have as great an impact as policy makers hope if they cannot overcome simple cash flow problems, as, for example, when a household must invest a substantial amount of money initially and slowly recover this investment over a long period of time. This would be the case, for example, when those who retrofit their homes against earthquake damage receive a small decrease each year in their premiums for home insurance. An even more significant concern about financial incentives is that they implicitly assume the overall cost of the adjustment is the *only* obstacle to adoption. Financial incentives can work as intended only if those in vulnerable populations can base their economic decisions on assumptions such as perfect information, perfect foresight, and utility maximization. As Chapter 4 indicated, empirical research has shown that support for these assumptions is limited, and that people consider requirements for time and effort, knowledge and skill, tools and equipment, and social cooperation, as well as the money that hazard adjustments cost.

There are other types of incentives in addition to financial incentives (Perry, 1979b). Recognizing that a financial incentive fills the gap between the financial cost of a hazard adjustment and what the household can afford, one can see that a technological incentive fills the gap between the time, effort, knowledge, and/or skill requirements of a hazard adjustment and amount of the corresponding resource that the household can expend. Thus, lists of qualified contractors or approved products are technological incentives because they supplement households' limited knowledge. Tool banks also provide a technological incentive when they loan specialized equipment that some homeowners need to retrofit their homes against damage from hazards such as hurricanes and earthquakes.

There are also other incentives, such as social recognition, that provide extrinsic rewards for adopting hazard adjustments. For example, a community could recognize the neighborhood association or business that had the highest increase in the adoption of hazard adjustment in the previous year. Recognition by senior elected officials such as a city mayor can be a powerful incentive for some people. Alternatively, community groups could be rewarded by other incentives, such as higher priority for local improvements like parks and other neighborhood amenities. This need not even involve allocating funds for projects that would not otherwise be built. Instead, the winning neighborhood might be scheduled for first priority in completion of a project that all neighborhoods will eventually receive.

By contrast, sanctions provide *extrinsic punishments* for not implementing a specific hazard adjustment. Of course, people need to be told that they are required to take an action before they can be punished for failing to take that action. This certainly involves communication and, in a sense, it involves risk communication because there rarely is perfect certainty that those who fail to take action will be caught and punished. However, the risk in this case is from a social hazard, not the environmental hazard, so sanctions do not involve quite the same sort of risk communication that we will be discussing throughout the remainder of this chapter. Regulations appear to be a simple, effective, and inexpensive method of ensuring the adoption of hazard adjustments because they only need to communicate a requirement, a date for compliance, and a sanction for noncompliance. However, regulations—especially "unfunded federal mandates"—are extremely unpopular politically and are the target of criticism from economists about the inefficiencies of "command and control" systems of societal decision making (Horwich, 1993). In addition, such mechanisms of behavioral control are vulnerable to criticisms, based on ample evidence, that they have serious organizational deficiencies. First, those who are subject to a new mandate must be informed of its requirements—a major task in itself. Second, mandates that are overly simplistic tend to be objectionable because they force some stakeholders into excessive levels of protection, while others escape with insufficient protection. Unfortunately, mandates that are complex enough to avoid these problems frequently are too complex for nonspecialists to understand or to implement. Finally, sanctions require monitoring to ensure compliance. For example, building code requirements must be enforced by having inspectors examine the work that has been done at each stage of the construction process. Inspections can be expensive and, even when they have been made, they sometimes fail to ensure compliance with regulations.

Technological innovations are, of course, the most attractive way of achieving risk reduction because they reduce the trade-off between efficacy and cost. In some cases, these advances provide greater efficacy at the same cost as existing methods of protection, whereas in other cases they provide the same level of efficacy at lower cost. In rare instances, there are simultaneous improvements in both cost and performance. In this sense, a technological innovation is much like a financial incentive providing a reward for the adoption of a hazard adjustment, but a technological innovation provides an intrinsic reward (i.e., the innovation itself provides more protection per dollar invested through increased efficiency), whereas a financial incentive provides an extrinsic reward because someone else (frequently government) must absorb the cost differential through a transfer payment. Although technological innovations are an extremely attractive solution, local government has little control over their availability. For example, communities in areas prone to wildfires might be interested in inexpensive roof shingles with greater fire resistance than conventional varieties, but local government can't develop and produce such an innovation. Instead, it usually can only promote the technological innovations produced by others.

When implemented individually, risk communication, incentives, sanctions, and technological innovations have limited effectiveness in reducing losses from environmental hazards. Thus, reducing the escalating trend of disaster losses will require the development of programs that integrate all of these mechanisms for achieving the adoption of hazard adjustments. That is, local officials must identify the existing mix of adjustments in their communities, assess the social forces maintaining that mix of adjustments, identify a more effective mix of hazard adjustments, and increase their community's capacity (or ability) and commitment (or motivation) to adopt and implement this mix of adjustments. One way of illuminating the ways in which implementation mechanisms can be linked to hazard adjustments can be seen in Table 5.1, which displays a matrix containing the implementation mechanisms (risk communication, incentives, sanctions, and technological innovations) in rows and the categories of hazard adjustments (hazard mitigation, preparedness for emergency response, and preparedness for disaster recovery) in columns. For example, risk communication should address information about the hazard regardless of type of hazard adjustment advocated, but each column contains specific information about that specific hazard adjustment—property protection in the case of hazard mitigation, population protection in the case of preparedness for emergency response, and asset protection in the case of preparedness for disaster recovery. The incentives for hazard mitigation and preparedness for emergency response are identical, but differ from the incentive for recovery preparedness (which is limited primarily to insurance subsidies, as in the federal flood insurance program). It is important to note that local jurisdictions

Table 5.1 Methods of Promoting Hazard Adjustments by Households and Businesses

	Hazard mitigation	*Response preparedness*	*Recovery preparedness*
Risk communication	Information on hazard vulnerability and property protection methods	Information on hazard vulnerability and population protection methods	Information on hazard vulnerability and financial asset protection methods
Incentives	Grants, loans, tax credits, rebates	Grants, loans, tax credits, rebates	Subsidized insurance*
Sanctions	Land use regulations, building codes	Required plans, staffing, and training	Required insurance*
Technological advances	New products and services for property protection	New products and services for communication, population protection, and property protection	

* Federal or state responsiblity

have limited control over incentives for recovery preparedness, because only the federal government seems to have enough money to subsidize hazard insurance.

There are significant opportunities for local sanctions to promote hazard adjustment adoption because the regulation of land use and building construction practices has historically been a prerogative of local government. Local jurisdictions also might establish emergency preparedness requirements for hazard planning, staffing, and training, but there has been greater reliance on this mechanism at the federal and state levels than at the local level. As was the case with incentives, regulations for recovery preparedness have been limited at the local level. However, insurance regulations are more likely to appear at the state level than at the federal level. Finally, technological innovations consist mostly of new products and services. In the case of hazard mitigation, these are principally for property protection (although reduction of property damage typically reduces casualties as well). Technological innovations in response preparedness focus mostly on communication (especially warning, but also continuing public information), population protection, and—to a lesser degree—property protection (especially post-impact actions to limit the amount of further damage).

In summary, incentives, sanctions, and technological innovations are attractive mechanisms for increasing the adoption of hazard adjustments that should be considered for use as supplements to risk communication, but not as substitutes for it. As the previous discussion indicates, incentives and sanctions generally transfer costs from risk area residents to government and, therefore, to the taxpayers who live outside the risk area. That is, incentives and sanctions frequently subsidize risk area occupancy, which might not be popular if those who are providing the subsidies are aware of the price they are paying. In any event, incentives and technological innovations involve voluntary compliance, so risk communication will be needed to ensure that risk area residents understand the need to adopt hazard adjustments. Consequently, an effective risk communication program is an essential component of any community's efforts to reduce its hazard vulnerability.

❖ RISK COMMUNICATION DURING THE CONTINUING HAZARD PHASE

As noted earlier, the continuing hazard phase involves a stable probability (usually low) that a catastrophic incident will threaten public safety, property, and the environment. This phase is characterized principally by hazard mitigation and emergency preparedness activities, although preparedness for disaster recovery also should be undertaken at this time (Schwab et al., 1998). There are five basic functions that should be addressed in the continuing hazard phase. Table 5.2 identifies these as strategic analysis, operational analysis, resource mobilization, program development, and program implementation. These five functions and the tasks associated with them are listed in the table as if they form a simple linear sequence, but, in fact, some of the tasks will be performed concurrently. In addition, the process will frequently be iterative. For example, some resource mobilization tasks might take place concurrently with the operational analysis, or tasks conducted during the operational analysis phase might be suspended temporarily in order to return to the strategic analysis and refine it.

Strategic Analysis

Task 1: Conduct a Community Hazard/Vulnerability Analysis

As noted in the discussion of Figure 5.1, environmental hazard managers need to understand the hazards to which the community is exposed, the geographic areas of the community that are at greatest risk, and the population segments and economic sectors that are the most vulnerable. Knowing the characteristics of the most significant hazards makes it possible to develop more effective community emergency

Table 5.2 Specific Tasks for the Continuing Hazard Phase

Strategic analysis
Conduct a community hazard/vulnerability analysis
Analyze the community context
Identify the community's perceptions of the hazards and hazard adjustments
Set appropriate goals for the risk communication program
Operational analysis
Identify and assess feasible hazard adjustments for the community and its households and businesses
Identify ways to provide incentives, sanctions, and technological advances
Identify the available risk communication sources in the community
Identify the available risk communication channels in the community
Identify specific audience segments
Resource mobilization
Obtain the support of senior appointed and elected officials
Enlist the participation of other government agencies
Enlist the participation of nongovernmental, nonprofit and private sector organizations
Work with the mass media
Work with neighborhood associations and service organizations
Program development for all phases
Staff, train, and exercise a crisis communications team
Establish procedures for communicating effectively in an escalating crisis and in emergency response
Plan to make use of informal communication networks
Establish procedures for controlling message distortion
Program implementation for the continuing hazard phase
Build source credibility by increasing expertise and trustworthiness
Use a variety of channels to disseminate hazard information
Present an appropriate risk communication program approach
Describe community or facility hazard adjustments being planned or implemented
Describe feasible household hazard adjustments
Evaluate performance

operations plans and to identify the most appropriate hazard adjustments. Knowing the geographic areas at greatest risk makes it possible to focus the risk communication program on specific target audiences. Knowing the population segments and economic sectors that are the most vulnerable provides further information about how to target the risk communication program, and it also suggests which incentives and sanctions might be best suited to increasing hazard adjustment adoption.

Task 2: Analyze the Community Context

The most comprehensive research on the practice of local environmental hazard management has been that undertaken by Drabek (1987, 1990), whose careful analysis of the problem has identified many effective managerial strategies. In particular, he has emphasized the need for emergency managers to continually study their communities. Indeed, if environmental hazard management is primarily a local activity, then the people in this field must know not only the characteristics of the local governmental system but also those of local households, businesses, and nongovernmental organizations. The latter include all of the context variables discussed in Chapters 3 and 4, including ethnic composition, communication channels, perceptions of authorities, levels of education, and income distribution.

If environmental hazards are not high in the community's priorities, as usually is the case (Rossi et al., 1982), environmental hazard managers need to begin with small programs, demonstrate their effectiveness, and build constituencies for environmental hazard management (Lindell, 1994c). In developing a risk communication program, environmental hazard managers need to realistically assess the resources that the community can afford to allocate to this activity, but they should not limit their assessment to the resources of a single agency. Instead, they should explore the ways that a variety of different organizations (e.g., the emergency management department, the police department, the fire department, the watershed management authority, and the public health department) might collaborate in developing a comprehensive program. As noted earlier, disaster planning committees and Local Emergency Planning Committees provide excellent frameworks within which to achieve this collaboration.

It also is important to be aware of state and federal mandates that can be used to justify increased efforts in risk communication. For example, the Environmental Protection Agency's implementation of the Superfund Amendments and Reauthorization Act of 1986 (SARA Title III) requires a community risk communication component. Similarly, some states have hazard notification regulations, such as California's requirement that prospective buyers be notified before purchasing residential property near a known earthquake fault (Palm, 1981). State resources can be accessed by referring to state hazard analysis websites (Hwang, Sanderson, & Lindell, 2001). Federal agencies such as the U.S. Geological Survey, National Weather Service, Environmental Protection Agency, and Federal Emergency Management Agency have many resources, including, for example, the Federal Emergency Management Agency's Talking About Disasters website at http://www.fema.gov/rrr/talkdiz.

Task 3: Identify the Community's Prevailing Perceptions of Hazards and Hazard Adjustments

Of the many hazards that are prevalent in modern society, the ones that seem to produce the greatest conflict are those that have a potential for inflicting significant harm on bystanders, such as the residents of areas near technological facilities. The general public perceives the risks of nuclear power plants and chemical facilities as being greater than those of other technologies and natural hazards (Lindell & Earle, 1983; Slovic, 1987), and the public differs from technologists by considering what Hance, Chess, and Sandman (1988) call the "outrage" dimensions of risk, including voluntariness, controllability by those exposed, fairness in the distribution of risks and benefits, trustworthiness of information sources, naturalness, familiarity, dread, detectability, and understanding by science. Thus, this line of research suggests that residents of most communities are likely to consider the risks of technological facilities to be greater than those of natural hazards, even if the hazards' annual fatality rate is the same (Slovic, 1987).

It is common to find that technological hazards generate a level of risk perception that exceeds what experts consider to be warranted, whereas natural hazards seem to elicit the opposite. Environmental hazard managers can begin to address this problem by explaining the community hazard/vulnerability analysis and their resulting assessments of risk area residents' personal likelihood and consequences of disaster impact. A major impediment to effective risk communication is the difficulty in explaining small probabilities of occurrence and small numbers of expected casualties per year. This has led some experts to propose risk comparisons that list the annual death rate (Morrall, 1986), the loss of life expectancy (Cohen & Lee, 1979), and the time to increase risk by one chance in a million (Crouch & Wilson, 1982). Unfortunately, these solutions seem to produce more problems than they solve (Covello, 1991). Specifically, such risk comparisons typically ignore the uncertainties in the estimates (which could differ significantly from one hazard to another) and, by comparing hazards only in terms of casualties, equate hazards that have what many people consider very different types of consequences. The problem is compounded when the experts presume that if people "have voluntarily accepted" the risks on the list that have higher fatality rates (often these are lifestyle risks such as automobile driving), they also "should accept" other risks on the list that have a lower fatality rate (often this is the risk of a technological facility that they are proposing to build and operate). Of course, this argument ignores the fact that the facility risk will be added to the lifestyle risk, not substituted for it, and that the facility risk often is estimated by risk analysts, whereas the lifestyle risk is computed actuarially from a very large database.

When attempting to place the risks into context, Covello (1991) cautions environmental hazard managers to recognize that risks are cumulative, and so each new hazard contributes to the total risk; to disclose assumptions; to include all significant health, safety, and environmental impacts; to include both short-term and long-term consequences; and to convey uncertainties by presenting estimates for the best case, expected case, and worst case. Hance and colleagues (1988) recommend that environmental hazard managers avoid making comparisons to other hazards that differ on outrage factors such as risk voluntariness, controllability, novelty, and detectability—especially if these comparisons seem to trivialize the risk under consideration. Instead, environmental hazard managers should be prepared to make comparisons to the same risk at previous points in time, to administrative standards, to risks in other communities, to risks of other environmental hazards, or to the risk estimates of other analysts. When the risks of long-term health effects such as cancer are presented, it might be useful to compare the risk due to a specific facility or activity to the background level of risk that is prevalent in the community—nonetheless acknowledging that even a single additional death is not inconsequential. Environmental hazard managers also should be prepared to indicate how people should respond to the risks that they are describing, and how they personally would respond to these risks. This is an especially appropriate point at which to identify hazard adjustments that can be adopted by households, because the research cited in Chapter 4 suggests that people have only modest awareness of appropriate hazard adjustments and there is certainly wide variation in people's ratings of the efficacy and resource requirements of these hazard adjustments. These findings indicate that environmental hazard managers should talk to local residents about the hazards in their community and the hazard adjustments the residents can use to protect themselves and their property from these hazards. Nonetheless, environmental hazard managers must be cautious about misleading people when their personal views differ from agency policy.

Regarding the topic of discussion in community meetings, Hance and colleagues (1988) recommend that environmental hazard managers reject a distinction between "perceived risk" and "real risk" in favor of a recognition that the latter are, in fact, scientifically estimated risks that are uncertain. Moreover, they advocate an acknowledgement of the legitimate role of people's values and feelings regarding environmental hazard management. This involves listening to, respecting, and acknowledging people's feelings and values regarding the issues under discussion. It also involves environmental hazard managers being aware of their own feelings and values, as well as the values of the agencies that they represent.

Task 4: Set Appropriate Goals for the Risk Communication Program

As Chapter 4 indicated, hazard awareness is an important first step in the process of hazard adjustment, as people need first to be informed about the hazards to which their community is exposed. This could include some information about physical science, engineering, public health, social science, and planning perspectives on environmental hazards. In addition, people need to be informed about the likelihood that events of different magnitudes will occur in their location. In the case of hurricanes, environmental hazard managers should ensure that residents of coastal communities understand the atmospheric processes that cause hurricanes, the long-term probabilities of their community being struck by hurricanes in Saffir-Simpson Categories 1-5 over the next 10 years, and the different types of threats (wind, tornadoes, storm surge, and inland flooding). However, as the research in previous chapters has shown, it also is necessary to ensure that local residents personalize the risk of casualties to themselves and their families, damage to their property, and disruption to their lives. To help people to personalize the risk, local environmental hazard managers should provide detailed maps showing areas at risk from wind and storm surge, as well as the vulnerability of different types of structures in the community to these threats. For example, hurricane vulnerability can be assessed by defining the areas that would be affected by hurricanes in Saffir-Simpson Categories 1-5 and displaying these risk areas on large-scale maps indicating local landmarks that will assist people to identify the locations of their homes and workplaces. These maps could be supplemented by drawings of different types of structures (e.g., mobile homes, typical single family residences, and typical multifamily structures) showing the level of damage that would be expected at each hurricane category.

In addition, environmental hazard managers need to foster people's sense of personal responsibility for self-protection in order to reach high levels of household hazard adjustment adoption. Thus, it will be important to remind people that there are limits to what local government and industry can do to mitigate environmental hazards and that there is much they can do to prevent damage to their homes and the likelihood of death or injury to themselves and their families. Finally, as the PADM indicates, the risk communication program should ensure that people are aware of the different types of hazard adjustments and have accurate beliefs about the efficacy and resource requirements of these hazard adjustments. As indicated in Chapter 4, there is strong theoretical and empirical support for the proposition that the probability of hazard adjustment adoption is higher if messages address attitudes toward the adjustments themselves than if these messages address only the hazard (Lindell & Whitney, 2000).

Risk communication about environmental hazards should be a progressive, long-term process in which the methods of risk communication should be guided by what research has revealed about the process of household hazard adjustment adoption. First, households move into and out of risk areas, requiring repeated efforts to ensure that newcomers are aware of the hazard. Second, multiple communication attempts over time that vary in the information presented should be used to produce frequent thoughts and discussions about local hazards, so a high level of hazard intrusiveness will stimulate action. Third, receiving essentially the same message from different sources via multiple channels will enhance people's belief in the accuracy of the messages. Fourth, each hazard requires many different adjustments because protection (structural protection, personal health and safety, financial stability) is hazard-specific and because hazards vary in the level of resources they require. Thus, disseminating information about the hazard itself, accompanied by a list of appropriate hazard adjustments, would be a daunting endeavor for environmental hazard managers and, indeed, one that could overload message recipients if all of the relevant information were presented concurrently. That is, presentation of a large number of hazard adjustments in a single hazard awareness campaign is unlikely to produce the immediate adoption of all of them, and it might be perceived as so overwhelming that it is rejected and none of the adjustments are adopted. Environmental hazard managers might even need to prioritize the hazard adjustment suggested in different campaigns—perhaps emphasizing the simplest adjustments first and more difficult ones later.

Moreover, environmental hazard managers should recognize that even the most scientifically sound and effectively implemented risk communication programs will not produce very high levels of household adoptions of hazard adjustments. The social psychology of protection is such that many variables, some of them well understood and others not, influence the hazard adjustment adoption process. Studies of the effects of information dissemination on household emergency preparedness have found that risk communication programs produce only small increments in the level of hazard adjustment adoption (Lindell & Perry, 2000). Thus, sustained risk communication programs will be needed to yield significant increased in hazard mitigation or emergency preparedness. A long-term perspective is not likely to demonstrate immediate results, but it can put environmental hazards on the political agenda, which can reinforce the results achieved at the household level (Birkland, 1997; Prater & Lindell, 2000). By taking a long-term perspective over many years—multiple sources, channels, and messages repeated over time—environmental hazard managers can reinforce previous messages and build a cumulative impact (Drabek, 1986; Dynes et al., 1972; Lindell & Perry, 1992; Perry & Nigg, 1985; Quarantelli, 1977). The recommendation to send multiple messages that reinforce this information over time is not a new one (see, e.g., Davenport & Waterstone, 1979; Perry & Nigg, 1985), but it has not been widely adopted. The advantage of a phased approach is that it frees the environmental hazard manager from the need to cover all the issues in a single effort, which has the potential for overloading risk area residents with information and decreasing their attention to and comprehension of these messages.

Operational Analysis

Task 1: Identify and Assess Feasible Hazard Adjustments for the Community and Its Households and Businesses

The purpose of this task is to address the problem that many people who know about their exposure to environmental hazards often don't know what to do to reduce their vulnerability (Lindell & Perry, 2000). Thus, authorities should develop a list of feasible hazard adjustments, describe these adjustments in terms of their efficacy and resource requirements, and provide a list of qualified vendors for any products or services that households will need to implement these hazard adjustments. To identify feasible hazard adjustments, local environmental hazard managers could access resources such as the American Red Cross website at http://www.redcross.org/services/disaster/beprepared, where they can find information about recommended household adjustments for a wide range of hazards. These can be evaluated in terms of resource requirements such as financial cost, time and effort, knowledge and skill, tools and equipment, and cooperation with others.

Task 2: Identify Ways to Provide Incentives, Sanctions, and Technological Innovations

Some hazard adjustments require a significant amount of household resources for implementation, so the level of adoption could be increased by incentives, sanctions, and/or technological innovations. As noted earlier, sanctions are appealing because they avoid the obvious costs associated with incentives and have been shown to be effective in situations such as the use of seat belts in automobiles (Escobedo, Chorba, & Remmington, 1992). However, they are less useful than they appear because they require constant monitoring for enforcement, even in the workplace (Lindell, 1994b). Because household hazard adjustments are inherently implemented in the home, it would be extremely difficult for community authorities to successfully ensure compliance with any mandate to adopt hazard adjustments.

By contrast, the financial cost of a hazard adjustment can be reduced by providing incentives such as grants, loans at subsidized interest rates, or tax credits. In most cases, this strategy is very expensive for local jurisdictions to implement, but there are cases where hazard adjustment adoption can be promoted by drawing incentives from another source. Specifically, Lindell (1995) observed that increasing the efficacy of sheltering in-place for toxic chemical releases by sealing homes more effectively also lowers their heating and air conditioning needs. Thus, opportunities exist for environmental hazard managers to collaborate with electric utilities to promote two objectives concurrently—increased toxic chemical safety and reduced power consumption.

An alternative incentive is for environmental hazard managers to reduce resource requirements such as knowledge and skill by providing specific plans or checklists for hazard adjustment implementation. For example, providing plans for homeowners to bolt their houses to their foundations makes this hazard adjustment feasible for do-it-yourselfers with only a modest level of construction experience, whereas a community tool bank makes this hazard adjustment feasible for those who lack the tools and equipment that are needed. Listing qualified vendors for services, tools, and materials reduces the amount of time and effort that would be required to locate such vendors. Similarly, environmental hazard managers could list any recent technological innovations in hazard adjustments (e.g., improved methods of retrofitting structures against damage) and publicize this information.

Task 3: Identify the Available Risk Communication Sources in the Community

The research reviewed in previous chapters indicates that sources can be categorized as authorities (local, state, and federal government agencies, facility operators, and scientists), mass media (especially newspapers, television, and radio), and peers (friends, relatives, neighbors, and coworkers). These sources are judged in terms of their credibility, which comprises perceived expertise and trustworthiness, but these credibility perceptions are likely to vary depending on whether a source is speaking about hazards or hazard adjustments. Within the latter category, sources are likely to be differentiated with respect to their credibility regarding disaster responses and long-term hazard adjustments and, within each of these categories, with respect to hazard adjustment efficacy and hazard adjustment resource requirements (Lindell, 1994b).

The best risk information sources will be credible because of their expertise regarding multiple hazards and their trustworthiness to multiple community groups. Previous hazard research has documented that official sources are generally the most credible, and that message recipients infer credibility from the source's credentials (e.g., job title and educational degrees), acceptance by other sources of known credibility, or previous history of job performance (Perry & Lindell, 1990b). Lindell and Perry (1992) found that the degree of expertise attributed to different sources varies from one hazard to another. Residents of a town near Mt. St. Helens felt they knew almost as much as official sources about a familiar hazard (i.e., the volcano hazard at Mt. St. Helens 5 years after the first major eruption). However, they felt that they knew significantly less than officials about unfamiliar hazards (toxic chemical hazards in transportation and radiological hazards from a nearby nuclear power plant). Moreover, there is reason to believe that perceptions of source characteristics vary by gender, ethnicity, and other demographic characteristics (Nigg, 1982; Perry, 1987; Perry & Nelson, 1991).

The issue of perceived source characteristics is especially important in connection with peer influence. Practitioners have found that people who are contacted by their peers are more likely to adopt hazard adjustments, alter the decisions of the organizations to which they belong, and bring pressure to bear on their governmental policy makers (Lindell, 1994b; Michaels, 1990). For example, a bank president whose basic operations were seriously damaged by an earthquake can speak persuasively to unaffected bank presidents about their potential losses and how to implement hazard adjustments. Peer sources such as this can affect their audiences through a number of social and psychological mechanisms. First, they can obtain greater access to the target audience and, thus, provide them with greater exposure to hazard-relevant information. Second, the source's similarity to the receiver is likely to increase the audience's attention to and comprehension of the message. Third, peers' definitions of a threat are more likely to be accepted because their credibility is based on personal experience in situations that the recipients believe to be very similar to their own. Fourth, a peer communicator is more likely to use vivid descriptions of events (which research has shown to be more memorable than pallid statistics). Finally, peers are more likely than authorities to provide more convincing descriptions of the efficacy or resource requirements of recommended hazard adjustments. All of these reasons suggest that environmental hazard managers should recruit peers of their audience members for their hazard awareness programs.

Source credibility has special implications among ethnic minorities, but most research on this topic has focused on Mexican Americans, African Americans, and Whites. The results of these studies indicate that authorities (particularly firefighters and police) tend to be regarded as credible by the majority of all three ethnic groups, except under special circumstances (Lindell & Perry, 1992). African Americans and Whites tended to be more skeptical of the mass media than are Mexican Americans. In general, Mexican Americans are more likely than African Americans or Whites to consider peers (friends, relatives, neighbors, or coworkers) to be the most credible sources. There is evidence, however, that the results vary by location (in this case, by city), which appears to reflect differences in routine or perhaps situational relationships between ethnic groups and specific authorities such as police. For example, an ethnic minority group in one community rated police as credible, whereas the same ethnic group in another community did not. Discussions with local informants revealed that in the community where police had low credibility, police had recently conducted an enhanced crime enforcement program in neighborhoods with a high proportion of minority residents. This program was interpreted as discriminatory enforcement against minorities.

The practical implication of these locational differences in source credibility is that environmental hazard managers must find out for themselves what are the patterns of credibility attribution in their own communities. As previously noted, there is no substitute for knowing which minority groups live and work in the community, if they are geographically concentrated (and where), and how they view alternative sources of information about environmental hazards and hazard adjustments. Such information can be gained from personal observation, informants, and census data. Perhaps the best information comes from environmental hazard managers' active outreach programs employed over a long period of time—for example, speaking at meetings of neighborhood associations and civic organizations and involving citizens in advisory committees. Not only does such community involvement provide environmental hazard managers with information about citizens' credibility attributions, but it also enhances authorities' visibility, fosters dialogue, and facilitates citizens' access to accurate risk information. Finally, the presence of differential credibility attributions among ethnic groups reinforces the use of peers as risk communication sources. Hence, individuals who are recognized as credible by particular ethnic groups, known as *opinion leaders*, should be recruited to participate as additional sources of risk information.

Task 4: Identify the Available Risk Communication Channels in the Community

The primary risk communication channels available in most communities are the electronic media such as radio and television (and, increasingly, websites) and print media such as local newspapers and magazines. Other print media that have been used in hazard awareness programs include brochures, posters, telephone book inserts, comic/coloring books, reports, and scientific journal articles. Additional communication channels include informal face-to-face conversations (drop-in hours at local libraries, newsletters, information booths at local events and shopping malls) and formal meetings with or without audiovisual presentations such as computer simulations, slide shows, and films (Hance et al., 1988; Mileti et al., 1990). Even though environmental hazard managers have access to all of these channels in principle, access to many of them is limited in practice because their costs frequently exceed agency budgets. For example, prominent advertisements typically cost far more than agency budgets allow, but even in these cases there are alternatives such as interviews that provide television programming during off-peak hours or newspaper coverage in feature columns. In addition, it is possible to obtain access through public service announcements on radio and television or inserts in newspapers and magazines. Such messages involve a minimum cost if, for example, an agency creates its own videotape presentation for television or prints a full-page insert for a newspaper. To gain access to these low-cost opportunities for publicity, environmental hazard managers must establish contacts with local media personnel. In addition, collaboration with private sector organizations can sometimes yield financial contributions that can be used to pay for low cost items such as brochures and posters. The ability to provide speakers for meetings of neighborhood associations or civic organizations depends on the staffing constraints of environmental hazard management agencies.

Task 5: Identify Specific Audience Segments

Environmental hazard managers face a significant dilemma in designing their hazard awareness programs. On the one hand, most risk communication programs have assumed a very homogeneous "public" and have done little to tailor information materials to different groups. One obvious reason for this strategy is that it is easier and cheaper to provide a generic program; another reason is that existing research can barely provide a basis for what to say to the "typical" person, let alone guidance on how to tailor messages to specific demographic groups. On the other hand, as indicated in previous chapters, individuals with different demographic characteristics are likely to have different interests and concerns, motives for undertaking hazard adjustments, and media preferences, so different approaches must be used with them. For example, methods of persuading middle class homeowners to buy flood insurance or invest in earthquake retrofits for their home will almost certainly need to be quite different from those used to reach school districts, large corporations, or hazards professionals. A variety of sources have emphasized the importance of tailoring information to the characteristics of each audience segment (Expert Review Committee, 1987; Hance et al., 1988; Nelson & Perry, 1991; Olson, Lagorio, & Scott, 1990). This advice has been implemented in a few hazard awareness programs that now target their information to specific audiences, but there is a conspicuous lack of detailed research on receiver characteristics to provide definitive guidance on this topic. The Bay Area Regional Earthquake Preparedness Project (1990) and Southern California Earthquake Preparedness Project operated by the California Office of Emergency Services have published guides and manuals for special groups including schools, hospitals, corporations, city managers, environmental hazard managers, and the news media (Eisner, 1990; Schulz, 1993).

The design of audience segmentation strategies should be based on local assessments of receiver characteristics, which we have defined broadly in terms of geographic (e.g., recency and frequency of hazard experience and proximity to the impact area) and socioeconomic (e.g., age, sex, education, income, and ethnicity) attributes. To identify specific audience segments, environmental hazard managers should use the data on vulnerable population segments and business sectors from the community hazard/vulnerability analysis. Specifically, they should use these analyses to identify risk areas (e.g., floodplains, hurricane risk areas, chemical facility Vulnerable Zones, and nuclear power plant Emergency Planning Zones), any distinctly cohesive neighborhoods within those risk areas, and especially any predominantly ethnic areas of those neighborhoods.

Of course, the first consideration in such analyses is to ensure that those at risk *receive* hazard-relevant information. Thus, environmental hazard managers should assess each audience segments' channel access and channel preference to identify the types of media used (e.g., radio) and, more specifically, the channels used (e.g., specific radio stations). Next, environmental hazard managers need to ensure that recipients *heed* and *comprehend* the messages. This step can be facilitated by determining each population segment's and business sector's perceptions of different information sources to assess their credibility. To the greatest extent possible, this information should be used during program implementation to ensure that each group hears from the sources that it considers to be most credible.

Message comprehension can be assured if environmental hazard managers determine whether there are any audience segments for whom there are language barriers. These are less likely to arise among older or more acculturated groups (except perhaps among Native Americans) or among groups whose socioeconomic status is similar to that of the majority population. However, language tends to be a very important issue for recent immigrants and for minority groups who have either resisted acculturation (which is most likely when there is a high level of ethnic identity) or experienced sufficient prejudice and discrimination to preclude acculturation. In such cases, language differences constitute an obvious limitation to understanding hazard-related information and, for that matter, tend to inhibit other forms of community participation as well. For all of these reasons, information about environmental hazards and hazard adjustments needs to be presented in a multilingual format, preferably across multiple channels. The existence of language barriers is linked to source and channel choice because communities with large minority groups often contain mass media channels that are language specific. In Los Angeles, San Francisco, and Seattle, for example, there are cable television channels, radio stations, newspapers, and magazines that communicate in Cantonese, Farsi, Japanese, Mandarin, Spanish, and Vietnamese. In jurisdictions with smaller minority populations, the number of channels will be far more limited—perhaps not including mass media at all—but the environmental hazard managers who know their communities should be able to identify some (even informal) mechanisms of native language communication.

Moreover, environmental hazard managers should assess the information needs of each population segment to determine what message content should be transmitted to them. Specific questions include whether they have adequate information about the hazards to which they are vulnerable, appropriate hazard adjustments, and the efficacy and resource requirements of those hazard adjustments. Finally, environmental hazard managers need to identify any audience segments that lack a sense of personal responsibility or self-efficacy for adopting hazard adjustments. Any groups that are low on these characteristics should be targeted for special attention during the implementation of the risk communication program.

Resource Mobilization

Task 1: Obtain the Support of Senior Appointed and Elected Officials

The research literature from a wide range of settings indicates that successful implementation of a new program in any type of organization needs the support of higher level management (Lindell, 1994c). In the public sector, obtaining the support of senior appointed and elected officials is also an important step toward obtaining the participation of other government agencies. Organizational support can be increased when middle managers recognize that top management attention is scarce in all organizations, so they must effectively "sell" the issues that they believe need a high priority. This means that environmental hazard managers must successfully identify community hazard vulnerability as an important issue and propose hazard mitigation, emergency preparedness, emergency response, and disaster recovery as effective solutions. Research by Dutton and Ashford (1993) suggests that this requires convincing top management of the following:

- Environmental hazards have the potential for inflicting significant casualties, damage, and disruption on the community.
- The community must take responsibility for protecting itself.
- Community agencies have the technical competence to manage these hazards effectively.
- The available solutions can be implemented at reasonable cost to reduce vulnerability to multiple hazards.

It is noteworthy that these recommendations are strikingly similar to those derived from the PADM, even though the research base for Dutton and Ashford's (1993) work was entirely different from that summarized in previous chapters.

Task 2: Enlist the Participation of Other Government Agencies

No matter how supportive senior appointed and elected officials would like to be, they are almost certain to have few additional resources to allocate to environmental hazard management, let alone to environmental risk communication. Consequently, environmental hazard managers should adopt an interorganizational perspective. There are at least two concerns here, the first of which is to be certain that each agency is aware of the risk communication programs being planned and implemented by other governmental (i.e., city, county, state, and federal) agencies, nongovernmental organizations, and hazardous technological facilities. This permits local environmental hazard managers to integrate their risk communication programs into a broader context. For example, local messages might be timed to reinforce message dissemination from relevant federal programs, or local messages might be structured to address local constraints, concerns, or other specific details. Furthermore, attention to the full range of messages being disseminated to local residents emphasizes the need for consistency and complementarity of content so that agencies can avoid creating an impression of competing or conflicting messages about a hazard (Ng & Hamby, 1997).

Another advantage of attending to the risk communication programs of other agencies lies in the interorganizational coordination that can be developed. As researchers have pointed out, local environmental hazard management goals are at times achieved more effectively through the development of coalitions that pool the resources of multiple agencies within local government (Drabek, 1990; Gillespie et al., 1993; Lindell et al., 1996). To elicit the active support of other government agencies, environmental hazard managers should identify ways in which collaboration can achieve the goals of both organizations. For example, environmental hazard managers could work with the police to ensure that Block Watch groups are provided with information about environmental hazards. Collaborative efforts such as this are very likely to be successful because local emergency management organizations have a long history of collaboration with police, fire, and emergency medical services organizations. However, collaboration with land use planners, transportation planners, building inspectors, or public health officials might be more difficult because environmental hazard managers rarely have experience in working with these agencies. Nonetheless, cooperation with land use planners is needed to ensure that zoning and subdivision regulations, capital development plans, and other activities minimize development in hazard-prone areas to the greatest extent possible. Transportation planners are needed to ensure that timely evacuation from those areas is feasible, whereas building inspectors are needed to ensure that the structures built in hazard-prone areas meet prevailing building codes. Finally, collaboration with public health officials will be needed to prepare for biohazards.

Task 3: Enlist the Participation of Nongovernmental and Private Sector Organizations

Nongovernmental organizations such as the American Red Cross and religious organizations such as the Salvation Army are active in household emergency response and, especially, disaster recovery. Some of these organizations routinely work with needy families and can identify the geographic areas in which there is a high concentration of population segments that are most likely to be vulnerable to disaster impact. These organizations can also help to identify methods of assisting households to prepare for emergencies, reduce the vulnerability of the structures in which they live, or find safer places to which they can move.

In addition, there are many disaster-relevant infrastructure organizations such as water, wastewater, fuel, and electric power utilities that can play a major role in promoting the adoption of hazard adjustments. Most of these respond to routine emergencies such as severe thunderstorms and winter storms, so they are aware of the demands that disasters can place on the community. In addition, these organizations routinely send bills to all of the residents of their service areas, a situation that provides environmental hazard managers with an opportunity to disseminate notices about sources and channels for obtaining further information about hazards and hazard adjustments.

Task 4: Work With the Mass Media

Collectively, the mass media comprise a variety of channels that routinely reach a large number of community residents. Consequently, a knowledge of media goals and operations, as well as familiarity with specific personnel in the news media, can set the stage for relationships in which information about environmental hazards adjustment can be disseminated and, in the process, the visibility and credibility of local environmental hazard management agencies can be enhanced. This is not to suggest that local environmental hazard managers should seek to co-opt or "manage" the local mass media, because this is likely to be ineffective and, possibly, counterproductive. The media, after all, serve functions in society that are distinctly different from those of environmental hazard managers (Burkhart, 1991). Rather, active contact with reporters and editors can allow environmental hazard managers access to channels with which citizens are familiar and that they routinely use for information. For example, environmental hazard managers in communities subject to seasonal hazards (e.g., winter snow, spring flooding and tornadoes, severe summer storms and hurricanes) can solicit interviews about appropriate hazard adjustments or provide news media channels with press releases or public service announcements with similar content. For less seasonal threats such as volcanic and earthquake hazards, feature editors can be provided with information that describes local environmental hazards, long-term hazard adjustments, and protective actions to be taken in emergencies, as well as opportunities for interviews on those topics. Similarly, arrangements can be made for newspaper and local magazine inclusion of periodic "hazard information inserts" directly constructed by environmental hazard managers. In a more general vein, environmental hazard managers can contact reporters about specific environmental hazard management activities, such as the performance of training activities, emergency drills, and full-scale response exercises. Cultivation of a cooperative relationship with the mass media through these mechanisms serves to diversify channels for the dissemination of risk information, as well as to increase the visibility of the environmental hazard management function in the community. Finally, reporters are well aware of their specialized audiences and tend to target them directly. This aspect of media coverage creates opportunities for environmental hazard managers to target messages to specific audience segments that are defined by gender, age, ethnicity (and language groups), and socioeconomic status.

It is important for environmental hazard managers to recognize that even though they consider environmental hazards to be a topic of vital concern for the community, reporters and editors will not automatically consider this information to be "newsworthy" during the continuing hazard phase. In order to increase the priority of this topic for the news media, many federal agencies, such as the National Weather Service, urge government officials to "declare" weeks for hazards such as tornadoes and hurricanes. Local environmental hazard managers can take advantage of the publicity generated by these agencies to contact their local media and arrange interviews in which they can provide supplementary information, but the amount of attention these events attract depends on competing demands—even on a slow news day these stories will receive little air time and will appear in the back pages of the newspaper.

One of the most important ways for local environmental hazard managers to collaborate with the news media is for them to work with reporters to develop the background materials that the reporters will need in an escalating crisis, an emergency response, or a disaster recovery. Environmental hazard managers should use their hazard/vulnerability analyses as the basis for developing plausible scenarios about the different types of emergencies that might confront their communities and analyze these scenarios to determine what types of information they want to disseminate to local residents in such situations. It also is important for environmental hazard managers to anticipate what types of information reporters are likely to seek during these events and to prepare fact sheets and other "boilerplate" that can be used no matter what specific conditions occur during an emergency.

Task 5: Work With Neighborhood Associations and Civic Organizations

Most communities have many neighborhood associations and civic organizations whose members participate when they perceive social and environmental problems in their community that they expect the organization to be successful in mitigating (Chavis & Wandersman, 1990; Florin & Wandersman, 1990). Such studies have found that participation in community groups is significantly related to three types of benefits—personal, social, and purposive—and their corresponding costs (Prestby, Wandersman, Florin, Rich, & Chavis, 1990). Moreover, members' sense of individual and collective self-efficacy is enhanced when these organizations are empowered by successfully influencing actions taken by the community. Unfortunately, there is a 50% mortality rate among voluntary community organizations during their first year of existence alone (Prestby & Wandersman, 1985).

Environmental hazard managers can help the leaders of these groups to ensure the survival of these organizations by working to increase members' organizational commitment (Whitney & Lindell, 2000). This can be achieved by increasing leader initiating structure (explaining what tasks to perform and how to perform them), leader consideration (recognizing the needs and limitations of each person), and perceived reward opportunities and by reducing role conflict (differing expectations regarding members' duties). In addition, environmental hazard managers can work with these organizations by providing them with opportunities to learn about environmental hazards and feasible adjustments to those hazards. Time is frequently available for this purpose during organizational meetings because most of these organizations meet regularly but are not always able to fill their meeting agendas.

Program Development

Task 1: Staff and Train a Crisis Communication Team

One important principle of risk communication is to establish a crisis communication team as part of a broader emergency preparedness program (Churchill, 1997; Fink, 1986). The crisis communication team forms a critical link between technical experts and the population at risk. Thus, the crisis communication team should have skill in communicating with both groups. Such communication might be directly with the public during public meetings, in which case the crisis communication team should have members who are skilled at facilitating large groups. Alternatively, risk communication messages might be transmitted through the mass media, in which case the risk communication team must be capable of responding effectively to the demands of reporters.

In either case, the crisis communication unit should be represented by a spokesperson who is technically competent to explain the situation clearly. As noted earlier, spokespeople will be perceived as credible if they have relevant credentials (e.g., job title and educational degrees), are accepted by other sources of known credibility, or have a demonstrated history of job performance that has enhanced their credibility (Lindell & Perry, 1992; Perry & Lindell, 1990a). It also will be helpful if they receive training from public relations experts (Hance et al., 1988).

The crisis communication team should have procedures to guide its activation and its initial contacts with the news media. In both cases, the procedures should be capable of being implemented at any time—24 hours a day, 365 days a year. The crisis communication team's procedures should include documentation of all emergency response related activities, especially an event log that records the information that was available and the criteria that were used to guide critical decisions such as those involving protective actions for the public. The crisis communication team should also prepare to monitor the information that is being disseminated by the news media; this can be accomplished by installing radios and television sets in the emergency operations center. They also should designate a rumor control center and ensure that it will be staffed by operators who are frequently updated on the status of the incident and the response to it. The procedures for the rumor control center should ensure that operators are frequently debriefed with information that answers questions frequently asked by callers. This will allow them to curtail the dissemination of any widespread misconceptions by addressing these issues in subsequent press releases and press briefings.

The crisis communication team should recognize that reporters are taught to describe events in terms of stories that are framed by five questions—who, what, when, where, and why (Churchill, 1997). Specifically, reporters will want to know what happened and what were the specific causes of the event. An important question that will require advance preparation is whether an incident like this has happened before and what actions were taken to prevent its recurrence (in the case of a technological hazard) or reduce the consequences (in the case of a natural hazard). Reporters also will want to know whether there were safeguards to prevent an incident (in the case of a technological hazard) and, if so, who was responsible for the safeguards and why they failed. Other questions will include who was (or will be) affected—including casualties, property damage, and economic disruption—and what authorities have done (and will do) to respond to the situation. It frequently is difficult to answer one or more of these questions because information is lacking. In such cases, it is important for the spokesperson to avoid speculation (and especially premature blame) but, rather, to admit that he or she does not know the answer and will find out as soon as possible. Even when authorities know that they have incomplete information, it usually is advisable to provide the news media with a brief statement, together with audiovisual materials, to summarize what is known about the incident.

When providing information to the news media, it is important to remember that reporters rarely have a scientific background, so technical details might be not only unnecessary but potentially confusing and thus counterproductive. To distinguish material that is informative from that which is useless or confusing requires advance preparation—especially advance contact with local reporters. Seeking informal contacts with or even formal interviews by reporters can provide environmental hazard managers with opportunities to assess reporters' hazard knowledge, provide them with additional information, and make suggestions about what types of materials would be useful to include in press kits and presentation aids. Moreover, inviting reporters to participate in drills and exercises will provide the crisis communication team with an understanding of reporters' information needs. This will not solve all problems; a major crisis such as the Three Mile Island nuclear power plant accident could draw reporters from around the country and even around the world. Reporters from national or international newspapers and television networks will not cover stories in exactly the same way as local reporters, but the most important information needs will be common to all categories of reporters.

Reporters frequently have little knowledge about scientific and technological processes, but they should be treated with respect because they have a difficult job to do. Specifically, they must be prepared to translate complex scientific concepts into terms that can be understood by any reasonably intelligent and literate citizen. Thus, environmental hazard managers who prepare briefing materials that facilitate this process will have a far better chance of getting their message to the public than those who continue to speak in technical jargon (McCallum & Anderson, 1991). Just as Chapter 3 advocated that officials translate warnings from English into the languages of ethnic minorities in order to ensure that the messages are translated correctly, agency officials also should translate their assessment of the situation from technical jargon into ordinary English to ensure that this message is also translated correctly. It is important to provide reporters with the best available information when they face a deadline, even if that information is not as reliable or current as one might prefer. This is because reporters themselves will use the best available information at the time they need it and might publish information that is even less reliable or current than what the authorities have available. Of course, it is useful to take notes (or tape discussions) with reporters to verify what has been said.

Finally, the communications plan and procedures should be tested by means of drills that test the crisis communication team alone, as well as by means of full scale exercises that test the integration of the crisis communication function into the overall emergency response organization. These drills and exercises should be based on scenarios that realistically portray the types of incidents that could occur, the likely emergency response actions of authorities, and, finally, the probable responses of the news media and the public. Each drill or exercise should be followed by a critique that evaluates the adequacy of the communications plan and procedures, as well as the staffing, training, and materials used.

Task 2: Establish Procedures for Maintaining an Effective Communication Flow During an Escalating Crisis or Emergency Response

All of the organizations participating in the risk communication program should establish procedures for coordinating the information they disseminate during crises and emergencies. It is especially important to routinize the flow of information among these organizations to ensure that each organization receives all the information it needs as promptly as possible. For many natural hazards (e.g., floods,

Table 5.3 Essential Incident Data

Date and time of report
Name, affiliation, and telephone number of information source
Location, type, and current status of the incident

- Derailment, containment failure, fire, explosion, liquid spill, gaseous release
- Hazardous material name, physical properties (gas, liquid, solid), environmental cues (sights, sounds, smells), and potential health effects
- Hazardous material release duration and quantity released
- Casualties and damage already incurred

Incident prognosis

- Potential for fire or explosion at site
- Potential for fire or explosion affecting residential, commercial, or industrial areas
- Hazardous material quantity available for release and expected release duration
- Locations and populations requiring protective action
- Types of protective actions recommended: evacuation, sheltering in-place, expedient respiratory protection, interdiction of food/water

Weather conditions (current and forecast wind speed and direction)
Chronology of important events in the development of the incident
Current status of response

- Facility/shipper/carrier actions: assessment, preventive, corrective, population protective actions
- Local/state/federal agency actions: assessment, preventive, corrective, population protective actions

Source: Adapted from the National Response Team (1987) and the U.S. Nuclear Regulatory Commission (1980).

tornadoes, and hurricanes) in which there is an escalating crisis and an emergency response, federal agencies such as the National Weather Service provide local environmental hazard managers with periodic updates on the status of the incident. Chemical and nuclear facility operators should establish procedures for providing similarly frequent and complete updates for incidents involving their facilities. The types of information that might be needed in an escalating crisis will depend on the circumstances, but recommendations regarding the content of incident notifications can be found in guidance for chemical (National Response Team, 1987) and nuclear (U.S. Nuclear Regulatory Commission, 1980) facilities and are summarized in Table 5.3. It is *advisable* that this table be adopted as a template because it is based on long experience with escalating crises and disaster responses. It is *essential* that facility operators and local environmental hazard managers discuss their information capabilities and needs and agree in advance what information will be exchanged when the need arises.

Task 3: Develop a Comprehensive Risk Communication Program

McGuire's (1985) system for analyzing message content can be defined in terms of the amount of material, speed of presentation, number of arguments, repetition, style, clarity, ordering, forcefulness, and extremity of the position advocated. Some of these characteristics can be measured objectively; for example, the amount of material can be measured in terms of the number of words, the speed of presentation can be measured in words per minute, and the number of arguments can be counted. Other characteristics are more ambiguous—repetition can be measured in terms of either the number of verbatim duplications of the message or the number of times an idea or argument is presented. Finally, characteristics such as the clarity and extremity of the arguments must be measured subjectively. As one might expect, there often are significant individual differences in receivers' perceptions of the subjective message characteristics, as well as in their reactions to all of these message characteristics.

At a somewhat broader level, Mileti and colleagues (Mileti & Peek, 2000; Mileti & Sorensen, 1987; Mileti et al., 1992) have defined warning message content in terms of information about the information source, the nature of the hazard, the impact location and time, guidance about recommended protective action, and frequency of repetition. Each of these messages can be further characterized in terms of stylistic characteristics, which include message specificity (the level of information detail), consistency (the compatibility of information within and between messages), and certainty (the stated or implied probability of an event's occurrence, as well as the source's apparent confidence in what he or she is saying). The stylistic characteristics also include clarity (the simplicity of the words used in the message), accuracy (the degree to which a source's statements are proven to be correct over time), sufficiency (the adequacy of the amount of information provided—neither too much nor too little), and channel (electronic, print, face-to-face).

Even more broadly, Sorensen and Mileti (1987) have classified hazard awareness programs in terms of number of different broad themes that can be interpreted according to the PADM. They noted that some programs, such as the educational model (which focuses on a few simplified concepts articulated by mascots such as the National Weather Service's Owlie Skywarn) and modeling (which relies on a movie star, a celebrity, or some other influential person to endorse hazard-relevant activities), place their emphasis on attracting attention and sharply restricting the complexity of the message content to promote comprehension and retention. The distinctive aspect of these strategies, the use of a likable or familiar source, is designed to enhance acceptance of the message.

Other types of programs focus more on message content. *Scientific information* programs attempt to disseminate technical data about the hazard agent. Although the information is correct and relevant to emergency response, it often seems complex and unfamiliar to nonspecialists. Because hazard information typically is not interesting to the general public during normal times and thus fails to attract attention or to be readily comprehended, such information is processed and retained by only a relatively small proportion of those who need it.

In contrast, *practical instructions* focus more on protective response (what to do in an emergency) than on the hazard itself. The very simplest form of practical instruction is the *prompt,* a sign that defines a single contingent action to take in the event of disaster (e.g., climb the canyon wall in case of a flash flood). Prompts, being shorter than instructional brochures, are more likely to attract attention and to be readily comprehended and retained for future use.

Attribute portrayal strategies are designed to emphasize the key advantages of recommended hazard adjustments, whereas *fear appeals* attract attention and motivate action by describing the potential personal consequences of disaster impact. Thus, attribute portrayals focus on the advantages of taking the recommended action, whereas fear appeals address the disadvantages of failing to take the recommended action. *Norm-oriented communications* differ from the previous two types of strategies in that such communications ignore the personal consequences of the hazard impact and emphasize the social incentives for adopting the recommended actions. They attempt to gain compliance by portraying the recommended action as something that is socially acceptable or even expected by others. Consequently, this strategy is directed toward what Fishbein and Ajzen (1975) call the message recipient's subjective norm.

The final strategy, *learning through participation,* has both cognitive and social reward components. The cognitive aspect involves the provision of step-by-step guidance for complex actions such as the development of a family emergency plan. When the participants encounter difficulties, they can consult a teacher for additional instructions before making further attempts. The social rewards come in the form of certificates, badges, stickers, or other devices that recognize the efforts that were required for completion of the task.

The fact that these different communication themes focus on different stages of the PADM suggests that these themes are not mutually exclusive and probably are not exhaustive. In turn, this implies that it might be possible to create more effective hazard awareness programs by presenting different themes in successive messages. That is, the more superficial themes, modeling and the educational model, rely on the peripheral route to persuasion (Petty & Cacioppo, 1986a) and thus involve heuristic processing (Chaiken, 1987). Such themes might be targeted to specific audiences or used in the initial stages of a campaign with the expectation that they will be followed by later messages with themes that rely on the central route to persuasion and thus involve systematic processing.

In evaluating the suitability of message content, the primary concern is that it should take into account the protective action decision process that determines the adoption of household hazard adjustments. Although adjustment adoption intentions and actual adoption depend on many additional variables, as described in previous chapters, the four key message content factors are perception of risk, perception of personal responsibility for action, beliefs about an adjustment's efficacy, and beliefs about its resource requirements. From this perspective, these variables become important targets for communication and one should consider their status in designing messages that are most likely to have an impact. We know that long-term risk—the probability of significant negative personal consequences from hazard impact—is difficult for most people to deal with. In particular, the statement that "there is a 1% probability of a damaging earthquake within the next year" has little impact on people's behavior, but cumulating probabilities over time by reporting that there is a 20% chance of an earthquake in the next 20 years does seem to make more of a difference in their risk perception (Kunreuther, 2001; Slovic, Fischhoff, & Lichtenstein, 1978). Thus, even communication programs that succeed in increasing the accuracy of people's risk perceptions are of no consequence if risk area residents fail to act on these risk perceptions by adopting effective hazard adjustments.

There are several implications of this conception of the hazard adjustment process. First, information about hazards and hazard adjustments needs to be presented in a form that attracts attention and is easily understood and retained, but even then,it will require periodic reinforcement over time. Second, risk communication programs should not overemphasize risk perception. Of course, it is important to communicate that a hazard exists and to accurately convey the probability of an event's occurrence and its personal consequences. Beyond this, however, detailed explanations of risk assessment processes and hazard agent dynamics are probably unnecessary for most people. Instead, environmental hazard managers need to emphasize the three other decision variables—perception of personal responsibility for action, beliefs about an adjustment's efficacy, and beliefs about its resource requirements.

In addition, environmental hazard managers should pay attention to message style factors, such as achieving clarity by choosing simple, nontechnical language and focusing the message on hazard consequences and hazard adjustments (Lindell & Perry, 1992). Specifically, Mileti (1993) explains that a hazard warning should address six issues: "a) what the risk is, b) where it is going to happen, c) when it is going to happen, d) what the effects will be, e) what people should do, and f) where to get information about it" (p. 148). Mileti's guidance raises a very important point. The six pieces of information are simple and can be communicated quickly (i.e., in a short time), no matter what the channel. For additional detail or elaboration, the people are referred to another specific place or person. It is important to remember that effective messages are short enough to avoid losing the receiver's attention because of seemingly irrelevant details that induce boredom. Moreover, long messages that send many details also have the potential for overloading receivers with so much information that they are unable to determine what is important and what is incidental. That is, the provision of too much information is probably as dysfunctional as the provision of insufficient or incomplete information. Nonetheless, it is important to recognize that what is "too long" will vary from one situation to another. Specifically, people's attention spans will be relatively short during the continuing hazard phase, but they can be expected to increase significantly during an emerging crisis or emergency response. People will pay attention to longer messages at times of elevated threat than when the danger is only a remote prospect.

In all cases, however, the production of brochures and other official written information should be multilingual. It is important to note, as Lindell and Perry (1992) have indicated, that translations need to be professionally executed to avoid complications arising from dialect variations within the same language group. Furthermore, when providing hazard information to non-English outlets, it is appropriate to provide it in both English and the target language to minimize information distortion that might be introduced if employees of a radio or television station, newspaper, or magazine perform a "freelance" translation of the English version. It is critically important to ensure—whether translating from English into one other language or many other languages—that all versions of the message are consistent and contain the same information.

As noted in Chapter 4, there is evidence that repeated official statements regarding the need for households likely to be struck by earthquakes to be self-sufficient for 72 hours have increased citizens' sense of personal responsibility for self-protection. Thus, a frank acknowledgement of the limits to governmental assistance might be useful in other contexts as well. Moreover, self-sufficiency is likely to increase when environmental hazard managers describe the ways in which households can protect themselves, together with specific descriptions of the resource requirements to implement these hazard adjustments.

Task 4: Plan to Make Effective Use of Informal Communication Networks

It is important for environmental hazard managers to recognize that peer communication takes place during all phases of a hazard—the continuing hazard phase, the escalating crisis phase, and the emergency response phase. They should plan to use these informal networks to increase the level of hazard adjustment adoption in their communities and to alert peers of those in these networks to dangerous situations. In particular, it is important to recognize that the information provided in any presentation to a neighborhood association or civic organization is likely to be passed on to other members who did not attend, as well as to friends, relatives, neighbors, and coworkers. Similarly, information that is disseminated to schoolchildren is also likely to be repeated at home.

Of course, environmental hazard managers must always be concerned that people receive *accurate* hazard adjustment information. Unfortunately, the mass media do not always relay the environmental hazard manager's message verbatim because of time pressures or wording that they consider to be beyond their audience's comprehension level. Even when the news media do present the message accurately, they sometimes distort it by proceeding to editorialize about it. Moreover, even the best intended friends, relatives, neighbors, and coworkers might misunderstand a message in the first place or inadvertently distort it through selective recall. The ability of environmental hazard managers to prevent such distortion is limited, especially in information exchanges among citizens themselves. One strategy for reducing distortion is to disseminate information through a range of official sources and channels, creating what Mileti (1993) calls a "supplemental barrage of information" (p. 148). The idea is to provide many opportunities for citizens to hear official messages via several channels, in the expectation that people will retain the common elements of these messages.

Environmental hazard managers also should plan to rely on these informal networks during emerging crises and emergency response. When information about an imminent hazard needs to be disseminated quickly, peers often relay the warning. Of course, this does not eliminate the responsibility that authorities have for establishing a timely and effective warning system. However, it does provide some degree of assurance that the warning system will reach a larger proportion of the population at risk, and that it will reach them more rapidly than would otherwise be expected.

Task 5: Establish Procedures for Obtaining Feedback From the News Media and the Public

As Figure 1.2 indicates, feedback is a critical part of any communication process because it provides receivers with an opportunity to confirm that they have comprehended the message, to reconcile inconsistencies within or between messages, or to obtain information that is not available in the messages they have received. Feedback is an inherent part of some communication channels, such as informal face-to-face discussions. It is somewhat more limited in public hearings where public comment might be limited to a few minutes at the end of a meeting (indeed, avoiding feedback is often a major objective of such "hearings") and, in any event, individual speakers are typically limited to 3 to 5 minutes apiece. This need for feedback is precisely the reason why many scholars recommend informal channels of communication (e.g., Committee on Risk Perception and Communication, 1989; Covello, 1987; Hance et al,

1988). Thus, if community or agency procedures require public hearings, these should be supplemented by less formal procedures such as advisory panels and meetings with neighborhood associations and civic organizations.

During emerging crises, there often is pressure to disseminate information rapidly via the electronic and print media, so opportunities for monitoring the degree of message distortion are somewhat limited. One highly effective strategy for performing this function is to monitor the news media by reading copies of local newspapers and listening radio and television broadcasts. When errors in media coverage are detected, environmental hazard managers can formulate a correction and transmit it to all media. Moreover, environmental hazard managers should establish specific procedures for obtaining feedback from citizens. One effective method is to provide a rumor control center with a telephone number or a website address that has been publicized in advance. People can contact this center to determine if the information they have received is correct or to obtain additional information that they need. If authorities monitor the questions that are being asked, they can determine if there are systematic patterns that need to be addressed in press releases to the mass media.

Time pressure is especially intense during emergency response, so it is important for environmental hazard managers to provide feedback mechanisms for those in imminent danger. Monitoring the news media and operating a rumor control center are especially important at this time because these activities ensure that those at risk receive accurate information initially and can confirm that information quickly. As noted in Chapter 3, research has shown that people who receive a warning message seek to verify, disconfirm, or extend the information in the message (Drabek, 1986). This behavior has been identified in connection with floods (Drabek, 1969; Perry et al., 1981), earthquakes (Mileti & Fitzpatrick, 1993; Turner et al., 1986), tornadoes (Mileti & Harvey, 1977; Moore et al., 1963), volcanic eruptions (Perry & Lindell, 1990a), and nuclear power plant accidents (Perry, 1985). Moreover, this pattern has been found in all of the ethnic groups on which research has been conducted. That is, African Americans, Whites, and Mexican Americans all tend to contact multiple information sources, but they tend to favor official sources in this process (Perry & Mushcatel, 1986). Lindell and Perry (1992) have argued that confirmation behavior represents an opportunity for environmental hazard managers to insert accurate information into citizen interactions regarding hazard information. The mechanism is similar in aim to rumor control centers; as part of all official hazard messages, environmental hazard managers can refer to other official sources that citizens can directly contact for additional information or explanation. Since the environmental hazard managers can select those other official sources that have the most congruent information, it is possible to ensure that those at risk receive consistent messages. An advantage of this strategy is that people can be referred to sources that involve both one-way and two-way communication. Examples of one-way communication are the use of websites (Hwang et al., 2001) and telephone book insertions (Perry, Greene, and Lindell, 1980). Two-way communications can be achieved by referring citizens to walk-in information resource centers and telephone call-in centers (Lindell & Perry, 1992).

Program Implementation During the Continuing Hazard Phase

Task 1: Build Source Credibility by Increasing Perceptions of Expertise and Trustworthiness

As noted previously, disaster researchers have found that those who think they are at risk from environmental hazards seek information from the news media (print and broadcast media) and peers (friends, relatives, neighbors, and coworkers), as well as from authorities (federal, state, and local government). In order to ensure that local authorities are considered to be the *most* credible source, they must take steps during the continuing hazard phase to enhance perceptions of their expertise and trustworthiness.

The members of the crisis communication team should ensure that its procedures are coordinated with all relevant agencies' emergency operations plans. This coordination can be verified by participating in joint training, drills, and full-scale exercises, so that team members willingly accept the involvement of other agencies and understand the roles they will play in an escalating crisis or emergency response. It is especially important that environmental hazard managers get to know their counterparts in other agencies so that they can coordinate the information they disseminate during escalating crises and emergency response. Collaborating with experts in other specialized agencies can help local environmental hazard managers to develop specialized knowledge about hazards, but *being seen* to collaborate with experts in other specialized agencies reinforces public perceptions of specialized competence. An effective way to achieve actual and perceived competence is to establish contacts with these organizations to produce joint messages, messages that reference each other, or, at least, messages that are consistent with each other.

It also is important for environmental hazard managers from each agency to develop a demonstrated history of effective job performance that enhances their credibility. In part, this experience can be gained during minor incidents such as severe storms and minor floods that cause localized damage and disruption of normal activities. However, credibility can also be enhanced by effective performance in public hearings or in meetings with advisory committees, neighborhood associations, and civic organizations. In such venues, agency spokespeople can enhance perceptions of their expertise by being fully prepared to explain the community's hazards, the process of hazard/vulnerability analysis, the accuracy of past hazard predictions, and the reasons for prediction errors. They also should describe environmental hazard management actions being undertaken by community agencies or facility operators, hazard adjustments that can be taken by individual households, and adjustments that can be implemented by neighborhood associations (e.g., Citizen Emergency Response Teams—see http://training.fema.gov/emiweb/CERT).

Of course, expertise is only one component of credibility; trustworthiness is also essential. According to Renn and Levine (1991), trust develops when messages are perceived to be accurate, objective, and complete. This can be expected when a source is fair, unbiased, complete, and accurate (Meyer, 1988; Trumbo & McComas, 2003). Similarly, Maeda and Miyahara (2003) contend that a trustworthy source is competent, open and honest, caring and concerned, and sympathetic. Accordingly, environmental hazard managers are advised to earn a community's trust by being competent, caring, honorable, and considering outrage factors when working with the public (Covello et al., 1989; Hance et al., 1988). It also is important to promote meaningful public involvement by involving the community in the continuing hazard phase (or early in the decision process of a new facility), avoiding secret meetings, and explaining the agency's procedures (especially what constraints on public participation are imposed by law and agency policy). Environmental hazard managers also should provide accurate information that is responsive to people's requests. In this regard, it is important to recognize the difference between the information that people think they need and the information that experts think is needed. Environmental hazard managers must learn to respond to both sets of information needs.

Finally, the need for multiple sources to collaborate in repeatedly transmitting a variety of messages over many different channels is reinforced by the variation in source credibility by hazard and audience segment (Mileti & Peek, 2001; Perry & Nigg, 1985; Sorensen, 2000). Such a strategy not only increases the likelihood that members of the target population will be exposed directly to the official messages, but it also sets the topic on the "public agenda" and increases the likelihood that this information will be transmitted through informal social networks.

Task 2: Use a Variety of Channels to Disseminate Hazard Information

Information channels differ significantly with respect to the types of information most suited to them, and messages tend to be channel-bound. Radio, face-to-face conversations, and oral presentations are limited to verbal information, whereas television, print media, computer simulations, slide shows, and films can convey numeric and graphic information as well as verbal information. The fact that messages disseminated through different media inherently have different characteristics implies that different channels could be selected to contribute to different stages of information processing. For example, radio or television spots might have their greatest impact in establishing initial hazard awareness (i.e., attracting attention to the problem) and maintaining its intrusiveness by means of frequent thought and discussion. By contrast, printed materials are most effective in providing the detailed information needed to establish a perception of threat and identifying suitable hazard adjustments. This function follows from their ability to be retained and reread to enhance comprehension and memory for important information such as definitions and checklists. The importance of written information has been underscored by research on floods (Perry et al., 1981) and earthquakes (Mileti & Fitzpatrick, 1993; Mileti et al., 1992).

Still other channels include public meetings and interactive (listener or viewer call-in) broadcast programs, which provide opportunities for two-way communication that are effective for answering unresolved questions but have the disadvantage that such communication is oral and thus less readily retained. The advantage of interactive channels is that their use is likely to enhance the receiver's personalization of the message, but large public meetings are especially likely to elicit theatrical demonstrations of outrage rather than sincere questions. Thus, when agency policies or particular circumstances require large public meetings, Hance and colleagues (1988) advocate considering the use of neutral moderators such as the League of Women Voters, structuring agendas so that public comment can be made before the end of the meeting (by which time most people have left), and breaking the meeting up into smaller working groups with specific topics to address. Hance and her colleagues also encourage environmental hazard managers to identify all of the interest groups that are likely to become involved and to have informal meetings with them early in the process, but to be sure to provide equal information access to all of them.

In addition to the channel boundedness of certain types of information (verbal, numeric, and graphic), environmental hazard managers should recognize that channel access is unevenly distributed in communities and can be compounded by variations in ethnicity and income. That is, people can vary in their access to different information channels because of individual preferences or because of limits imposed by the absence of resources (e.g., funds to purchase a computer with Internet access) or personal skills (e.g., a lack of English facility eliminates many mass media sources). Typically, variation in resources and personal skills do not eliminate channel access altogether but, instead, concentrate it on a narrower range of channels (for example, some segments of the population might use only Chinese language radio, television, and newspapers).

Simple individual preferences also restrict the access that each channel provides to different community groups, so cross-channel linkages might be required. In this way, a radio listener who is interested in an initial message can be directed to another channel, such as a neighborhood meeting or library reference section, for more detailed information. Studies of ethnicity and channel preference, although limited in number, indicate that patterns of preference can be identified (Nelson & Perry, 1991; Perry & Nelson, 1991). Thus, Whites tend to prefer that environmental hazard information be communicated via print media such as brochures and newspaper articles rather than via oral media such as speakers at organizations, neighborhood meetings, and local television. By contrast, Mexican Americans tend to express a preference for information sent via oral media such as local radio, local television, and neighborhood meetings rather than print media such as newspapers and brochures. However, they also tend to give low ratings to speakers at organizational meetings. The preferences of African Americans are more difficult to summarize, but they tend to prefer local radio, newspapers, and brochures to speakers at organizations, neighborhood meetings, and television. As was the case with credibility attributions, channel preferences for some of the ethnic groups have also been found to vary from one community to another.

These data reflect the same scientific and practical limitations as data on source credibility variations. That is, only a small number of ethnic groups have been studied, yet there is clearly variation within ethnic groups in their channel preference. Given these limitations, the appropriate strategy for disseminating hazard-relevant information is to use a range of channels that is as wide as is feasible, given the available information about different groups' channel access and preferences. This simple approach solves the problem of variation in channel preference by casting a wide net over the available channels. If enough channels are used, environmental hazard managers are likely to reach all members of a community that has even the most varied pattern of channel preferences.

To maximize channel diversity within realistic resource limitations, environmental hazard managers can draw on existing research for two important pieces of guidance. First, it is known that radio, newspapers, and direct mail brochures are channels that are reasonably popular with at least the three ethnic groups for whom adequate data are available. Newspapers and brochures are particularly useful since they provide a written record of hazard adjustment information that can be retained and retrieved at a later date.

Existing data emphasize that neighborhood meetings are preferred by at least one ethnic group and probably by others, such as recent immigrant groups. A problem with existing data on channel preferences is that the range of socioeconomic groups studied is limited. Thus, the conclusion that few individuals choose speakers at associations and organizations might be reflecting only lower and moderate income groups. Among higher income groups, it is known that association memberships (fraternal organizations, professional groups, community leadership programs, etc.) are frequently sought out for a variety of reasons, including professional and personal contacts. Thus, community outreach programs can provide access to these groups as well.

Task 3: Describe Community or Facility Hazard Adjustments Being Planned or Implemented

In many communities, there are environmental hazard management actions being planned or implemented by local government agencies or, in the case of some technological hazards, by hazardous facility operators. Local residents should be informed of any hazard mitigation actions being taken to reduce the probability of an incident so they will understand that their risk is being reduced. Of course, it is unlikely that all of them will believe that these measures will be wholly effective in protecting them and, indeed, environmental hazard managers should acknowledge that there is no mitigation action that can guarantee complete safety. That is, land use and building construction practices can reduce, but not eliminate, the threat of natural hazards. The same can be said about the use of land use practices and engineered safety features in connection with technological hazards. In addition, environmental hazard managers should describe any emergency preparedness actions being taken to facilitate an active response to an incident and any recovery preparedness actions to support a rapid restoration of the community to normal patterns of social and economic functioning after an incident occurs. A major objective of such descriptions is to assure local residents that the authorities are taking responsibility for taking action to reduce the risk to local residents and also to facilitate action by local residents to protect themselves.

Task 4: Describe Feasible Household Hazard Adjustments

Even when hazard mitigation actions have been implemented to reduce the likelihood of incidents ranging from floods to accidental chemical releases, some local residents will not be satisfied that these actions will provide an adequate level of safety. In such cases, environmental hazard managers should inform risk area residents of hazard adjustments that they could take to protect themselves. For example, households can mitigate flood risk by adopting a variety of floodproofing measures (Federal Emergency Management Agency, 1986), prepare for airborne releases of toxic chemicals by reducing air infiltration in their homes (Lindell & Perry, 1992), or drink bottled or boiled water in the event of groundwater contamination of local wells.

In some cases, the most cost-effective (and, sometimes, the only available) hazard adjustments are those taken by households. For example, earthquakes cannot be prevented (as engineered safety features can prevent chemical releases) or controlled (as levees can control floods). Consequently, the most effective methods for reducing earthquake casualties and damage is by household hazard adjustments, such as bolting heavy items with a high center of gravity (e.g., refrigerators, water heaters) to the walls. In such cases, environmental hazard managers should promote the adoption of the most feasible hazard adjustments by beginning with the ones that are most effective, most generally useful, and lowest in resource requirements. In particular, there will be a multiple use dimension or "generic" utility to a given mitigation or preparedness measure when it provides protection against multiple hazards; for example, storing extra medications and devising a family evacuation plan are measures that can be used in connection with hurricanes, volcanic eruptions, hazardous materials incidents (including nuclear power plant accidents), floods, and wildland fires. As noted previously, this approach is supported by research showing that people who believe that a given hazard adjustment has multiple uses are more likely to adopt it (Lindell & Prater, 2002; Russell et al., 1995).

Task 5: Evaluate Program Effectiveness

It is important to evaluate the effectiveness of any risk communication program by measuring the degree to which it has achieved its objectives (Stallen, 1991). An evaluation of program effectiveness is the logical complement to the goal-setting activity undertaken in the strategic analysis. Thus, environmental hazard managers should determine how to measure the goals that they have set, how to collect the data needed, and how to determine if the data indicate that the goals have been achieved. This comparison process can then serve as the basis for determining whether changes need to be made in the risk communication program.

As we have indicated numerous times throughout this volume, a primary goal of environmental risk communication should be to promote household adoption of hazard adjustments. Thus, the first step in the program evaluation will usually be to identify the hazard adjustments whose adoption the program is seeking to increase. The remaining steps will depend on the resources available. If resources are limited, the evaluation will probably be limited only to assessing the adoption of hazard adjustments and will be able to collect a limited amount of data—for example, distributing checklists of hazard adjustments at meetings of neighborhood associations and civic organizations and asking respondents to indicate which ones they have adopted. More sophisticated designs would also assess people's perceptions of the attributes of these hazard adjustments and their perceptions of the hazards to which they are vulnerable. Such assessment would identify impediments to hazard adjustment adoption, as well as information source perceptions, channel access, and channel preference. In addition, more sophisticated designs would collect data from a random sample of the population rather than the biased samples that result from systematic differences in meeting attendees, nonattending members, and nonmembers of these organizations. Of course, the best evaluation designs will use pretest-posttest or treatment-control group designs (Cook et al., 1991). Such evaluations are possible, even for environmental hazard managers who are not trained in program evaluation, if a professor in a nearby college or university is willing to conduct the evaluation as part of a class project.

❖ RISK COMMUNICATION DURING AN ESCALATING CRISIS OR EMERGENCY RESPONSE

It is important to recognize that there is a difference between a state of chronic hazard and an escalating crisis, but the time at which the transition takes place is rarely well defined. It helps to consider the definition of an *escalating crisis*—a situation in which there is a significantly increased probability of an incident occurring that will threaten the public's health, safety, and/or property. Unfortunately, the problem is that the probability of occurrence is never completely objective and so the determination of whether a crisis exists will also be subjective rather than objective. As a practical matter, a crisis exists if authorities (including technological facility operators), *or* the news media, *or* a significant proportion of those in the community believe that there is an increased risk. Asserting that a crisis exists if any of these groups defines the situation as such follows from the basic principle that "perception is reality." If the news media or local residents believe that there is a crisis, then there is a crisis unless authorities can convince them otherwise. This might make it seem as if any abnormal situation will inevitably become an escalating crisis, but such is not necessarily the case. The crucial point is that authorities must be prepared to explain specifically why a situation is or is not a crisis.

Classifying the Situation

Authorities can exert some control over the definition of the situation by establishing specific criteria in advance of an incident that systematically define elevated conditions of threat. For example, the National Weather Service has established an emergency classification system that consists of watches and warnings, whereas the U.S. Nuclear Regulatory Commission (1980) classifies an incident as an Unusual Event, an Alert, a Site Area Emergency, or a General Emergency. The number of categories in the emergency classification system should correspond to meaningful differences in the levels of response by local authorities (and facility personnel, in the case of technological facilities), but the number of categories is less important than the fact that the emergency classification system has been established in advance, is defined as objectively as possible, and is agreed to by all responding

Table 5.4 Specific Tasks for the Escalating Crisis and Emergency Response Phases

Activate the crisis communication team promptly
Determine the appropriate time to release sensitive information
Select the communication channels that are appropriate to the situation
Maintain source credibility with the news media and the public
Provide timely and accurate information to the news media and the public
Evaluate performance through post-incident critiques

organizations (Lindell & Perry, 1992). By establishing a set of objective indicators of environmental or plant conditions that are linked to specific response actions, authorities commit themselves in advance to taking those actions under those conditions—a situation that indicates that decisions are being made on the basis of rational scientific considerations, not the exigencies of the moment.

Program Implementation During an Escalating Crisis or Emergency Response

Once authorities have determined that environmental conditions have exceeded the criteria listed in the emergency classification system, they need to implement the predetermined response actions. Many of these actions will include further emergency assessment, expedient hazard mitigation, population protection, and incident management (Tierney et al., 2001). One of the most important incident management actions is risk communication, and this will consist of the six tasks listed in Table 5.4, each of which is described in more detail below.

Task 1: Activate the Crisis Communication Team Promptly

When any of the criteria in the emergency classification system have been exceeded, the crisis communication team should be activated promptly and should prepare to disseminate information even if it does not need to release that information immediately. Members of the team should contact all appropriate authorities and open all necessary communication links to ensure that all sources of information and expertise are brought to bear on the situation. In particular, the crisis communication team should ensure that the spokespeople of all relevant government agencies, nongovernmental organizations, and technological facilities coordinate their contacts with the news media and community organizations. This does not mean that all responding organizations must agree on all press releases or all statements before community organizations, although it is preferable that this be the case. However, it is essential that all organizations be aware of the information that is being disseminated by other organizations. This will provide them with an opportunity to identify any disagreement and prepare appropriate explanations before they are contacted by the news media.

Environmental hazard managers should review the information in press kits and any background materials they have prepared for briefing the news media in press conferences or community groups in public hearings. They should also contact personnel in their agencies who are peripherally related to the crisis (e.g., plant workers and clerical support staff) to brief them about the situation. Such personnel might have incomplete or outdated information about the situation, but they may be interviewed by reporters as they leave their workplaces. In addition, such agency personnel (or others) are likely to pass important information on to their families who might, in turn, pass the information on to their friends and neighbors. Not only is the information likely to be widely disseminated before authorities realize it, but it might be distorted into a form that is very difficult to correct.

During the initial stages of an escalating crisis or emergency response, environmental hazard managers should take care to review their communication objectives (Churchill, 1997). These objectives should become the criteria according to which all later press releases, press conferences, and public meetings should be evaluated. In most environmental emergencies, the principal objectives will be to promote appropriate protective action by those whom the authorities believe to be in the most immediate danger and also to promote active monitoring of the situation by those who might later be determined to be at risk. An objective should not be to prevent "panic," which disaster researchers have found to be extremely rare (Drabek, 1986; Lindell & Perry, 1992). Nor should authorities ridicule what they consider to be unnecessary protective action by those who *think* they are at risk, as long as such actions do not impede the protection of those whom the authorities believe *are* at risk. It is especially important for authorities to avoid attempting to promote one protective action by criticizing another. For example, some misguided attempts have been made to promote sheltering in-place by asserting that people are exposing themselves to major traffic accident risks if they evacuate. Not only is this incorrect (the accident risks in evacuation appear to be no greater than those of normal driving; Lindell & Perry, 1992), but it is likely to lead those at risk to believe that there is nothing they can do to protect themselves.

Task 2: Determine the Appropriate Time to Release Sensitive Information

When environmental hazard managers, but not others, can detect the subtle environmental cues that indicate the onset of an emergency, they must determine when to alert others of the danger. In the case of volcanic eruptions, this might be indicated by increases in the number of earthquakes or the amount of gases released. In the case of a nuclear power plant accident, this might be indicated by the failure of critical plant safety systems. Thus, the crisis communication team needs to be guided by procedures that define when information is to be released. There are no universal rules for determining when to release information because even experts disagree (Kasperson, 1987). On the one hand, early releases of information often are characterized by a significant degree of uncertainty, so there is a possibility that crisis conditions might never materialize or that they will be less severe than initially expected. Consequently, authorities frequently withhold information in order to avoid unnecessary disruption. The disadvantage of delaying the release of information is that this can be misinterpreted as a "cover-up" if the data are leaked (Hance et al., 1988) and, as noted earlier, there are many ways in which such leaks can occur. It also is important to respond appropriately to reporters' questions when they become aware that something important is happening. Statements of "no comment" are almost certain to be interpreted as meaning that authorities have important information that is being withheld.

By contrast, an early release of information tends to enhance the credibility of the information source and to increase a source's control over the agenda. In particular, being the first to break bad news provides an opportunity to put the information into an appropriate context. In addition, controlling the timing of a press release can have a significant impact on the amount of attention it receives. A press release distributed on a slow news day might receive substantially more coverage in the news media than the same information released on a busy day or on a Friday afternoon.

Task 3: Select the Communication Channels That Are Appropriate to the Situation

One of the most significant differences between a continuing hazard and an escalating crisis is that the latter is "newsworthy," so environmental hazard managers will generally have little difficulty in obtaining the news media coverage they sought, usually unsuccessfully, during the continuing hazard phase. As always, news media coverage needs to be monitored to ensure that reporters are accurately disseminating the information released by environmental hazard managers, yet this procedure alone cannot ensure that those at risk are receiving, heeding, and comprehending the information they need. Thus, environmental hazard managers need to promote dialogue through two-way communication, preferably in small groups rather than massive public hearings. This will help them to understand public risk perceptions and explain risks more effectively (Hance et al., 1988).

Even though an escalating crisis or an emergency response will prompt the news media to seek information, environmental hazard managers should not rely only on reporters' requests for interviews to determine when and what information to disseminate. Instead, they should initiate communication with reporters through press releases and press conferences. Typically, press releases afford the most control over the agenda, whereas interviews provide the least control. Despite the lack of control over the questions being asked, interviews are sometimes preferable to press conferences, because the latter can present a rather chaotic image when a spokesperson attempts unsuccessfully to respond to reporters fiercely competing with each other for the right to ask the next question. Thus, an interview's advantages of a quiet setting can more than offset its loss of control over the agenda under discussion (Fink, 1986). Whatever the method of communicating through the news media to the public, environmental hazard managers should take the initiative in defining the time and content of their messages.

Task 4: Maintain Source Credibility With the News Media and the Public

During an escalating crisis or emergency response, environmental hazard managers should obtain timely and accurate data from within their own and other agencies and make their recommended actions consistent with the analyses. If the available data are incomplete, they should be honest about what is and is not known. A candid confession of ignorance might be uncomfortable at the time, but it is less potentially dangerous to the environmental hazard manager's credibility than making up an answer that is later found out to be incorrect.

A related principle is that environmental hazard managers should recognize that the news media have many sources of information other than authorities. Consequently, it is important for environmental hazard managers to respond to reporters when they need information for an imminent deadline, because reporters will obtain the best information they can from whatever sources are available at the time that they need to file their stories (Churchill, 1997). In addition, it is important to recognize that there is a significant amount of competition among media organizations, so environmental hazard managers must take care to ensure that they do not inadvertently handicap those stations and newspapers who provide responsible and ethical coverage of the situation. Thus, it is important to disseminate the available information to representatives of all news media simultaneously. This avoids the appearance of favoritism that can arise from exclusive interviews and also ensures that information is disseminated as widely as possible as soon as possible.

Accordingly, it is often better to explain that data has been or is being collected, describe how it is being or will be analyzed, and indicate the date on which the results of the analyses will be released. Hance and colleagues (1988) have noted that agencies should present some management options when the data reveal environmental problems, but practitioners differ in their beliefs about the balance between analyzing these options thoroughly and presenting tentative options that provide a starting point for input from the community. The advantage of thorough analysis is that it can provide local residents with definitive data about any residual risks (i.e., the risks remaining after mitigation, preparedness, or response actions have been implemented) and well-defined solutions that have been endorsed by all relevant authorities. By contrast, the advantage of presenting tentative options is that the process remains open to input regarding the methods of analysis, the alternative management strategies considered, and the appropriate values to be considered in evaluating these alternatives. Thus, decisions about which of these courses to pursue must depend on the willingness and ability of all stakeholders to accept ambiguity and participate in a (possibly) protracted process of identifying and selecting an appropriate management strategy.

Trust is a major issue in risk communication because there tends to be so little of it to begin with and what there is can be lost so easily. As Kasperson (1987) noted, trust in institutions has been decreasing for some time and television anchors tend to be among the few people other than independent scientists who are generally trusted. Television anchors are trusted because they are familiar, authoritative, and have developed a track record of accuracy over time. Some public safety and health authorities have also become trusted for similar reasons, but this is less common. Frequently, those who must communicate information about environmental risks are stereotyped as representatives of their organizations, and unless the stereotype is positive at the outset, it can be difficult to build trust during a crisis. This is the reason why it is so important for environmental hazard managers to forestall public stereotypes about their agencies, and thus themselves, by working with community groups on multiple environmental issues before crises arise and publicizing the accomplishments of their agencies in handling these problems. As was the case during the continuing hazard phase, agencies can acquire trust by working during an escalating crisis or emergency response with other agencies that have already gained the public's trust. In addition, it is also important to recognize that "the public" is not a monolithic entity, so some experts emphasize the need for explicitly addressing the concerns of different population segments.

Consequently, environmental hazard managers should listen to what other participants (including activist groups) say, promise only what they can deliver, and follow up on the promises they have made (Hance et al., 1988). It also is important to recognize the role that opinion leaders play in influencing the opinions of others (e.g., Covello, 1987). This is consistent with the findings of previous chapters that integration into kin and community networks influences all stages of the protective action decision process from information receipt to hazard adjustment adoption.

Task 5: Provide Timely and Accurate Information About the Hazard to the News Media and the Public

According to Churchill (1997), news releases should be no longer than 2 pages and should consist of simple short sentences in plain English and in other languages as required to serve the population at risk. They should contain a dateline (date and location of release), the organizational source (including point of contact) for the information, a summary lead that provides a one sentence abstract of the press release, the text of the press release, and a brief description of any attachments. These should be supplemented by fact sheets, which contain the basic background information that is appropriate to any incident. For a case such as increased volcanic activity than might result in an eruption, the news release would indicate the agency that was issuing the press release, the spokesperson to contact for further information, a summary lead indicating the nature of the incident (e.g., "U.S. Geological Survey officials announce increased threat of eruption at Mt. St. Helens"), and text that addresses the *who, what, when, where,* and *why* of that incident. There should be attachments, including information such as a biographical summary about the spokesperson; photographs of the mountain, the detection equipment, or the Emergency Operations Center; and fact sheets about volcanic processes, procedures for assessing eruption risks, and emergency response plans—especially warning and evacuation plans.

In deciding how to present the material, it is important to assess the audience's level of technical sophistication so that the presentation can be made neither too technical for people to understand nor so simplistic that the audience is insulted. In general, it is important to presume that the average member of the audience is intelligent but uninformed about environmental risks. Thus, environmental hazard managers should avoid acronyms and use ordinary English words rather than technical jargon to explain basic concepts. Nonetheless, environmental hazard managers should expect that some members of the audience will be trained in relevant scientific disciplines, so they should be prepared to respond to individual audience members during question-and-answer sessions after the formal presentation and to distribute more technically advanced materials on request.

Environmental hazard managers should anticipate the possibility of confrontational tactics of the news media or some members of the public. If they are confronted with differing interpretations from other experts, they should be prepared to calmly reiterate their own scientific qualifications and support their own position on the dispute and explain what they believe are the weaknesses in alternative positions. However, they should not engage in ad hominem attacks on others because this will just destroy their own credibility. If they find that a community does not accept a risk, environmental hazard managers should not conclude that people don't understand the risk. Instead, the community might reasonably believe that the benefits of preparing for it simply do not justify the costs that they must incur in doing so.

In connection with benefits, Hance and colleagues (1988) caution about explicitly addressing jobs provided as a benefit that offsets the risk, and they recommend that environmental hazard managers be prepared to address the issue of monetary or other forms of compensation but leave it to the community to raise if they so choose. However, environmental hazard managers should be prepared to discuss ways that a community can monitor and control the risk.

Environmental hazard managers should be prepared to describe the process by which risks were assessed (including ways in which cautious estimates were used in different steps of the analysis), and what the risks are (in terms of quantities released, ambient concentrations, individual exposures via different pathways, probabilities of adverse effects, and expected levels of impact over different time periods). Environmental hazard managers also should be prepared to acknowledge the uncertainties in the data and even be ready to state that they don't know the answer to a question when this is the case. However, they also should be prepared to state what will be done to obtain an answer to the question.

Task 6: Evaluate Performance Through Post-Incident Critiques

To improve their performance, organizations must learn from their experience. Thus, each incident in which environmental hazard managers must disseminate risk information to the news media or the public should be followed by a thorough critique of the performance (Lindell & Perry, 1992; National Response Team, 1987). All members of the crisis communication team should review the goals of the risk communication program, the event logs kept during the incident, and other available documentation to identify deficiencies in organizational performance. Experience in drills, exercises, and incidents has demonstrated the importance of focusing on the performance of the organization rather than the performance of individuals because this enhances a spirit of cooperation. Thus, each participant should be encouraged to follow up on any deficiencies by identifying the ways in which these can be corrected by improvements in plans, procedures, training, facilities, equipment, or materials and supplies.

References

Aguirre, B. (1991). Evacuation in Cancun during Hurricane Gilbert. *International Journal of Mass Emergencies and Disasters, 9,* 31-45.

Aguirre, B., Anderson, W. A., Balandran, S., Peters, B., & White, H. (1991). *Sarasota, Texas, tornado May 22, 1987.* Washington, DC: National Academy Press.

Ajzen, I. (1987). Attitudes, traits and actions. In L. Berkowitz (Ed.), *Advances in experimental social psychology* (pp. 459-473). New York: Academic Press.

Ajzen, I. (1991). The theory of planned behavior. *Organizational Behavior and Human Decision Processes, 50,* 179-211.

Allbaugh, J. (2002). The new direction of FEMA. *The Natural Hazards Observer, 26,* 1-4.

Alvirez, S., & Bean, T. (1976). Participation of Blacks, Puerto Ricans and Whites in voluntary associations. *Social Forces, 556,* 1053-1071.

Anderson, W. A. (1969). Disaster warning and communication in two communities. *Journal of Communication, 19,* 92-104.

Angel, R., & Tienda, M. (1982). Determinants of extended household structure: Cultural pattern or economic need? *American Journal of Sociology, 87,* 1360-1383.

Asch, S. (1951). Effects of group pressure upon the modification and distortion of judgments. In H. Guetzkow (Ed.), *Groups, leadership and men* (pp. 177-190). Pittsburgh, PA: Carnegie Press.

Ashford, N. A., Gobbell, J. V., Lachman, J., Matthiesen, M., Minzner, A., & Stone, R. (1993). *The encouragement of technological change for preventing chemical accidents: Moving firms from secondary prevention and mitigation to primary prevention.* Cambridge: Massachusetts Institute of Technology Center for Technology, Policy and Industrial Development.

Babchuk, N., & Ballweg, J. (1971). Primary extended kin relations of Negro couples. *Sociological Quarterly, 2,* 69-77.

Baker, E. J. (1979). Predicting response to hurricane warnings. *Mass Emergencies, 4,* 9-24.

Baker, E. J. (1980). Coping with hurricane evacuation difficulties. In E. J. Baker (Ed.), *Hurricanes and coastal storms: Awareness, evacuation and mitigation* (pp. 23-30). Tallahassee: Florida State University.

Baker, E. J. (1991). Hurricane evacuation behavior. *International Journal of Mass Emergencies and Disasters, 9,* 287-310.

Baker, E. J. (1993). Empirical studies of public response to tornado and hurricane warnings in the United States (pp. 65-74). In J. Nemec, J. Nigg, & F. Siccardi (Eds.), *Prediction and perception of natural hazards.* London: Kluwer Academic.

Baker, E. J., & Patton, D. (1974). Attitudes toward hurricane hazards on the Gulf Coast. In G. White (Ed.), *Natural hazards* (pp. 30-38). Oxford, UK: Oxford University Press.

Bandura, A. (1977). *Social learning theory.* Englewood Cliffs, NJ: Prentice Hall.

Barton, A. (1969). *Communities in disaster.* New York: Doubleday.

Bates, F., Fogelman, C., Parenton, V., Pittman, R., & Tracy, G. (1963). *The social and psychological consequences of natural disaster.* Washington, DC: National Academy of Sciences-National Research Council.

Bauman, D. (1983). Determination of the cost effectiveness of flood hazard information programs. *Papers and Proceedings of Applied Geography Conferences, 6,* 292-305.

Bay Area Regional Earthquake Preparedness Project. (1990). *Putting the pieces together.* Oakland, CA: Bay Area Regional Earthquake Preparedness Project.

Beach, L. R. (1990). *Image theory: Decision making in personal and organizational contexts.* New York: John Wiley.

Beach, L. R., & Mitchell, T. R. (1978). A contingency model for the selection of decision strategies. *Academy of Management Review, 3,* 439-449.

Bennett, R. (1973). Living conditions and everyday needs of the elderly with particular reference to social isolation. *International Journal of Aging and Human Development, 4,* 179-198.

Bernert, E. H., & Ikle, F. (1952). Evacuation and cohesion of urban groups. *American Journal of Sociology, 58,* 133-138.

Bianchi, S., & Farley, R. (1979). Racial differences in family living arrangements and economic well-being. *Journal of Marriage and the Family, 41,* 537-551.

Birkland, T. A. (1997). *After disaster: Agenda setting, public policy and focusing events.* Washington, DC: Georgetown University Press.

Blaikie, P., Cannon, T., Davis, I., & Wisner, B. (1994). *At risk: Natural hazards, people's vulnerability, and disasters.* London: Routledge.

Blalock, H. (1969). *Theory construction.* Englewood Cliffs, NJ: Prentice Hall.

Blalock, H. (1982). *Conceptualization and measurement in the social sciences.* Beverly Hills, CA: Sage.

Blanchard-Boehm, R. D. (1998). Understanding public response to increased risk from natural hazards. *International Journal of Mass Emergencies and Disasters, 16,* 247-278.

Blong, R. J. (1984). *Volcanic hazards: A sourcebook on the effects of eruptions.* New York: Academic Press.

Bolin, R. (1976). Family recovery from natural disaster. *Mass Emergencies, 1,* 267-277.

Bolin, R., & Bolton, P. (1986). *Race, religion and ethnicity in disaster recovery.* Boulder: University of Colorado Institute of Behavioral Science.

Bolin, R., & Klenow, D. (1983). Older people in disaster. *Journal of Aging, 26,* 29-45.

Bond, M. (1999). Unity in diversity. In J. Adamopoulos & Y. Kashima (Eds.), *Social psychology and cultural context* (pp. 17-44). Thousand Oaks, CA: Sage.

Bonilla-Silva, E. (1999). The new racism. In P. Wong (Ed.), *Race, ethnicity and nationality in the United States* (pp. 55-101). Boulder, CO: Westview.

Boswell, T., & Curtis, J. (1984). *The Cuban-American experience.* Totowa, NJ: Rowman & Allenheld.

Bourque, L. B., Reeder, L., Cherlin, A., Raven, B., & Walton, D. (1973). *The unpredictable disaster in a metropolis.* Los Angeles: Survey Research Center, University of California, Los Angeles.

Brehm, J., & Cohen, A. (1962). *Explorations in cognitive dissonance.* New York: John Wiley.

Brinkmann, W. (1975). *Hurricane hazard in the United States.* Boulder: University of Colorado Institute of Behavioral Science.

Britton, N., Kearney, G., & Britton, K. (1983). Disaster response. In J. Oliver (Ed.), *Insurance and natural disaster management* (pp. 260-332). Townsville, Queensland, Australia: James Cook University of North Queensland.

Brodbeck, M. (1968). Models, meaning, and theories. In M. Brodbeck (Ed.), *Readings in the philosophy of the social sciences* (pp. 579-600). New York: Macmillan.

Brunacini, A. V. (1985). *Fire command.* Quincy, MA: National Fire Protection Association.

Bullard, R. (1994). *Dumping in Dixie.* Boulder, CO: Westview.

Bunge, M. (1998). *Social science under debate.* Toronto: University of Toronto Press.

Burger, J. M., & Palmer, M. (1992). Changes in and generalization of unrealistic optimism following experiences with stressful events: Reactions to the 1989 California earthquake. *Personality and Social Psychology Bulletin, 18,* 39-43.

Burkhart, F. (1991). *Media, emergency warnings and citizen response.* Boulder, CO: Westview.

Burton, I. (1972). Cultural and personality variables in the perception of natural hazards. In J. Wohlwill & D. Carson (Eds.), *Environment and the social sciences* (pp. 101-120). Washington, DC: American Psychological Association.

Burton, I., & Kates, R. (1964). The perception of natural hazards in resource management. *Natural Resources Journal, 3,* 412-441.

Burton, I., Kates, R., & White, G. (1978). *The environment as hazard.* Oxford, UK: Oxford University Press.

Burton, I., Kates, R., & White, G. (1993). *The environment as hazard* (2nd ed.). New York: Guilford.

Burton, I., Kliman, M., Powell, D., Schmidt, L., Timmerman, P., Victor, P., Whyte, A., & Wojick, J. (1981). *The Mississauga evacuation: Final report to the Ontario Ministry of the Solicitor General.* Toronto: University of Toronto Institute for Environmental Studies.

Canon, L. (1964). Self confidence and selective exposure to information. In L. Festinger (Ed.), *Conflict, decision and dissonance* (pp. 83-96). Stanford, CA: Stanford University Press.

Capek, S. M. (1993). The environmental justice frame. *Social Problems, 40,* 5-24.

Carter, M., Clark, J., Leik, R., & Fine, G. (1977). *Social factors affecting the dissemination of and response to warnings.* Paper presented at the 11th Technical Conference on Hurricanes and Tropical Meteorology, Miami Beach, FL.

Center for Natural Phenomena Engineering. (1994). *Earthquake risk reduction in the United States.* Oak Ridge, TN: Oak Ridge National Laboratories.

Chaiken, S. (1980). Heuristic versus systematic information processing and the use of source versus message cues in persuasion. *Journal of Personality and Social Psychology, 39,* 752-766.

Chaiken, S. (1987). The heuristic model of persuasion. In M. Zanna, J. Olson, & C. Herman (Eds.), *The Ontario symposium* (pp. 3-39). Hillsdale, NJ: Lawrence Erlbaum.

Chaiken, S., Liberman, A., & Eagly, A. (1989). Heuristic and systematic information processing within and beyond the persuasion context. In J. Uleman & J. Bargh (Eds.), *Thought, motivation and action* (pp. 81-101). New York: Guilford.

Chapman, L., & Chapman, J. (1969). Illusory correlation as an obstacle to the use of valid psychodiagnostic signs. *Journal of Abnormal Psychology, 74,* 271-280.

Chavis, D. M., & Wandersman, A. (1990). Sense of community in the urban environment: A catalyst for participation and community development. *American Journal of Community Psychology, 18,* 55-82.

Christensen, L., & Ruch, C. (1978). Assessment of brochures and radio and television presentations on hurricane awareness. *Mass Emergencies, 3,* 209-216.

Churchill E. R. (1997). Effective media relations. In E. K. Noji (Ed.), *The public health consequences of disasters* (pp. 122-132). London: Kluwer Academic.

Clifford, R. (1958). *The Rio Grande flood.* Washington, DC: National Academy of Sciences-National Research Council.

Cohen, B. L., & Lee, I. (1979). A catalog of risks. *Health Physics, 36,* 707-722.

Cohen, S., & Kapsis, R. (1978). Participation of Blacks, Puerto Ricans, and Whites in voluntary associations. *Social Forces, 56,* 1053-1071.

Committee on Preparedness, Awareness and Public Education. (1993). *Preparedness, awareness and public education.* Memphis, TN: National Science Foundation Central United States Earthquake Consortium.

Committee on Risk Perception and Communication. (1989). *Improving risk communication.* Washington, DC: National Research Council, National Academy of Sciences.

Committee on Socio-Economic Effects of Earthquake Prediction. (1978). *A program of studies on the socio-economic effects of earthquake predictions.* Washington, DC: National Research Council, National Academy of Sciences.

Cook, T., Campbell, D., & Peracchio, L. (1991). Quasi experimentation. In M. Dunnette & L. Hough (Eds.), *Handbook of industrial and organizational psychology* (pp. 491-576). Palo Alto, CA: Consulting Psychologists.

Cottrell, F. (1974). *Aging and the aged.* Dubuque, IA: William C Brown.

Covello, V. T. (1987). Case studies of risk communication: Introduction. In J. C. Davies, V. T. Covello, & F. W. Allen (Eds.), *Risk communication* (pp. 63-65). Washington, DC: The Conservation Foundation.

Covello, V. T. (1991). Risk comparisons and risk communication: Issues and problems in comparing health and environmental risks. In R. E. Kasperson & P. J. M. Stallen (Eds.), *Communicating risks to the public: International perspectives* (pp. 79-124). London: Kluwer Academic.

Covello, V. T., & Allen, F. W. (1988). *Seven cardinal rules for risk communication.* Washington, DC: U.S. Environmental Protection Agency.

Covello, V. T., McCallum, D. B., & Pavlova, M. T. (1989). *Effective risk communication.* New York: Plenum.

Cross, J. A. (1980). Residents' concerns about hurricane hazard within the lower Florida Keys. In E. J. Baker (Ed.), *Hurricanes and coastal storms* (pp. 61-66). Tallahassee: Florida State University.

Crouch, E., & Wilson, R. (1982). *Risk/benefit analysis.* Cambridge MA: Ballinger.

Crowfoot, J. E., & Wondolleck, J. (1990). Citizen organizations and environmental conflict. In J. E. Crowfoot & J. Wondolleck (Eds.), *Environmental disputes* (pp. 301-330). Washington, DC: Island.

Cutter, S., & Barnes, K. (1982). Evacuation behavior at Three Mile Island. *Disasters, 6,* 116-124.

Cyert, R., & March, J. (1963). *A behavioral theory of the firm.* Englewood Cliffs, NJ: Prentice Hall.

Daines, G. E. (1991). Planning, training, and exercising. In T. E. Drabek & G. J. Hoetmer (Eds.), *Emergency management: Principles and practice for local government* (pp. 161-200). Washington DC: International City Management Association.

Danzig, E., Thayer, P., & Galanter, L. (1958). *The effects of a threatening rumor on a disaster-stricken community.* Washington, DC: National Academy of Sciences.

Dash, N., Peacock, W. G., & Morrow, B. (1997). And the poor get poorer. In W.G. Peacock, B. Morrow, & H. Gladwin (Eds.), *Hurricane Andrew* (pp. 206-225). New York: Routledge.

Davenport, S., & Waterstone, P. (1979). *Hazard awareness guidebook.* Austin: Texas Coastal and Marine Council.

Davis, M. S. (1989). Living along the fault line. *Urban Resources, 5,* 8-14.

Dexter, J. R., Willeke, G. E., & James, L. D. (1979). Social aspects of flooding. In *Proceedings of the specialty conference on legal, institutional and social aspects of irrigation and drainage and water resources planning and management* (pp. 65-80). Blacksburg, VA: American Society of Civil Engineers.

Diggory, J. (1956). Some consequences of proximity to a disease threat. *Sociometry, 19,* 7-53.

Dooley, D., Catalano, R., Mishra, S., & Serxner, S. (1992). Earthquake preparedness: predictors in a community survey. *Journal of Applied Social Psychology, 22,* 451-470.

Douglas, D., Westley, B., & Chaffee, S. (1970). An information campaign that changed community attitudes. *Journalism Quarterly, 47,* 479-487.

Douglas, M., & Wildavsky, A. (1982). *Risk and culture.* Berkeley: University of California Press.

Dow, K. & Cutter, S. L. (2002). Emerging hurricane evacuation issues: Hurricane Floyd and South Carolina. *Natural Hazards Review, 3,* 12-18.

Drabek, T. E. (1968). *Disaster in aisle 13.* Columbus: The Ohio State University Disaster Research Center.

Drabek, T. E. (1969). Social processes in disaster. *Social Problems, 16,* 336-347.

Drabek, T. E. (1983). Shall we leave? *Emergency Management Review, 1,* 25-29.

Drabek, T. E. (1986). *Human system responses to disaster: An inventory of sociological findings.* New York: Springer-Verlag.

Drabek, T. E. (1987). *The professional emergency manager.* Boulder: University of Colorado Institute of Behavioral Science.

Drabek, T. E. (1990). *Emergency management: Strategies for maintaining organizational integrity.* New York: Springer-Verlag.

Drabek, T. E. (1996). *Disaster evacuation behavior: Tourists and other transients* (Monograph No. 58). Boulder: University of Colorado Institute of Behavioral Science Program on Environment and Behavior.

Drabek, T. E. (1999). Understanding disaster warning responses. *Social Science Journal, 36,* 515-523.

Drabek, T. E., & Boggs, K. (1968). Families in disaster: Reactions and relatives. *Journal of Marriage and the Family, 30,* 443-451.

Drabek, T. E., Key, W., Erickson, P., & Crowe, J. (1975). The impact of disaster on kin relationships. *Journal of Marriage and the Family, 37,* 481-494.

Drabek, T. E., & Stephenson, J. (1971). When disaster strikes. *Journal of Applied Social Psychology, 1,* 187-203.

Dutton, J. E., & Ashford, S. J. (1993). Selling issues to top management. *Academy of Management Review, 18,* 397-428.

Duval, T. S., & Mulilis, J. P. (1999). A person-relative-to-event approach to negative threat appeals and earthquake preparedness: A field study. *Journal of Applied Social Psychology, 29,* 495-516.

Dynes, R. R., & Quarantelli, E. L. (1976). The family and community context of individual reactions to disaster. In H. Parad, H. L. L. Resnik, & L. Parad (Eds.), *Emergency and disaster management* (pp. 231-244). Bowie, MD: The Charles Press.

Dynes, R. R., Quarantelli, E. L., & Kreps, G. (1972). *A perspective on disaster planning.* Columbus: The Ohio State University Disaster Research Center.

Dynes, R. R., & Wenger, D. (1971). Factors in community perception of water resources. *Water Resources Bulletin, 7,* 644-651.

Eagly, A. H., & Chaiken, S. (1993). *The psychology of attitudes.* Ft. Worth, TX: Harcourt, Brace.

Edwards, M. L. (1991). *Public response to the earthquake prediction.* Unpublished master's thesis, Department of Sociology, University of Delaware, Newark, DE.

Edwards, M. L. (1993). Social location and self-protective behavior. *International Journal of Mass Emergencies and Disasters, 11,* 293-304.

Edwards, W. (1954). The theory of decision making. *Psychological Bulletin, 41,* 380-417.

Eisner, R. K. (1990). Beyond planning: Learning from the Loma Prieta Earthquake. *U.C. Berkeley College of Environmental Design News, 8,* 6-9.

Endo, R., & Neilsen, J. (1979). Social responses to natural hazard predictions. *Western Sociological Review, 10,* 59-69.

Erikson, K. (1976). *Everything in its path.* New York: Simon & Schuster.

Escobedo, L.G., Chorba, T. L., & Remmington, P. L. (1992). The influence of safety belt laws on self-reported safety belt use in the United States. *Accident Analysis and Prevention, 24,* 643-653.

Expert Review Committee. (1987). *The National Earthquake Hazard Reduction Program.* Washington, DC: FEMA Office of Earthquakes and Natural Hazards.

Farley, J. E. (1998). *Earthquake fears, predictions and preparations in mid-America.* Carbondale: Southern Illinois University Press.

Farley, J. E., Barlow, H., Finkelstein, M., & Riley, L. (1991). *Earthquake hysteria.* Paper presented at the annual meeting of the Midwest Sociological Society, Des Moines, IA.

Farley, J. E., Barlow, H. D., Finkelstein, M., & Riley, L. (1993). Earthquake hysteria before and after: A survey and follow-up on public response to the Browning forecast. *International Journal of Mass Emergencies and Disasters, 11,* 305-322.

Faupel, C., Kelley, S., & Petee, T. (1992). The impact of disaster education on disaster preparedness for Hurricane Hugo. *International Journal of Mass Emergencies and Disasters, 10,* 5-24.

Fazio, R. (1985). How do attitudes guide behavior? In R. Sorrentino & E. Higgins (Eds.), *The handbook of motivation and cognition* (pp. 204-243). New York: Guilford.

Federal Emergency Management Agency. (1986). *Design manual for retrofitting flood-prone residential structures.* Washington, DC: Author.

Federal Emergency Management Agency. (1996). *Guide for all-hazard emergency operations planning.* Washington, DC: Author.

Federal Emergency Management Agency. (1997). *Multi-hazard identification and risk assessment.* Washington, DC: Author.

Federal Emergency Management Agency. (2003). *Federal response plan: Interim.* Washington, DC: Federal Emergency Management Agency.

Feldman, J. (1999). The social cognitive approach to culture and psychology. In J. Adamopoulos & Y. Kashima (Eds.), *Social psychology and cultural context* (pp. 43-62). Thousand Oaks, CA: Sage.

Feldman, J., & Lindell, M. K. (1990). On rationality. In I. Horowitz (Ed.), *Organization and decision theory* (pp. 88-113). Boston: Kluwer Academic.

Festinger, L. (1957). *A theory of cognitive dissonance.* Stanford, CA: Stanford University Press.

Festinger, L. (1964). *Conflict, decision and dissonance.* Stanford, CA: Stanford University Press.

Fink, S. (1986). *Crisis management: Planning for the inevitable.* New York: AMACOM.

Fishbein, M., & Ajzen, I. (1975). *Belief, attitude, intention and behavior.* Reading, MA: Addison-Wesley.

Fishbein, M., & Ajzen, I. (1981). Acceptance, yielding and impact. In R. Petty, T. Ostrom, & T. Brock (Eds.), *Cognitive responses in persuasion* (pp. 339-359). Hillsdale, NJ: Lawrence Erlbaum.

Fishbein, M., & Stasson, M. (1990). The role of desires, self-predictions, and perceived control in the prediction of training session attendance. *Journal of Applied Social Psychology, 20,* 173-198.

Fiske, S. T., & Taylor, S. E. (1991). *Social cognition* (2nd ed.). New York: McGraw-Hill.

Fitzpatrick, C., & Mileti, D. (1991). Motivating public evacuation. *International Journal of Mass Emergencies and Disasters, 9,* 137-152.

Florin, P., & Wandersman, A. (1990). An introduction to citizen participation, voluntary organizations, and community development: Insights for empowerment through research. *American Journal of Community Psychology, 18,* 41-54.

Flynn, C. B. (1979). *Three Mile Island telephone survey.* Washington, DC: Nuclear Regulatory Commission.

Flynn, C. B., & Chalmers, J. (1980). *The social and economic effects of the accident at Three Mile Island.* Tempe, AZ: Mountian West Research Corporation.

Flynn, J., Peters, E., Mertz, C. K, & Slovic, P. (1998). Risk, media, and stigma at Rocky flats. *Risk Analysis, 18,* 715-727.

Fowlkes, M., & Miller, P. (1987). Chemicals and community at Love Canal. In B. Johnson and V. Covello (Eds.), *The social and cultural construction of risk* (pp. 109-128). New York: Reidel.

Frey, D. (1986). Recent research on selective exposure to information. *Advances in Experimental Social Psychology, 19,* 41-80.

Friedman, M., & Savage, L. (1948). The utility analysis of choices involving risk. *Journal of Political Economy, 56,* 279-304.

Friedsam, H. J. (1962). Older persons in disaster. In G. Baker & D. Chapman (Eds.), *Man and society in disaster* (pp. 19-29). New York: Basic Books.

Fritz, C. E. (1961a). Disaster. In R. K. Merton & R. A. Nisbet (Eds.), *Contemporary social problems* (pp. 651-694). New York: Harcourt, Brace & World.

Fritz, C. E. (1961b). *Disaster and community therapy.* Washington, DC: National Research Council-National Academy of Sciences.

Fritz, C. E. (1968). Disasters. In L. Gardiner (Ed.), *International encyclopedia of the social sciences* (pp. 1120-1126). New York: The Free Press.

Fritz, C. E., & Marks, E. (1954). The NORC studies of human behavior in disaster. *Journal of Social Issues, 10,* 26-41.

Fritz, C. E., & Mathewson, J. (1957). *Convergence behavior in disasters.* Washington, DC: National Academy of Sciences-National Research Council.

Fritz, C. E., & Williams, H. B. (1957). The human being in disasters. *Annals of the American Academy of Political and Social Science, 309,* 42-51.

Garcia, E. M. (1989). Earthquake preparedness in California. *Urban Resources, 5,* 15-19.

Geertz, C. (1973). *The interpretation of culture.* New York: Basic Books.

Georgas, J. (1999). Family in cross-cultural psychology. In J. Adamopoulos & Y. Kashima (Eds.), *Social psychology and cultural context* (pp.163-175).Thousand Oaks, CA: Sage.

Gillespie, D., Colignon, R., Banerjee, M., Murty, S., & Rogge, M. (1993). *Partnerships for community preparedness.* Boulder: Institute of Behavioral Science, University of Colorado.

Gillespie, D., & Perry, R. W. (1976). An integrated systems and emergent norm approach to mass emergencies. *Mass Emergencies, 1,* 303-312.

Girard, C., & Peacock, W. G. (1997). Ethnicity and segregation: Post-hurricane relocation. In W. G. Peacock, B. Morrow, & H. Gladwin (Eds.), *Hurricane Andrew: Gender, ethnicity and the sociology of disasters* (pp. 191-205). New York: Routledge.

Gladwin, H. & Peacock, W. G. (1997). Warning and evacuation: A night for hard houses. In W. G. Peacock, B. H. Morrow, & H. Gladwin (Eds.), *Hurricane Andrew: Gender, ethnicity and the sociology of disasters* (pp. 52-74). London: Routledge.

Glass, A. (1970). The psychological aspects of emergency situations. In C. Abram (Ed.), *Psychological aspects of stress* (pp. 11-22). Springfield, IL: Charles C Thomas.

Glass, R., Craven, R., Bregman, D., Stoll, B., Horowitz, N., Kerndt, P., & Winkle, J. (1980). Injuries from the Wichita Falls tornado. *Science, 207,* 734-738.

Goldenberg, S. (1992). *Thinking methodologically.* New York: HarperCollins.

Green, K., Neal, D., & Quarantelli, E. L. (1989). *The relationships of disaster-related emergent citizen groups to other organizations.* Newark: University of Delaware, Disaster Research Center.

Greene, M., & Gori, P. (1982). *Earthquake hazards information dissemination: A study of Charleston, South Carolina.* Reston, VA: U.S. Geological Survey.

Greene, M., Perry, R. W., & Lindell, M. K. (1981). March, 1980 eruptions of Mt. St. Helens: Citizen perceptions of volcano hazard. *Disasters, 5,* 49-66.

Greenway, A. R. (1998). *Risk management planning handbook.* Rockville, MD: Government Institutes Press.

Gruntfest, E. (1977). *What people did during the Big Thompson flood.* Boulder: University of Colorado Institute of Behavioral Research.

Gruntfest, E., Downing, T., & White, G. (1978). Big Thompson flood exposes need for better flood reaction system. *Civil Engineering, 78,* 72-73.

Gudykunst, W. B. (1998). *Bridging differences: Effective intergroup communication.* Thousand Oaks, CA: Sage.

Gudykunst, W. B., & Kim, Y. (1997). *Communicating with strangers.* New York: McGraw-Hill.

Gutteling, J. M., & Wiegman, O. (1996). *Exploring risk communication.* Boston: Kluwer Academic.

Haas, J. E., & Trainer, P. (1974). Effectiveness of the tsunami warning system in selected coastal towns in Alaska. In *Proceedings of the Fifth World Conference on Earthquake Engineering* (pp. 85-99). Rome: International Association on Earthquake Engineering.

Haas, J. E., Cochrane, H., & Eddy, D. (1977). Consequences of a cyclone for a small city. *Ekistics, 44,* 45-51.

Hamilton, R., Taylor, R. M., & Rice, G. (1955). *The social psychological interpretation of the Udall, Kansas tornado.* Wichita, KS: University of Wichita Press.

Hance, B., Chess, C., & Sandman, P. (1988). *Improving dialogue with communities.* New Brunswick: New Jersey Department of Environmental Protection.

Handmer, J., & Penning-Roswell, E. (1990). *Hazards and the communication of risk.* Brookfield, VT: Gower.

Hanson, S., Vitek, J. D., & Hanson, P. O. (1979). Natural disaster: Long range impact on human response to future disaster threats. *Environment and Behavior, 11,* 268-284.

Harding, D. M., & Parker, D. J. (1974). Flood hazard at Shrewsbury, United Kingdom. In G. White (Ed.), *Natural hazards* (pp. 43-52). New York: Oxford University Press.

Harris, M. (1979). *Cultural materialism.* New York: Random House.

Harris, P. (1996). Sufficient grounds for optimism. *Journal of Social and Clinical Psychology, 15,* 9-52.

Hass, R. G. (1981). Effects of source characteristics on cognitive response and persuasion. In R. E. Petty, T. M. Brock, & T. C. Ostrom (Eds.), *Cognitive responses in persuasion* (pp. 43-52). Hillsdale, NJ: Lawrence Erlbaum.

Hawkes, G., & Stiles, M. (1986). Attitudes about pesticide safety. *California Agriculture, 40,* 19-22.

Healy, R. J. (1969). *Emergency and disaster planning.* New York: John Wiley.

Helweg-Larsen, M. (1999). The lack of optimistic biases in response to the 1994 Northridge earthquake: The role of personal experience. *Basic and Applied Social Psychology, 21,* 119-129.

Hershiser, M., & Quarantelli, E. L. (1976). The handling of dead in a disaster. *Omega, 7,* 195-208.

Hill, R., & Hansen, R. (1962). Families in disaster. In G. Baker & D. Chapman (Eds.), *Man and society in disaster* (pp. 53-69). New York: Basic Books.

Hodge, D. C., Sharp, V., & Marts, M. (1979). Contemporary responses to volcanism. In P. Sheets & D. Grayson (Eds.), *Volcanic activity and human ecology* (pp. 221-248). New York: Academic Press.

Hodge, D. C., Sharp, V., Marts, M., Sheridan, F., MacGregor, J., & Cullen, J. (1978). *Social implications of volcano hazard: Case studies in the Washington Cascades and Hawaii.* Washington, DC: National Science Foundation.

Hofstede, G., & Bond, M. (1984). Hofstede's culture dimensions. *Journal of Cross-Cultural Psychology, 15,* 417-433.

Hogarth, R., & Kunreuther, H. (1993). *Decision making under ignorance.* Philadelphia: University of Pennsylvania Risk Management and Risk Processes Center.

Horwich, G. (1993). The role of the for-profit private sector in disaster mitigation and response. *International Journal of Mass Emergencies and Disasters, 11,* 189-205.

Houts, P. S., Cleary, P., & Hu, T. (1988). *The Three Mile Island crisis.* University Park: The Pennsylvania State University Press.

Houts, P. S., Lindell, M. K., Hu, T., Cleary, P., Tokuhata, G., & Flynn, C. (1984). The protective action decision model applied to evacuation during the Three Mile Island crisis. *International Journal of Mass Emergencies and Disasters, 14,* 27-39.

Hovland, C., Janis, I., & Kelley, H. (1953). *Communication and persuasion.* New Haven, CT: Yale University Press.

Hutton, J., & Mileti, D. E. (1979). *Analysis of adoption and implementation of community land use regulations for floodplains.* San Francisco: Woodward-Clyde.

Hutton, R. R. (1982). Advertising and the Department of Energy's campaign for energy conservation. *Journal of Advertising, 11,* 27-39.

Hwang, S. N., & Lindell, M. K. (2003). *Assessing the effects of environmental amenities and disamenities on housing prices using GIS techniques.* College Station: Texas A&M University Hazard Reduction & Recovery Center.

Hwang, S. N., Sanderson, W., & Lindell, M. K. (2001). State emergency management agencies' hazard analysis information on the internet. *International Journal of Mass Emergencies and Disasters, 19,* 85-108.

Ives, S. M., & Furuseth, O. (1983). Immediate response to headwater flooding in Charlotte, North Carolina. *Environment and Behavior, 15,* 512-525.

Jackson, E. L. (1977). Public response to earthquake hazard. *California Geology,* 30, 278-280.

Jackson, E. L. (1981). Response to earthquake hazard. *Environment and Behavior, 13,* 387-416.

Jackson, E. L., & Mukerjee, T. (1974). Human adjustment to the earthquake hazard of San Francisco, California. In G. White (Ed.), *Natural hazards* (pp.160-166). New York: Oxford University Press.

James, L. R. Mulaik, S. A. & Brett, J. M. (1982). *Causal analysis: Assumptions, models, and data.* Beverly Hills, CA: Sage.

Janis, I. (1962). Psychological effects of warnings. In G. Baker & D. Chapman (Eds.), *Man and society in disaster* (pp. 255-92). New York: Basic Books.

Janis, I., & Mann, L. (1977). *Decision making.* New York: The Free Press.

Jardine, G., & Hrudey, S. (1997). Mixed messages in risk communication. *Risk Analysis, 17,* 489-498.

Jarvik, M. (1951). Probability learning and a negative recency effect in the serial anticipation of alternative symbols. *Journal of Experimental Psychology, 41,* 291-297.

Johnson, B. (1991). Risk and culture research: Some cautions. *Journal of Cross Cultural Psychology, 22,* 141-149.

Johnson, E., & Eagly, A. (1989). Effects of involvement on persuasion: A meta-analysis. *Psychological Bulletin, 106,* 290-314.

Kahneman, D., & Tversky, A. (1979). Prospect theory: An analysis of decision under risk. *Econometrica, 47,* 263-291.

Kaplan, A. (1964). *The conduct of inquiry.* San Francisco: Chandler.

Kartez, J. D., & Lindell, M. K. (1987). Planning for uncertainty. *American Planning Association Journal, 53,* 487-498.

Kasperson, R. (1987). Panel discussion on "Trust and credibility: The central issue?" In J. C. Davies, V. T. Covello, & F. W. Allen (Eds.), *Risk communication* (pp. 43-62). Washington, DC: The Conservation Foundation.

Kasperson, R., & Stallen, P. J. M. (1991). Risk communication: The evolution of attempts. In R. E. Kasperson & P. J. M. Stallen (Eds.), *Communicating risks to the public: International perspectives* (pp. 1-12). London: Kluwer Academic.

Kates, R. (1976). *Risk assessment of environmental hazards.* Paris: Scientific Committee on Problems of the Environment.

Kates, R. (1977). Experiencing the environment as hazard. In S. Wapner, S. Cohen, & B. Kaplan (Eds.), *Experiencing the environment* (pp. 133-156). New York: Plenum.

Keeney, R. (1982). Decision analysis. *Operations Research, 30,* 803-838.

Keesing, R. (1974). Theories of culture. *Annual Review of Anthropology, 3,* 73-97.

Kennedy, C., Fossum, J., & White, B. (1983). An empirical comparison of within-subjects and between-subjects expectancy theory models. *Organizational Behavior and Human Performance, 32,* 124-143.

Kennedy, W. C. (1970). Police departments: organizations and tasks in a disaster. *American Behavioral Scientist, 13,* 354-361.

Kent, D. (1971). The Negro aged. *The Gerontologist, 11,* 48-51.

Ketchum, J., & Whittaker, H. (1982). Hazards analysis. *Comprehensive Emergency Management Bulletin, 2,* 1-17.

Killian, L. M. (1952). The significance of multi-group membership in disaster. *American Journal of Sociology, 57,* 309-314.

Kramer, W., & Bahme, C. (1992). *Fire officer's guide to disaster control.* Saddlebrook, NJ: Pennwell.

Krimsky, S., & Plough, A. (1988). *Environmental hazards: Communicating risks as a social process.* Dover, MA: Auburn House.

Kroeber, A., & Kluckhohn, C. (1952). *Culture.* New York: Random House.

Kubasek, N., & Silverman, G. (2000). *Environmental law.* Upper Saddle River, NJ: Prentice Hall.

Kunreuther, H. (1993). Earthquake insurance as a hazard reduction strategy. In Committee on Socio-Economic Impacts (Ed.), *1993 National earthquake conference: Socio-economic effects* (pp. 191-210). Memphis, TN: Central United States Earthquake Consortium.

Kunreuther, H. C. (2001). Protective decisions: Fear or prudence. In S. J. Hoch & H. C. Kunreuther (Eds.), *Wharton on making decisions* (pp. 259-272). New York: John Wiley.

Kunreuther, H., Ginsberg, R., & Handmer, J. (1993). *Reducing losses from natural hazards through insurance and mitigation.* Philadelphia: University of Pennsylvania Risk Management and Risk Processes Center.

Kunreuther, H., Ginsberg, R., Miller, L., Sagi, P., Slovic, P., Borkan, B., & Katz, N. (1978). *Disaster insurance protection: Public policy lessons.* New York: John Wiley.

Lachman, R., Tatsuoka, M., & Bonk, W. (1961). Human behavior during the tsunami of May 1960. *Science, 133,* 1405-1409.

Lansing, J., & Kish, L. (1957). Family life cycle as an independent variable. *American Sociological Review, 22,* 512-519.

Lasswell, H. (1948). The structure and function of communication in society. In L. Bryson (Ed.), *Communication of ideas.* (pp. 43-71). New York: Harper.

Latané, B., & Darley, J. M. (1970). *The unresponsive bystander: Why doesn't he help?* New York: Appleton-Century-Crofts.

Lazarus, R. (1966). *Psychological stress and the coping process.* New York: McGraw-Hill.

Lazarus, R. (1991). *Emotion and adaptation.* New York: Oxford University Press.

Lazarus, R. S., & Folkman, S. (1984). *Stress, appraisal, and coping.* New York: Springer.

Leonard, V. A. (1973). *Police pre-disaster preparation.* Springfield, IL: Charles C Thomas.

Leventhal, H. (1970). Findings and theory in the study of fear communications. In L. Berkowitz (Ed.), *Advances in experimental social psychology* (pp. 119-186). New York: Academic Press.

Lieberson, S. (1982). *Making it count.* Los Angeles: University of California Press.

Lieberson, S. (1985). Unhyphenated whites in the United States. *Ethnic and Racial Studies, 8,* 158-180.

Lifton, R., & Olson, E. (1976). The human meaning of total disaster. *Psychiatry, 39,* 1-18.

Lillibridge, S. R. (1997). Managing the environmental health aspects of disasters: Water, human excreta, and shelter. In E. Noji (Ed.), *The public health consequences of disasters* (pp. 65-78). New York: Oxford University Press.

Lindblom, C. (1959). The science of muddling through. *Public Administration Review, 19,* 79-99.

Lindell, M. K. (1994a). Perceived characteristics of environmental hazards. *International Journal of Mass Emergencies and Disasters, 12,* 303-326.

Lindell, M. K. (1994b). Motivational and organizational factors affecting implementation of worker safety training. In M. J. Colligan (Ed.), *Occupational medicine state of the art reviews: Occupational safety and health training* (pp. 211-240). Philadelphia: Hanley & Belfus.

Lindell, M. K. (1994c). Are Local Emergency Planning Committees effective in developing community disaster preparedness? *International Journal of Mass Emergencies and Disasters, 12,* 159-182.

Lindell, M. K. (1995). Assessing emergency preparedness in support of hazardous facility risk analyses: An application at a U.S. hazardous waste incinerator. *Journal of Hazardous Materials, 40,* 297-319.

Lindell, M. K., & Barnes, V. E. (1986). Protective response to technological emergency: Risk perception and behavioral intention. *Nuclear Safety, 27,* 457-467.

Lindell, M. K., & Brandt, C. J. (2000). Climate quality and climate consensus as mediators of the relationship between organizational antecedents and outcomes. *Journal of Applied Psychology, 85,* 331-348.

Lindell, M. K., Bolton, P., Perry, R. W., Stoetzel, G., Martin, J., & Flynn, C. (1985). *Planning concepts and decision criteria for sheltering and evacuation in a nuclear power plant emergency.* Washington, DC: Atomic Industrial Forum.

Lindell, M. K., & Earle, T. (1983). How close is close enough? *Risk Analysis, 3,* 245-254.

Lindell, M. K., & Perry, R. W. (1983). Nuclear power plant emergency warning: How would the public respond? *Nuclear News, 26,* 49-53.

Lindell, M. K., & Perry, R. W. (1987). Warning mechanisms in emergency response systems. *International Journal of Mass Emergencies and Disasters, 5,* 137-153.

Lindell, M. K., & Perry, R. W. (1990). Effects of the Chernobyl accident on public perceptions of nuclear plant accident risks. *Risk Analysis, 10,* 393-399.

Lindell, M. K., & Perry, R. W. (1992). *Behavioral foundations of community emergency planning.* Washington, DC: Hemisphere.

Lindell, M. K., & Perry, R. W. (1993). Risk area residents' changing perceptions of volcano hazard at Mt. St. Helens. In J. Nemec, J. Nigg, & F. Siccardi (Eds.), *Prediction and perception of natural hazards* (pp. 159-166). London: Kluwer Academic.

Lindell, M. K., & Perry, R. W. (1996). Identifying and managing conjoint threats. *Journal of Hazardous Materials, 50,* 31-46.

Lindell, M. K., & Perry, R. W. (1997). Hazardous materials releases in the Northridge earthquake. *Risk Analysis, 17,* 147-156.

Lindell, M. K., & Perry, R. W. (2000). Household adjustment to earthquake hazard. *Environment and Behavior, 32,* 590-630.

Lindell, M. K., & Perry, R. W. (2001). Community innovation in hazardous materials management: Progress in implementing SARA Title III in the United States. *Journal of Hazardous Materials, 88,* 169-194.

Lindell, M. K., Perry, R. W., & Greene, M. R. (1983). Individual response to emergency preparedness planning near Mt. St. Helens. *Disaster Management, 3,* 5-11.

Lindell, M. K., & Prater, C. S. (2000). Household adoption of seismic hazard adjustments: A comparison of residents of two states. *International Journal of Mass Emergencies and Disasters, 18,* 317-338.

Lindell, M. K., & Prater, C. S. (2002). Risk area residents' perceptions and adoption of seismic hazard adjustments. *Journal of Applied Social Psychology, 32,* 2377-2392.

Lindell, M.K., Prater, C.W., Perry, R.W. & Wu, J.Y. (2002). EMBLEM: *An empirically-based large scale evacuation time estimate model.* College Station: Texas A&M University Hazard Reduction & Recovery Center.

Lindell, M. K., Prater, C. W., Sanderson, W. G., Jr., Lee, H. M., Zhang, Y., Mohite, A., & Hwang, S. N. (2001). *Texas Gulf coast residents' expectations and intentions regarding hurricane evacuation.* College Station: Texas A&M University Hazard Reduction & Recovery Center.

Lindell, M. K., & Whitney, D. J. (2000). Correlates of household seismic hazard adjustment adoption. *Risk Analysis, 20,* 13-25.

Lindell, M. K., Whitney, D. J., Futch, C. J., & Clause, C. S. (1996). The Local Emergency Planning Committee: A better way to coordinate disaster planning. In R. T. Sylves & W. L. Waugh, Jr. (Eds.), *Disaster management in the U.S. and Canada: The politics, policymaking, administration and analysis of emergency management.* Springfield, IL: Charles C Thomas.

Lion, R., Meertens, R. M., & Bot, I. (2002). Priorities in information desire about unknown risks. *Risk Analysis, 22,* 765-776.

Liverman, D., & Wilson, J. (1981). The Mississagua train derailment and evacuation. *Canadian Geographer, 25,* 365-375.

Logan, J., & Molotch, H. (1987). *Urban fortunes.* Berkeley: University of California Press.

Logue, J., Melick, M., & Struening, E. (1981). A study of health and mental status following a major natural disaster. In R. Simmons (Ed.), *Research in community and mental health* (pp. 217-274). Greenwich, CT: JAI.

Lorge, I., Fox, D., Davitz, J., & Brenner, M. (1958). A survey of studies contrasting the quality of group performance and individual performance, 1920-1957. *Psychological Bulletin, 55,* 337-372.

Lowrance, W. W. (1976). *Of acceptable risk.* Los Altos, CA: William Kaufman.

Lundgren, R., & McMakin, A. (1998). *Risk communication: A handbook for communicating environmental, safety and health risks.* Columbus, OH: Battelle.

Mack, R., & Baker, G. (1961). *The occasion instant.* Washington, DC: National Academy of Sciences-National Research Council.

Maddox, J., & Rogers, R. (1983). Protection motivation and self-efficacy. *Journal of Experimental Social Psychology, 19,* 469-479.

Maeda, Y., & Miyahara, M. (2003). Determinants of trust in industry, government and citizen's groups in Japan. *Risk Analysis, 23,* 303-310.

Major, A. M. (1999). Gender differences in risk and communication behavior in response to an earthquake prediction. *International Journal of Mass Emergencies and Disasters, 17,* 313-338.

Makosky, F. (1977). *The forecast office's severe weather role.* Paper presented at the Tenth Conference on Severe Local Storms, Tallahassee, FL.

May, P. J. (1985). *Recovering from catastrophes: Federal disaster relief policy and politics.* Westport, CT: Greenwood.

May, P. J. (1991). Addressing public risks. *Journal of Policy Analysis and Management, 10,* 263-285.

May, P. J., & Williams, W. (1985). *Disaster policy implementation.* New York: Plenum.

McAdoo, H. P. (1999). Families of color. In H. P. McAdoo (Ed.), *Family ethnicity* (pp. 3-15). Thousand Oaks, CA: Sage.

McCallum, D. B., & Anderson, L. (1991). Communicating about pesticides in drinking water. In R. E. Kasperson & P. J. M. Stallen (Eds.), *Communicating risks to the public: International perspectives* (pp. 237-262). London: Kluwer Academic.

McGuire, W. J. (1969). The nature of attitudes and attitude change. In G. Lindsey and E. Aronson (Eds.), *Handbook of social psychology* (pp. 329-348). Reading, MA: Addison-Wesley.

McGuire, W. J. (1985). The nature of attitudes and attitude change. In G. Lindzey & E. Aronson (Eds.), *Handbook of social psychology* (pp. 233-256). New York: Random House.

McKenna, T. J. (2000). Protective action recommendations based upon plant conditions. *Journal of Hazardous Materials, 75,* 145-164.

McLuckie, B. (1970). *Warning systems in disaster.* Columbus: The Ohio State University Disaster Research Center.

McPherson, H. J., & Saarinen, T. (1977). Flood plain dwellers' perceptions of the flood hazard in Tucson, Arizona. *The Annals of Regional Science, 9,* 25-40.

Menninger, W. C. (1952). Psychological reactions in an emergency. *American Journal of Psychiatry, 109,* 128-130.

Meyer, P. (1988). Defining and measuring credibility of newspapers: Developing an index. *Journalism Quarterly, 65,* 567-574, 588.

Michaels, S. (1990). *BAREPP Survey of Information Users.* Oakland, CA: Bay Area Regional Earthquake Preparedness Project.

Middleton, R., & Putney, A. (1970). Racial and cultural variations among American families. *Journal of Marriage and the Family, 42,* 887-903.

Midlarsky, E. (1968). Aiding responses: An analysis and review. *Merrill-Palmer Quarterly, 14,* 229-260.

Mileti, D. S. (1974). *A normative causal model analysis of disaster warning response.* Boulder: University of Colorado Department of Sociology.

Mileti, D. S. (1975). *Natural hazards warning systems in the United States.* Boulder: University of Colorado Institute of Behavioral Science.

Mileti, D. S. (1993). Communicating public risk information. In J. Nemec, J. Nigg, & F. Siccardi (Eds.), *Prediction and perception of natural hazards* (pp. 143-152). London: Kluwer Academic.

Mileti, D. S. (1999). *Disasters by design.* Washington, DC: Joseph Henry.

Mileti, D. S., & Beck, E. (1975). Communication in crisis. *Communication Research, 2,* 24-49.

Mileti, D. S., & Darlington, J. (1997). The role of searching in shaping reactions to earthquake risk information. *Social Problems, 44,* 89-103.

Mileti, D. S., Drabek, T., & Haas, J. E. (1975). *Human systems in extreme environments.* Boulder: University of Colorado Institute of Behavioral Science.

Mileti, D. S., & Fitzpatrick, C. (1993). *The great earthquake experiment.* Boulder, CO: Westview.

Mileti, D. S., Fitzpatrick, C., & Farhar, B. C. (1992). Fostering public preparations for natural hazards. *Environment, 34,* 16-39.

Mileti, D. S., & Harvey, P. (1977). *Correcting for the human factor in tornado warnings.* Paper presented at the Tenth Annual Conference on Severe Local Storms, Norman, OK.

Mileti, D. S., Hutton, J., & Sorenson, J. H. (1981). *Earthquake prediction response and options for public policy.* Boulder: University of Colorado Institute for Behavioral Science.

Mileti, D. S., & O'Brien, P. (1992). Warnings during disasters. *Social Problems, 39,* 40-57.

Mileti, D. S., & Peek, L. (2000). The social psychology of pubic response to warnings of a nuclear power plant accident. *Journal of Hazardous Materials, 75,* 181-194.

Mileti, D. S., & Sorensen, J. H. (1987). Why people take precautions against natural disasters. In N. Weinstein (Ed.), *Taking care: Why people take precautions* (pp. 296-320). New York: Cambridge University Press.

Mileti, D. S., & Sorenson, J. H. (1988). Planning and implementing warning systems. In M. Lystad (Ed.), *Mental health response to mass emergencies* (pp. 321-345). New York: Brunner/Mazel.

Mileti, D. S., Sorensen, J. H., & O'Brien, P. W. (1992). Toward an explanation of mass care shelter use in evacuations. *International Journal of Mass Emergencies and Disasters, 10,* 25-42.

Mirowsky, J., & Ross, C. (1980). Minority status, ethnic culture and distress. *American Journal of Sociology, 86,* 479-495.

Mitchell, T., & Beach, L. (1990). Toward an understanding of intuitive and automatic decision making. *Organizational Behavior and Human Decision Processes, 47,* 1-20.

Moore, H. E. (1958). *Tornadoes over Texas.* Austin: University of Texas Press.

Moore, H. E., Bates, F., Lyman, M., & Parenton, V. (1963). *Before the wind: A study of response to Hurricane Carla.* Washington, DC: National Academy of Sciences-National Research Council.

Morrall, J. (1986). A review of the record. *Regulation, 10,* 25-34.

Morrow, B. (1997). Streching the bonds: The families of Andrew. In W. G. Peacock, B. Morrow, & H. Gladwin (Eds.), *Hurricane Andrew: Ethnicity, gender, and the sociology of disasters* (pp. 141-170). New York: Routledge.

Moscovici, S., & Facheaux, C. (1972). Social influence, conformity bias and the study of active minorities. In L. Berkowitz (Ed.), *Advances in experimental social psychology* (Vol. 6, pp. 149-202). London: Academic Press.

Mulilis, J. P., & Duval, T. S. (1995). Negative threat appeals and earthquake preparedness. *Journal of Applied Social Psychology, 25,* 1319-1339.

Mulilis, J. P., & Duval, T. S. (1997). The PrE model of coping with threat and tornado preparedness behavior: The moderating effects of felt responsibility. *Journal of Applied Social Psychology, 27,* 1750-1766.

Mulilis, J. P., & Lippa, R. A. (1990). Behavioral change in earthquake preparedness due to negative threat appeals. *Journal of Applied Social Psychology, 20,* 619-638.

Murton, B., & Shimaburkuro, S. (1974). Human adjustment to volcanic hazard in Puna District, Hawaii. In G. F. White (Ed.), *Natural hazards: Local, national and global* (pp. 151-159). New York: Oxford University Press.

National Governors' Association. (1987). *Comprehensive emergency management.* Washington, DC: National Governors' Association Emergency Preparedness Project.

National Response Team. (1987). *Hazardous materials emergency planning guide.* Washington, DC: Author.

Neal, D. M., Perry, J., & Hawkins, R. (1982). Getting ready for blizzards: Preparation levels in the winter of 1977-1978. *Sociological Focus, 15,* 67-76.

Nelson, C., Coovert, M., Kurtz, A., Fritzsche, B., Crumley, C., & Powell, A. (1989). *Models of hurricane evacuation behavior.* Tampa: University of South Florida Department of Psychology.

Nelson, L. S., & Perry, R. W. (1991). Organizing public education for technological emergencies. *Disaster Management, 4,* 21-26.

Neuwirth, K., Dunwoody, S., & Griffin, R. J. (2000). Protection motivation and risk communication. *Risk Analysis, 20,* 721-734.

Ng, K. L., & Hamby, D. M. (1997). Fundamentals for establishing a risk communication program. *Health Physics, 73,* 473-482.

Nigg, J. M. (1982). Awareness and behavior: Public response to prediction awareness. In T. F. Saarinen (Ed.), *Perspectives on increasing hazard awareness* (pp. 36-51). Boulder: University of Colorado Institute of Behavioral Science.

Nisbett, R., & Ross, L. (1980). *Human inference: Strategies and shortcomings of social judgment.* Englewood Cliffs, NJ: Prentice Hall.

Norris, F. H., Smith, T., & Kaniasty, K. (1999). Revisiting the experience-behavior hypothesis: The effects of Hurricane Hugo on hazard preparedness and other self-protective acts. *Basic and Applied Psychology, 21,* 27-47.

O'Keefe, D. (1990). *Persuasion.* Thousand Oaks, CA: Sage.

Oliver-Smith, A. (1996). Anthropological research on hazards and disasters. *Annual Review of Anthropology, 25,* 303-28.

Oliver-Smith, A. (1998). Global changes and the definition of disaster. In E. L. Quarantelli (Ed.), *What is a disaster?* (pp. 177-194). London: Routledge.

Olsen, M. E. (1970). Social and political participation of Blacks. *American Sociological Review, 35,* 682-697.

Olsen, M. E. (1978). *The process of social organization.* New York: Holt, Rinehart & Winston.

Olson, R., Lagorio, H., & Scott, S. (1990). *Knowledge transfer in earthquake engineering.* Berkeley: University of California Press.

Oram, A. (1966). The reappraisal of the social and political participation of Negroes. *American Journal of Sociology, 72,* 32-46.

Otway, H. (1973). Risk estimation and evaluation. In *Proceedings of the IIASA Planning Conference on Energy Systems* (pp. 11-19). Laxenburg, Austria: International Institute for Applied Systems Analysis.

Palm, R. (1981). *Real estate agents and special studies zone disclosure.* Boulder: University of Colorado Institute of Behavioral Science.

Palm, R., & Hodgson, M. (1992). *After a California earthquake: Attitude and behavior change.* Chicago: University of Chicago Press.

Palm, R., Hodgson, M., Blanchard, R., & Lyons, D. (1990). *Earthquake insurance in California.* Boulder, CO: Westview.

Payne, J. (1982). Contingent decision behavior. *Psychological Bulletin, 92,* 382-402.

Peacock, W. G., & Girard, C. (1997). Ethnic and racial inequalities in hurricane damage and insurance settlements. In W. G. Peacock, B. Morrow, & H. Gladwin (Eds.), *Hurricane Andrew: Ethnicity, gender, and the sociology of disasters* (pp. 171-190). New York: Routledge.

Perrow, C. (1984). *Normal accidents: Living with high-risk technologies.* New York: Basic Books.

Perry, H. S., & Perry, S. (1959). *The schoolhouse disasters: Family and community as determinants of the child's response to disaster.* Washington, DC: National Academy of Sciences-National Research Council.

Perry, R. W. (1976). Attitude scales as behavior estimation devices. *Journal of Social Psychology, 100,* 137-142.

Perry, R. W. (1979a). Evacuation decision making in natural disaster. *Mass Emergencies, 4,* 25-38.

Perry, R. W. (1979b). Incentives for evacuation in natural disaster. *Journal of the American Planning Association, 45,* 440-447.

Perry, R. W. (1981). Personal communication to R.W. Perry from B. Bena, Director, Cowlitz County Department of Emergency Services. Seattle, WA: Battelle Human Affairs Research Centers.

Perry, R. W. (1983a). Environmental hazards and psychopathology. *Environmental Management, 7,* 543-552.

Perry, R. W. (1985). *Comprehensive emergency management: Evacuating threatened populations.* Greenwich, CT: JAI.

Perry, R. W. (1987). Racial and ethnic minority citizens in disasters. In R. Dynes & C. Pelanda (Eds.), *The sociology of disasters* (pp. 87-99). Gorizia, Italy: Franco Angelli.

Perry, R. W. (1990). Volcanic hazard perceptions at Mt. Shasta. *The Environmental Professional, 12,* 312-318.

Perry, R. W. (2000). Diffusion theories. In E. Borgatta & R. Montgomery (Eds.), *Encyclopedia of sociology* (pp. 674-681). New York: Macmillan.

Perry, R. W., & Greene, M. (1982). *Citizen response to volcanic eruptions.* New York: Irvington.

Perry R. W., Greene, M., & Lindell, M. K. (1980). Enhancing evacuation warning compliance. *Disasters, 4,* 433-449.

Perry, R. W., & Hirose, H. (1991). *Volcano management in the United States and Japan.* Greenwich, CT: JAI.

Perry, R. W., & Lindell, M. K. (1987). Source credibility in volcano hazard information. *Volcano News, 25,* 8-10.

Perry, R. W., & Lindell, M. K. (1989). Communicating threat information for volcano hazards. In L. Walters, L. Wilkins, & T. Walters (Eds.), *Bad tidings: Communication and catastrophe* (pp. 47-62). Hillsdale, NJ: Lawrence Erlbaum.

Perry, R. W., & Lindell, M. K. (1990a). *Living with Mt. St. Helens: Human adjustment to volcano hazards.* Pullman: Washington State University Press.

Perry, R. W., & Lindell, M. K. (1990b). Predicting long-term adjustment to volcano hazard. *International Journal of Mass Emergencies and Disasters, 8,* 117-136.

Perry, R. W., & Lindell, M. K. (1991). The effects of ethnicity on evacuation decision-making. *International Journal of Mass Emergencies and Disasters, 9,* 47-68.

Perry, R. W., & Lindell, M. K. (1997a). Aged citizens in the warning phase of disasters. *International Journal of Aging and Human Development, 44,* 257-267.

Perry, R. W., & Lindell, M. K. (1997b). Earthquake planning for government continuity. *Environmental Management, 21,* 89-96.

Perry, R. W., Lindell, M. K., & Greene, M. (1980). *Human response to volcanic eruptions: Mt. St. Helens, May 18, 1980.* Seattle, WA: Battelle Human Affairs Research Centers.

Perry, R. W., Lindell, M. K., & Greene, M. (1981). *Evacuation planning in emergency management.* Lexington, MA: Heath-Lexington.

Perry, R. W., Lindell, M. K., & Greene, M. (1982a). Crisis communications: Ethnic differentials in interpreting and acting on disaster warnings. *Social Behavior and Personality, 10,* 97-104.

Perry, R. W., Lindell, M. K., & Greene, M. (1982b). Threat perception and public response to volcano hazard. *Journal of Social Psychology, 116,* 199-204.

Perry, R. W., & Montiel, M. (1997). Conceptualizando riesgo para disastres sociales. *Desastres Sociedad, 6,* 67-72.

Perry, R. W., & Mushcatel, E. (1986). *Minority citizens in disasters.* Athens: University of Georgia Press.

Perry, R. W., & Nelson, L. (1991). Ethnicity and hazard information dissemination. *Environmental Management, 15,* 581-587.

Perry, R. W., & Nigg, J. (1985). Emergency management strategies for communicating hazard information. *Public Administration Review, 45,* 72-77.

Peters, R., Covello, V., & McCallum, D. (1997). The determinants of trust and credibility in environmental risk communication. *Risk Analysis, 17,* 43-54.

Petty, R., & Cacioppo, J. (1986a). *Communication and persuasion.* New York: Springer-Verlag.

Petty, R., & Cacioppo, J. (1986b). The elaboration likelihood model of persuasion. In L. Berkowitz (Ed.), *Advances in experimental social psychology* (pp. 123-205). New York: Academic Press.

Petty, R., & Cacioppo, J. (1990). Involvement and persuasion. *Psychological Bulletin, 107,* 367-374.

Prater, C. S., & Lindell, M. K. (2000). The politics of hazard mitigation. *Natural Hazards Review, 1,* 73-82.

Prater, C., Wenger, D., & Grady, K. (2000). *Hurricane Bret post storm assessment: A review of the utilization of hurricane evacuation studies and information dissemination.* College Station: Texas A&M University Hazard Reduction & Recovery Center.

Prestby, J. E., & Wandersman, A. (1985). An empirical exploration of a framework of organizational viability: Maintaining block organizations. *Journal of Applied Behavioral Sciences, 21,* 287-305.

Prestby, J. E., Wandersman, A., Florin, P., Rich, R. C., & Chavis, D. M. (1990). Benefits, costs, incentive management and participation in voluntary organizations: A means to understanding and promoting empowerment. *American Journal of Community Psychology, 18,* 117-150.

Quarantelli, E. L. (1960). A note on the protective function of the family in disasters. *Marriage and Family Living, 22,* 263-264.

Quarantelli, E. L. (1965). Mass behavior and government breakdown in major disaster. *Police Yearbook, 21,* 105-112.

Quarantelli, E. L. (1977). Social aspects of disasters and their relevance to pre-disaster planning. *Disasters, 1,* 98-107.

Quarantelli, E. L. (1980). *Evacuation behavior and problems.* Columbus: The Ohio State University Disaster Research Center.

Quarantelli, E. L. (1984). *Sociobehavioral responses to chemical hazards.* Newark: University of Delaware Disaster Research Center.

Quarantelli, E. L. (1985). *Emergent citizens groups in disaster preparedness and recovery activities.* Newark: University of Delaware Disaster Research Center.

Quarantelli, E. L. (1995). What is a disaster? *International Journal of Mass Emergencies and Disasters, 13,* 221-229.

Quarantelli, E. L., & Taylor, V. (1977). *Some views on the warning problem in disasters as suggested by sociological research.* Paper presented at the American Meteorological Society Conference on Severe Local Storms, Norman, OK.

Rabin, R. (1978). Dealing with disasters: Some thoughts on the adequacy of the legal system. *Stanford Law Review, 30,* 281-298.

Raven, B. (1965). Social influence and power. In I. Steiner & M. Fishbein (Eds.), *Current studies in social psychology* (pp. 371-382). New York: Holt, Rinehart & Winston.

Raven, B. (1993). The bases of power. *Journal of Social Issues, 49,* 227-251.

Renn, O., & Levine, D. (1991). Credibility and trust in risk communication. In R. E. Kasperson & P. J. M. Stallen (Eds.), *Communicating risks to the public: International perspectives* (pp. 175-218). London: Kluwer Academic.

Reynolds, P. D. (1971). *A primer in theory construction.* Boston: Allyn & Bacon.

Riad, J. K., Norris, F. H., & Ruback, R. B. (1999). Predicting evacuation in two major disasters: Risk perception, social influence and access to resources. *Journal of Applied Social Psychology, 29,* 918-934.

Rogers, E. (1984). *Diffusion of innovations.* New York: The Free Press.

Rogers, E. (1987). The diffusion of innovations perspective. In N. Weinstein (Ed.), *Taking care* (pp. 121-157). New York: Cambridge University Press.

Rogers, G. O., & Sorensen, J. H. (1988). Diffusion of emergency warnings. *Environmental Professional, 10,* 185-198.

Rogers, G. O., & Sorensen, J. H. (1989). Warning and response in two hazardous materials transportation accidents in the U.S. *Journal of Hazardous Materials, 22,* 57-74.

Rogers, R. (1975). A protection motivation theory of fear appeals and attitude change. *Journal of Psychology, 91,* 93-114.

Rogers, R. W., & Mewborn, C. (1976). Fear appeals and attitude change: Effects of a threat's noxiousness, probability of occurrence, and efficacy of coping response. *Journal of Personality and Social Psychology, 34,* 54-61.

Rogers, R. (1983). Cognitive and physiological processes in fear appeal and attitude change. In J. Cacioppo & R. Petty (Eds.), *Social psycho-physiology* (pp. 171-189). New York: Guilford.

Rosenberg, M. J. (1956). Cognitive structure and attitudinal effect. *Journal of Abnormal and Social Psychology, 53,* 367-372.

Rosenthal, I. (1990). Communicating with the public about major accident hazards: Legitimacy, credibility and risk. In H. Gow & H. Otway (Eds.), *Communicating with the public about major accident hazards* (pp. 173-187). New York: Elsevier.

Rossi, P. H., Wright, J. D., Webber-Burdin, E., Pietras, M., & Diggins, W. F. (1982). *Natural hazards and public choice: The state and local politics of hazard mitigation.* New York: Academic Press.

Rowe, W. (1977). *An anatomy of risk.* New York: John Wiley.

Ruch, C., & Christensen, L. (1980). *Hurricane message enhancement.* College Station: Texas A and M University Center for Strategic Technology.

Ruggles, S. (1994). The origins of African-American family structure. *American Sociological Review, 59,* 136-151.

Russell, L. A., Goltz, J. D., & Bourque, L. (1995). Preparedness and mitigation activities before and after two earthquakes. *Environment and Behavior, 27,* 744-770.

Saarinen, T. (1982). *Perspectives on increasing hazard awareness.* Boulder, CO: Natural Hazards Research Applications and Information Center.

Saarinen, T., & Sell, J. (1985). *Warning and response to the Mt. St. Helens eruption.* Albany: State University of New York Press.

Sahlins, M. (1976). *Culture and practical reason.* Chicago: University of Chicago Press.

Schulz, P. (1993). Education, awareness and information transfer issues. In *Improving earthquake mitigation* (pp. 159-175). Washington, DC: Federal Emergency Management Agency.

Schwab, J., Topping, K. C., Eadie, C. C., Deyle, R. E., & Smith, R. A. (1998). *Planning for post-disaster recovery and reconstruction* (PAS Report 483/484). Chicago: American Planning Association.

Sheppard, B., Hartwick, J., & Warshaw, P. (1988). The theory of reasoned action: A meta-analysis of past research with recommendations for modifications and future research. *Journal of Consumer Research, 15,* 325-343.

Sherman, S., & Corty, E. (1984). Cognitive heuristics. In R. Wyer & T. Srull (Eds.), *Handbook of social cognition* (pp. 189-286). Hillsdale, NJ: Lawrence Erlbaum.

Showalter, P. S. (1993). Prognostication of doom: An earthquake prediction's effect on four small communities. *International Journal of Mass Emergencies and Disasters, 11,* 292-297.

Simon, H. (1957). *Administrative behavior.* New York: Macmillan.

Simon, H. (1959). Theories of decision making in economics and behavioral sciences. *American Economic Review, 49,* 253-283.

Simpson-Housley, P., & Bradshaw, P. (1978). Personality and the perception of earthquake hazard. *Australian Geographical Studies, 16,* 65-72.

Sims, J., & Bauman, D. (1972). The tornado threat: Coping styles of the North and the South. *Science, 176,* 1386-1392.

Sims, J., & Bauman, D. (1983). Educational programs and human response to natural hazards. *Environment and Behavior, 15,* 165-189.

Singer, E. (1981). Reference groups and social evaluations. In M. Rosenberg & R. Turner (Eds.), *Social psychology* (pp 66-93). New York: Basic Books.

Sjoberg, G. (1962). Disasters and social change. In G. Baker & D. Chapman (Eds), *Man and society in disaster* (pp. 356-384). New York: Basic Books.

Slovic, P. (1987). Perception of risk. *Science, 236,* 280-285.

Slovic, P., Fischhoff, B., & Lichtenstein, S. (1978). Accident probabilities and seat belt usage. *Accident Analysis and Prevention, 10,* 281-285.

Slovic, P., Fischhoff, B., & Lichtenstein, S. (1980). Facts and fears: Understanding perceived risk. In R. Schwing & W. Albers (Eds.), *Societal risk assessment: How safe is safe enough?* (pp. 161-178). New York: Plenum.

Slovic, P., Kunreuther, H., & White, G. (1974). Decision processes, rationality and adjustments to natural hazards. In G. F. White (Ed.), *Natural hazards* (pp. 80-86). New York: Oxford University Press.

Smith, V., & Johnson, F. (1988). How do risk perceptions respond to information? *Review of Economics and Statistics, 50,* 1-8.

Sorenson, J. H. (1983). Knowing how to behave under the threat of disaster. *Environment and Behavior, 15,* 438-457.

Sorensen, J. H. (1986). *Evacuations due to chemical accidents.* Oak Ridge, TN: Oak Ridge National Laboratory.

Sorenson, J. H. (1991). When shall we leave: Factors affecting the timing of evacuation departures. *International Journal of Mass Emergencies and Disasters, 9,* 153-164.

Sorenson, J. H. (2000). Hazard warning systems: Review of 20 years of progress. *Natural Hazards Review, 1,* 119-125.

Sorensen, J. H., & Mileti, D. S. (1987). Programs that encourage the adoption of precautions against natural hazards: Review and evaluation. In N. Weinstein (Ed.), *Taking care: Why people take precautions* (pp. 321-339). New York: Cambridge University Press.

Sorenson, J. H., & Richardson, B. (1984). Risk and uncertainty as determinants of human response in emergencies. In *Proceedings of the annual meetings of the Society for Risk Analysis* (pp. 23-34). Knoxville, TN: Society for Risk Analysis.

Sorensen, J. H., & White, G. (1980). Natural hazards: A cross cultural perspective. In I. Altman, A. Rapoport, & J. F. Wohlwill (Eds.), *Human behavior and the environment: Advances in theory and research* (pp. 89-95). New York: Plenum.

Sotomayer, M. (1971). Mexican-American interaction with social systems. *Social Casework, 52,* 316-322.

Southern California Earthquake Data Center. (n.d.). Putting down roots in earthquake country. Retrieved April 25, 2003, from http://www.scecdc.scec.org/eqcountry.html

Stallen, P. J. M. (1991). Developing communications about risks of major industrial accidents in the Netherlands. In R. E. Kasperson & P. J. M. Stallen (Eds.), *Communicating risks to the public: International perspectives* (pp. 55-66). London: Kluwer Academic.

Stallings, R. A. (1971). *Communications in natural disaster.* Columbus: The Ohio State University Disaster Research Center.

Stallings, R. A. (1991). Ending evacuations. *International Journal of Mass Emergencies and Disasters, 9,* 183-200.

Stallings, R. A. (1995). *Promoting risk: Constructing the earthquake threat.* New York: Aldine de Gruyter.

Stallings, R. A. (1998). Disaster and the theory of the social order. In E. L. Quarantelli (Ed.), *What is a disaster?* (pp. 127-145). London: Routledge.

Staples, R. (1976). *Introduction to Black sociology.* New York: McGraw-Hill.

Staples, R., & Mirande, A. (1980). Racial and cultural variations among American families: A decennial review of the literature on minority families. *Journal of Marriage and the Family, 42,* 887-903.

Steele, G. A., Lyons, M., & Smith, D. (1979). *Area Agency on Aging: Disaster contingency planning.* Tallahassee: Florida Research Center.

Streeter, C. (1991). Redundancy in social systems: Implications for warning and evacuation planning. *International Journal of Mass Emergencies and Disasters, 9,* 167-182.

Sullivan, R., Mustart, D., & Galehouse, J. (1977). Living in earthquake country. *California Geology, 30,* 3-8.

Svensen, O. (1981). Are we all less risky and more skillful than our fellow drivers? *Acta Psychologica, 47,* 143-148.

Texas Governor's Division of Emergency Management. (2002). *Coastal Bend study area hurricane storm atlas.* Austin, TX: Author.

Tierney, K. (1978). *Emergent norm theory as theory.* Columbus: The Ohio State University Disaster Research Center.

Tierney, K. J. (1988). Social aspects of the Whittier Narrows earthquake. *Earthquake Spectra, 4,* 11-23.

Tierney, K., Lindell, M. K., & Perry, R. W. (2001). *Facing the unexpected: Disaster preparedness and response in the United States.* Washington, DC: Joseph Henry.

Titmuss, R. (1950). *Problems of social policy.* London: HMSO.

Tomeh, A. (1973). Formal voluntary organizations: Participation correlates and interrelationships. *Sociological Inquiry, 43,* 80-122.

Toole, M. J. (1997). Communicable diseases and disease control. In E. Noji (Ed.), *The public health consequences of disasters* (pp. 79-100). New York: Oxford University Press.

Trainer, P., & Hutton, J. (1972). *An approach to the differential distribution of deaths in disasters.* Paper presented at the annual meeting of the Midwest Council on Social Research in Aging, Kansas City, Kansas.

Triandis, H. (1980). Values, attitudes and interpersonal behavior. In H. E. Howe, Jr. (Ed.), *Nebraska symposium on motivation, 1979.* (Vol. 27, pp. 195-259). Lincoln: University of Nebraska Press.

Triandis, H. (1995). *Individualism-collectivism.* Boulder, CO: Westview.

Trumbo, C. W., & McComas, K. A. (2003). The function of credibility in information processing for risk perception. *Risk Analysis, 23,* 343-353.

Turner, J. (1991). *Social influence.* Pacific Grove, CA: Brooks/Cole.

Turner, R., & Kiecolt, K. (1984). Responses to uncertainty about risk: Mexican-American, Black, and Anglo beliefs about the manageability of the future. *Social Science Quarterly, 65,* 665-679.

Turner, R., & Killian, L. (1972). *Collective behavior.* Englewood Cliffs, NJ: Prentice Hall.

Turner, R., Nigg, J., & Heller-Paz, D. (1986). *Waiting for disaster.* Los Angeles: University of California Press.

Turner, R., Nigg, J., Paz, D., & Young, B. (1979). *Earthquake threat: The human response in Southern California.* Los Angeles: University of California at Los Angeles, Institute for Social Science Research.

Turner, R., Nigg, J., Paz, D., & Young, B. (1981). *Community response to earthquake threat in Southern California: Part 10 summary and recommendations.* Los Angeles: University of California at Los Angeles, Institute for Social Science Research.

Tversky, A., & Kahneman, D. (1971). Belief in the law of small numbers. *Psychological Bulletin, 76,* 105-110.

Tversky, A., & Kahneman, D. (1974). Judgment under uncertainty. *Science, 185,* 1124-1131.

Tversky, A., & Kahneman, D. (1981). The framing of decisions and the psychology of choice. *Science, 211,* 453-458.

Tversky, A., & Kahneman, D. (1986). Judgment under uncertainty. In H. Arkes & K. Hammond (Eds.), *Judgment and decision making* (pp. 38-55). New York: Cambridge University Press.

Tyhurst, J. S. (1957). Psychological and social aspects of civilian disaster. *Canadian Medical Association Journal, 76,* 385-393.

Urbanik, T. (2000). Evacuation time estimates for nuclear power plants. *Journal of Hazardous Materials, 75,* 165-180.

Urbanik, T., Desrosiers, A., Lindell, M. K., & Schuller, C. R. (1980). *Analysis of techniques for estimating evacuation times for emergency planning zones* (BHARC-401/80-017, NUREG/CR-1745). Washington, DC: U.S. Nuclear Regulatory Commission.

U.S. Nuclear Regulatory Commission. (1980). *Criteria for preparation and evaluation of radiological emergency response plans and preparedness in support of nuclear power plants* (NUREG-0654). Washington, DC: Author.

Vaughn, E. (1995). The significance of socioeconomic and ethnic diversity for the risk communication process. *Risk Analysis, 15,* 169-180.

Vaughn, E., & Nordenstam, B. (1991). The perception of environmental risks among ethnically diverse groups. *Journal of Cross-Cultural Psychology, 22,* 29-60.

Vaughn, E., & Seifert, M. (1992). Variability in the framing of risk issues. *Journal of Social Issues, 48,* 118-135.

Vogt, B. M., & Sorensen, J. H. (1987). *Evacuation in emergencies.* Oak Ridge, TN: Oak Ridge National Laboratory.

Vroom, V. H. (1964). *Work and motivation.* New York: John Wiley.

Wanous, J., Keon, T., & White, J. (1983). Expectancy theory and occupational/organizational choices. *Organizational Behavior and Human Performance, 32,* 66-86.

Warrick, R. A. (1981). *Four communities under ash.* Boulder: University of Colorado Institute for Behavioral Science.

Waterstone, M. (1978). *Hazard mitigation behavior of urban flood plain residents.* Boulder, CO: Natural Hazards Research Applications and Information Center.

Watson, W., & Maxwell, R. (1977). *Human aging and dying.* New York: St. Martin's.

Weber, E., & Hsee, C. (1998). Cross cultural differences in risk perception, but cross cultural similarities in attitudes towards perceived risk. *Management Science, 44,* 1205-1217.

Weinstein, N. (1989). Effects of personal experience on self-protective behavior. *Psychological Bulletin, 105,* 31-50.

Weinstein, N. (1993). Testing four competing theories of health-protective behavior. *Health Psychology, 12,* 324-333.

Weinstein, N., & Nicolich, M. (1993). Correct and incorrect interpretations of correlations between risk perceptions and risk behaviors. *Health Psychology, 12,* 235-245.

Weller, J., & Quarantelli, E. L. (1973). Neglected characteristics of collective behavior. *American Journal of Sociology, 79,* 665-685.

Wenger, D. E. (1980). A few empirical observations concerning the relationship between the mass media and disaster knowledge: A research report. In Committee on Disasters and the Mass Media, *Disasters and the mass media: Proceedings of the Committee on Disasters and the Mass Media workshop, February, 1979* (pp. 241-253). Washington DC: National Academy of Sciences.

Wenger, D. E., Faupel, C., & James, T. (1980). *Disaster beliefs and emergency planning.* Newark: University of Delaware, Disaster Research Center.

White, G. (1972). Human response to natural hazard. In *Perspectives on benefit-risk decision making* (pp. 43-57). Washington, DC: National Academy of Sciences-National Academy of Engineering.

Whitney, D. J., & Lindell, M. K. (2000). Member commitment and participation in local emergency planning committees. *Policy Studies Journal, 28,* 467-484.

Whitney, D. J., Lindell, M. K., & Nguyen, D. H. (in press). Earthquake beliefs and adoption of seismic hazard adjustments. *Risk Analysis.*

Wicker, A. (1969). Attitudes versus actions. *Journal of Social Issues, 25,* 41-78.

Wilkson, D. (1999). Reframing family ethnicity in America. In H. McAdoo (Ed.), *Family ethnicity* (pp. 16-62). Thousand Oaks, CA: Sage.

Williams, H. (1964). Human factors in warning and response systems. In H. Grosser (Ed.), *The threat of impending disaster* (pp. 96-109). Cambridge: MIT Press.

Wilson, D. J. (1987). Stay indoors or evacuate to avoid exposure to toxic gas. *Emergency Preparedness Digest, 14,* 19-24.

Wilson, D. J. (1989). Variation of indoor shelter effectiveness caused by air leakage variability of houses in Canada and the USA. In T. S. Glickman & A. M. Ujihara (Eds.), *Proceedings of the conference on in-place protection during chemical emergencies* (pp. 189-199). Washington, DC: Resources for the Future.

Windham, G., Posey, E., Ross, P., & Spencer, B. (1977). *Reactions to storm threat during Hurricane Eloise.* State College: Mississippi State University.

Withey, S. (1962). Reaction to uncertain threat. In G. Baker & D. Chapman (Eds.), *Man and society in disaster* (pp. 93-123). New York: Basic Books.

Witt, J. L. (1995). *National mitigation strategy.* Washington, DC: Federal Emergency Management Agency.

Wong, P. (1999). Race, ethnicity and nationality in the United States. In P. Wong (Ed.), *Race, ethnicity and nationality in the United States* (pp. 293-314). Boulder, CO: Westview.

Wood, R., & Bandura, A. (1989). Social cognitive theory of organizational management. *Academy of Management Review, 14,* 361-383.

Worth, M. F., & McLuckie, B. F. (1977). *Get to high ground: The warning process in the Colorado flood.* Columbus: Disaster Research Center, Ohio State University.

Wright, C., & Hyman, H. (1966). Who belongs to voluntary associations? In W. Glaser & D. Sills (Eds.), *The government of associations* (pp. 239-248). Totowa, NJ: Bedminster.

Wright, G., & Phillips, L. (1980). Cultural variation in probabilistic thinking: Alternative ways of dealing with uncertainty. *International Journal of Psychology, 15,* 239-257.

Yates, J. (1990). *Judgment and decision making.* Englewood Cliffs, NJ: Prentice Hall.

Yinger, M. (1994). *Ethnicity.* Albany: State University of New York Press.

Zeigler, D., Brunn, S., & Johnson, J. (1981). Evacuation from a nuclear technological disaster. *Geographical Review, 71,* 1-16.

Zeigler, D., & Johnson, J. (1984). Evacuation behavior in response to nuclear power plant accidents. *Professional Geographical, 36,* 207-215.

Zhang, Y., Prater, C. S., & Lindell, M. K. (2003). *Risk area map reading accuracy and evacuation from Hurricane Bret.* College Station: Texas A&M University Hazard Reduction & Recovery Center.

Index

About the Authors

Michael K. Lindell is the Director of the Hazard Reduction & Recovery Center (HRRC) at Texas A&M University and has 30 years of experience in the field of emergency management, conducting research on community adjustment to floods, hurricanes, earthquakes, volcanic eruptions, and releases of radiological and toxic materials. He worked for many years as an emergency preparedness contractor to the U.S. Nuclear Regulatory Commission and has provided technical assistance on radiological emergency preparedness for the International Atomic Energy Agency, the Department of Energy, and nuclear utilities. In addition, he has trained as a Hazardous Materials Specialist at the Michigan Hazardous Materials Training Center and worked on hazardous materials emergency preparedness with State Emergency Response Commissions, Local Emergency Planning Committees, and chemical companies. In the past few years, Lindell directed HRRC staff performing hurricane hazard analysis and evacuation planning for the entire Texas Gulf coast. He has made over 120 presentations before scientific societies and short courses for emergency planners, as well as being an invited participant in workshops on risk communication and emergency management in this country and abroad. Lindell has also written extensively on emergency management and is the author of over 120 technical reports and journal articles, as well as 5 books.

Ronald W. Perry completed his Ph.D. in Sociology at the University of Washington. He joined Arizona State University in 1983 as Professor of Public Affairs. Perry has been engaged in the study of natural and technological hazards and disasters since 1971. His principal interests are in warning behavior, public education, and community preparedness. In 1997 he began studying incident management systems and emergency operations centers. He has published 14 books and more than 100 journal articles in these areas of interest. Perry currently serves on the Arizona Domestic Preparedness Terrorism Task Force, the U.S. Veteran's Health Administrations Task Force on Emergency Healthcare, the Arizona Council for Earthquake Safety, and the steering committee of the Phoenix Metropolitan Medical Response System. In 1996 Perry was given the Award for Excellence in Emergency

Management by the Arizona Emergency Services Association. In 1999 he received both the Award for Outstanding Environmental Achievement by a Team from the U.S. Environmental Protection Agency and a Certificate of Recognition from Vice President Al Gore's National Partnership for Reinventing Government. In 2003 the City of Phoenix selected him to receive the Pearce Memorial Award for Contributions to Hazardous Incident Management.